The History of Houston County
Texas

THE HISTORY
OF
HOUSTON COUNTY
TEXAS

Together with Biographical Sketches of Many Pioneers and Later Citizens of Said County, Who Have Made Notable Contributions to its Development and Progress.

By Armistead Albert Aldrich

Southern Historical Press, Inc.
Greenville, South Carolina

Copyright 1943
By: Armistead Albert Aldrich

All rights reserved. No part of this publication may be reproduced, stored in a retrieval system, transmitted in any form, posted on to the web in any form or by any means without the prior written permission of the publisher.

Please direct all correspondence and orders to:

www.southernhistoricalpress.com
or
SOUTHERN HISTORICAL PRESS, Inc.
PO BOX 1267
Greenville, SC   29601
southernhistoricalpress@gmail.com

ISBN #978-1-63914-014-5

Printed in the United States of America

MOTTO FOR PIONEERS

"Is there no action worth my mood,
No deed of daring high and pure,
That shall, when I am dead endure,
A well spring of perpetual good?"
                    Thomas Bailey Aldrich.

DEDICATION

TO THE MEMORY OF MY PIONEER GRANDFATHER,

COLLIN ALDRICH,

WHO FOUGHT BRAVELY FOR THE INDEPENDENCE OF TEXAS, AND TO THE MEMORY OF THE OTHER PIONEERS OF HOUSTON COUNTY, WHO FOUGHT WITH HIM AT SAN JACINTO, AND ACHIEVED THE FREEDOMS WHICH WE ENJOY TODAY,

AND

TO THE MEMORY OF THAT PEERLESS SOLDIER OF THE CROSS,

REVEREND, SAMUEL FISHER TENNEY,

MY PASTOR FOR MORE THAN HALF A CENTURY, WHOSE INFLUENCE SHAPED MY LIFE MORE THAN ANY OTHER AGENCY, THIS UNPRETENTIOUS VOLUME IS AFFECTIONATELY DEDICATED,

BY THE AUTHOR.

INTRODUCTION

To properly trace the history of Houston County back to the beginning, it would be necessary to go back to the days when Columbus discovered America. The author does not deem it proper or necessary to go back that far to present to the people of his native county such a history as will meet the demands of those for whom the present work is intended. His object is to preserve and honor the memory of the pioneers of Houston County, who blazed the way through the wilderness and won their freedom from the savage Indians and hostile Spaniards and Mexicans, who preceded them in this favored land. The Indians were here and roamed the forests where we now live and prosper, long before the advent of the first white man. The Spanish and French both asserted title to the country, of which Houston County now constitutes a part, and it was the conflict between these two people that led to the earliest development of this County. Students of History are familiar with the story of La Salle, who met his tragic death at the hands of his own companions, while endeavoring to find the Mississippi River, on a journey that would have taken him through what later became known as Houston County, and some assert that he even passed through this territory and met his tragic death in what is now Cherokee County, lying east of the Neches River. The writer would not undertake to rob Navasota of the distinction that it claims as having been near the spot of La Salle's death. Since the matter is shrouded in so much mystery, the writer will allow the neighbor City of Navasota to pre-empt all the glory that she desires from the claims made by her on account of the tragic death of the distinguished Frenchman. Citizens of Houston County will share with Navasota in paying tribute to the gallant La Salle, and will give due reverence to the splendid statue and monument to his memory that now adorns her principal street. The writer believes that the real history of Houston County should begin with the founding of the Spanish Missions in 1690, which all historians agree were established upon the soil that now constitutes the present bounds of Houston County. He will leave to other historians of more pretentious works the details of the struggles between the French and Spaniards over the territory of the Lone Star State, and content himself with chronicling events transpiring in connection with the founding of said missions and those that have occurred since that time. He is of the opinion that these will be of sufficient volume to fill the history of a single county. He sends forth this little history with the devout wish that it may prove of interest to the descendents of the pioneers and of those who have chosen to find a home within the limits of old Houston County, and are interested in the story of her making.

A. A. ALDRICH.

EDENS-MADDEN MASSACRE

No history of Houston County would be complete, without an account of the terrible massacre that occurred in October 1838, known as the Edens-Madden Massacre, which occurred at the home of John Edens, on San Pedro Creek, about 12 or 13 miles North East of Crockett. At that time many of the citizens of that locality were absent from home, having volunteered under Captain W. T. Sadler, a soldier of San Jacinto, to accompany Major Mabbitt in the Cordova-Kickapoo Expedition. A number of the families of the community were removed for safety to John Edens home and were left under his protection and three other old men—James Madden, Martin Murchison and Elisha Moore. The others present in the house were: Mrs. John Edens and her daughter, Emily; Mrs. John Murchison, Mrs. W. T. Saddler, her daughter, Mrs. James Madden and two little sons, aged seven and nine years; Mrs. Robert Madden and daughter, Mary; and a negro woman about sixty years of age, named Betsy or Patsy.

The John Edens home later became the home of Judge D. H. Edens, and where he lived and died. The house consisted of two log rooms, separted by a covered passageway. The women occupied one room and the men the other.

"On the fatal night, about the 19th day of October, 1838, after all the inmates had retired, the house was attacked by Indians. The assault was made on the room occupied by the women and children. The savages broke down the door and rushed in, using knives and tomahawks. Mrs. Murchison and her daughter, Mrs. Saddler, were instantly killed. Mrs. John Edens, mortally wounded, escaped from the room and crossed two fences, to die in the adjoining field. Of Mary, daughter of Robert Madden; Emily, daughter of John Edens, each three years old, and the two little sons of James Madden, no tidings were ever heard, whether carried into captivity or burned to ashes, was never known, but every presumption is in favor of the latter. The room was speedily set on fire. The men did not open the door into the passage. Mrs. Robert Madden dangerously wounded, rushed into the room of the men, falling on a bed. One by one, or rather two by two, the four men ran the gauntlet and escaped, supposing all the others were dead. Early in the assault, Patsy (or Betsy) seized a little girl of John Edens, yet living and the beloved wife of James Duke, swiftly bore her to the house of Mr. Davis, a mile and a half distant, and then moved by an inspiration that should embalm her memory in every generous heart, as swiftly returned as an angel of mercy to any who might survive. She arrived in time to enter the rapidly consuming house and rescue the unconscious Mrs. Robert Madden, but an instant before the roof fell in. Placing her on her own bed in her unmolested cabin in the yard, she sought elsewhere for deeds of mercy and found Mrs. James Madden under the eaves of the crumbling walls, doomed to speedy cremation. She gently bore her to the same refuge, and by them watched, bathed, poulticed and nursed—aye! prayed!—till the morrow brought succor." . . . .

"Mrs. James Madden thus rescued from the flames, bore upon her person three ghastly wounds from a tomahawk, one severing her collar bone, two ribs cut asunder near the spine, and a horrible gash in the back. But it is gratifying to record that both these wounded ladies recovered, and in 1883 were living near Augusta, Houston County, objects of affectionate esteem by their neighbors. On the day following this horrid slaughter, the volunteers, the husbands and neighbors of the victims, returned from the battle of Kickapoo, in time to perform the last rites to the fallen and nurse the wounded. The late venerable Captain William Yancey, of Palestine, Robert Madden and Elder Daniel Parker and others of the Edens and other old families of that vicinity, were among them."

CONTENTS

		PAGE
Introduction		vii
Edens-Madden Massacre		ix

CHAPTER		
I	Old Spanish Missions in Houston County	1
II	Houston County, Its Creation and Organization	7
III	Houston County Courthouses	30
IV	Houston County Newspapers	38
V	Schools in Houston County	63
VI	Lodges, Fraternities and Civic Clubs in Houston County	82
VII	Crockett Churches	99

BIOGRAPHIES

Captain Isaac Adair	121
Col. Earle Adams	121
Armistead Albert Aldrich	122
Albert Augustus Aldrich	123
Collin Aldrich	123
Collin Aldrich, Jr.	124
Oliver Cromwell Aldrich	125
Jacob Allbright	125
Murdock McIntosh Baker	126
Doctor James G. Barbee	127
Fielding Harvey Bayne	128
Doctor Stephen Thomas Beasley	129
H. W. Beeson	130
Dr. Jehu Armistead Beeson	131
William V. Berry	132
John Andrew Box	133
C. W. Bracken	133
Mendel Bromberg	134
Judge James Russell Burnett	135
Daniel M. Coleman	137
James Collins	137
James P. Collins	138
Doctor John Collins	139
John Collins, Jr.	139
General Thomas P. Collins	140

Bradford Davis	146
Mrs. Lucy Atkinson Collins	142
Judge Leroy W. Cooper	142
Doctor W. F. Corley	144
James M. Daniel	145
Colonel W. W. Davis	146
Miss Adina De Zavala	147
William Dickerson	148
Colonel George English	149
Captain John English	150
The Gossett Family	152
Edward Alexander Gause	154
James H. Gillespie	155
James Madison Hall	155
Captain John L. Hall	156
Joshua J. Hall and Mahala L. Hall	157
The Hallmark Family	158
Judge James T. Heflin	159
Dr. James Hunter	160
Tilman Ingram	161
William Johnson	161
Doctor William George Washington Jowers	162
Adam Columbus King	164
Rev. Samuel Alexander King	164
The Kyle Family	165
A. LeGory	166
Colonel John Long	167
George Brinson Lundy	168
James William Madden	169
N. J. Mainer	170
The Masters Family	171
John McConnell	172
The McLean Family	173
William McLean	174
Doctor Francis Lewis Meriwether	175
Col. Steward Alexander Miller	175
Armistead Thompson Monroe	177
Judge George F. Moore	178
Daniel Murchison	180
Daniel McIntosh Murchison	181
Col. D. A. Nunn	182
Mrs. Helen Williams Nunn	183
Hon. William B. Page	185
Hon. Nat Patton	185
Mrs. Maud Sims Pence	186
Cyrus Halbert Randolph	187
Judge Robert N. Read	188
The Rice Family	189

Captain John T. Smith	190
Zachariah Stidham	191
The Stokes Family	192
Judge William M. Taylor	193
Monroe Thomas	194
The Thompson Family	195
William Vicory Tunstall	196
Judge William Benjamin Wall	196
Judge Frank Alvan Williams	198
Dr. Albert Woldert	198
Major John Wortham	199
William Branch Worthington	202
Index	203

LIST OF ILLUSTRATIONS

BETWEEN PAGES

Section of Pictures (1) . . . . . . xvi and 1

Armistead Albert Aldrich.

First Baptist Church; First Methodist Church; David Crockett Memorial Building; First Christian Church; First Presbyterian Church.

Post Office, Replica of Spanish Mission (San Francisco de los Tejas); Old Courthouse of Houston County; Catholic Mission San Francisco de los Tejas; Houston County Courthouse.

Old Crockett Academy; Wooden Courthouse of Houston County built in 1869.

Lanier Edmiston; Mrs. C. L. Edmison; C. L. Edmiston.

Group picture with J. B. Stanton; W. B. Stanton, W. B. Worthington; Rev. R. Gage Lloyd; John LeGory; George W. Crook; James W. Arledge, Thomas W. Thompson, and A. A. Aldrich.

William H. Moore; Major John Smith; Mrs. Louisa Matlock Coleman; Albert Augustus Aldrich.

Mrs. Sarah M. Tenney; Rev. Samuel Fisher Tenney; Adam C. King; Rev. Samuel Alexander King.

Donation certificate of Collin Aldrich.

BETWEEN PAGES

Section of Pictures (2) . . . . . 128 and 129

Cynthia Ann Parker and Child; Hon. Isaac Parker.

Cyrus H. Randolph; Gen. John F. Beavers; H. F. Craddock; Mrs. Nancy Jane (Burton) Hail.

Capt. A. D. Elam and Mrs. A. D. Elam; Andrew Edwards Gossett; Mrs. Nannie Hanson Stuart; Edward Augustus Gause.

Judge L. W. Cooper; Mrs. Dolly E. Worthington; William B. Worthington; Judge Samuel Morris Thompson.

Gen. Thomas P. Collins; James P. Collins; Mrs. Emma Collins; Mrs. Mary Collins Douglas.

Major John Wortham; Steward Alexander Miller; Mrs. Lucy Atkinson Collins; A. LeGory.

Henry J. Arledge; Monroe Thomas; Daniel McIntosh Murchison; Mrs. Maud Sims Pence.

George B. Lundy; W. B. Page; William McLean.

Major John Spence; Capt. John H. Wootters; J. G. Barbee; Col. George English.

Joshua J. Hall; Mrs. Adele Robbins Spence; John Collins, Jr.; Mahala Roberts Hall.

Mrs. Rebecca Miller; Jacob Allbright; Mrs. Kitty Burnett; Dr. Albert Woldert.

Mrs. Amelia Vann Collins; Hon. J. W. Madden; Joe Adams; John McConnell.

J. M. Hall; A. H. Wootters; William J. Foster; W. H. L. Burton.

Mrs. Willie Rice; Joseph Rice; Eliza Jane Aldrich; Oliver Cromwell Aldrich.

Dr. Stephen T. Beasley and son; George Washington Hallmark and wife; Mrs. Virginia Barbeee Frymier; Daniel M. Coleman.

Mrs. Helen Williams Nunn; Col. David Alexander Nunn; Judge Frank A. Williams; Mrs. Corinne Nunn Corry.

BETWEEN PAGES

Section of Pictures (3) . . . . . 160 and 161

Hon. Charles Collins Stokes; Mrs. Lucy Hancock Stokes; Charles Stokes; Dr. Edgar B. Stokes.

Lodowick E. Downes; Major James C. Wootters; Judge James Taylor Heflin; Dr. S. J. Collins.

William Johnson; Col. Armistead Thompson Monroe; J. R. B. Barbee; Wilson E. Hail.

Mrs. Emma Adams and Col. Earle Adams; Rev. J. L. Spears; Dr. John Collins.

Mendel Bromberg; M. M. Baker; Judge George F. Moore; Daniel Murchison.

Dr. William H. Denny; Dr. James L. Lipscomb; James R. Burnett; Captain John T. Smith.

John W. Arledge; Judge William B. Wall; F. H. Bayne; Miss Adina DeZavala.

Mrs. Isabelle Taylor; Rev. R. Gage Lloyd; W. M. Taylor; Hon. Nat Patton.

	BETWEEN PAGES
Section of Pictures (4)	192 and 193

Sam Houston

David Crockett.

A Group Picture: Mrs. T. D. Craddock; Mrs. Dan McLean; Mrs. Lucy Collins; Mrs. W. A. R. French; Mrs. H. J. Castleberg; Mrs. S. F. Tenney; Mrs. Emma Adams Castleberg; Mrs. A. R. Spence; Mrs. Gussie Worthington Shivers; Mrs. Mabel Hail; Mrs. Denny Arledge; Mrs. Sue Wootters; Mrs. Hennie Millar; Mrs. Mary C. Douglas; Mrs. Virginia Frymier; Mrs. Angeline Craddock; Mrs. Bettie Chamberlain; Mrs. J. L. Lipscomb; Mrs. Nannie Morrison; Mrs. J. H. Wootters; Mrs. Geo. W. Crook (with back to camera); Mrs. Florence J. Arledge; Mrs. John R. Foster; Mrs. Margaret Grace; Mrs. Mary Wootters Morris; Miss Missouri Adcock; Mrs. Julia Barbee; T. D. Craddock; Alfred Lee Foster; Marian Foster; Mrs. Margaret Woodson.

Armistead Albert Aldrich

UPPER LEFT: First Baptist Church, Crockett, Texas. UPPER RIGHT: First Methodist Church, Crockett, Texas. CENTER: David Crockett Memorial Building. LOWER LEFT: First Christian Church, Crockett, Texas. LOWER RIGHT: First Presbyterian Church, Crockett, Texas.

Upper Left: Post Office at Crockett, Texas. Upper Right: Replica of Spanish Mission, San Francisco de los Tejas. Lower Left: Old Courthouse of Houston County erected in 1883. Lower Center: Catholic Mission San Francisco de los Tejas, Crockett, Texas. Lower Right: Houston County Courthouse, erected in 1939.

ABOVE: Old Crockett Academy. BELOW. Wooden Courthouse of Houston County. Built in 1869, and destroyed by fire in November, 1882.

ABOVE: Lanier Edmiston, Mrs. C. L. Edmiston and C. L. Edmiston.
BELOW LEFT TO RIGHT: J. B. Stanton. W. B. Worthington. Rev. R. Gage Lloyd. John LeGory. George W. Crook. James W. Arledge. Thomas W. Thompson. A. A. Aldrich.

UPPER LEFT: William H. Moore. UPPER RIGHT: Major John Smith. LOWER LEFT: Mrs. Louisa Matlock Coleman. LOWER RIGHT: Albert Augustus Aldrich.

UPPER LEFT: Mrs. Sarah M. Tenney. UPPER RIGHT: Rev. Samuel Fisher Tenney. LOWER LEFT: Adam C. King. LOWER RIGHT: Rev. Samuel Alexander King.

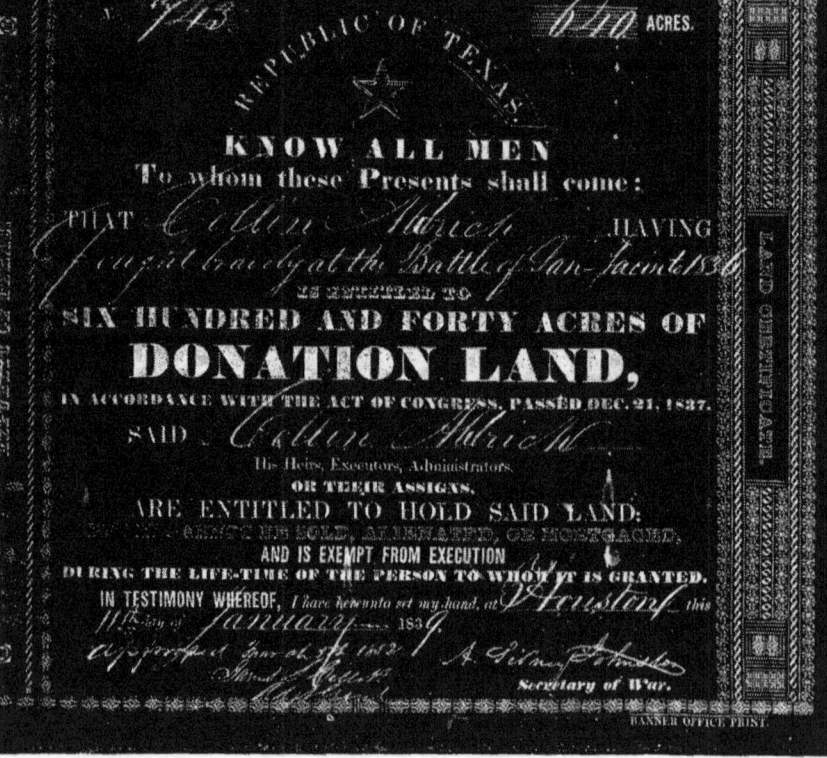

Donation Certificate of Collin Aldrich

THE HISTORY OF HOUSTON COUNTY

CHAPTER I

Old Spanish Missions in Houston County

The founding of the first two Spanish Missions in Texas, on the soil of what afterwards became Houston County, can be traced directly to the explorations of Robert Cavelier, Sieur de la Salle, afterwards known simply as La Salle. It was through him, and the expedition headed by him, that the King of France asserted claim to all the territory drained by the Mississippi River, including the territory embraced within the bounds of Texas. The French claim originated in the fact that on April 9, 1682, La Salle reached the mouth of the Mississippi River, on a journey down that stream from Canada, and set up a column, bearing the arms of France, with an inscription: "Louis the Great, King of France and of Navarre, reigns. April 9, 1682." and, with much ceremony shouted to his retinue and to the wandering Indians: "Long live the King" and proclaimed, that in the name of the King, he took possession of all the land drained by the Mississippi River. After this he returned to France and obtained permission to settle a colony at the mouth of the Mississippi, in order that he might hold all of his discoveries for France. Later, on July 24, 1684, La Salle set sail for America with four ships on which he carried about 300 soldiers, priests, mechanics and women and was well supplied with all the equipment necessary to found a city and protect it with arms. However, on this return trip, in search of the mouth of the Mississippi River, he missed his reckoning and finally landed in Matagorda Bay, on the Texas Coast of the Gulf of Mexico, which he mistook for the mouth of the Mississippi River. A few miles from the mouth of the Lavaca River, he erected a settlement, which he named Fort St. Louis. A short time afterwards he left this little fort and started, with seventeen men, to find the Mississippi River. It was on this expedition that he was murdered, by members of his own company, at a place which was claimed to be near the present site of the Navasota, and which some writers assert was near the Neches River, in what is now Cherokee County. The writer inclines to the view that Navasota had a better claim to being near the site of this miserable tragedy. This gives us a brief view of the French claim to the territory now known as Texas.

The Spanish claim is based upon the fact that Columbus discovered America and, in addition thereto, the conquest of Mexico by Cortes, and by the explorations of Cabeza de Vaca and Coronado, and other explorers. As a result of these conflicting claims between France and Spain the Viceroy of Mexico, then a part of the Spanish possessions in America, decided to establish a Mission in Texas, and in 1690, at the request of the Indians, did establish a Mission, San Francisco de los Tejas, in the land of the Tejas, at a place known to be within the bounds of Houston County. The Mission received its name from the tribe of Indians then inhabiting that part of Texas, who were known as the Tejas Indians. The word Tejas, which means "friendly," gave its name to all the territory now known as Texas.

The Spanish became alarmed at La Salle's Colony on Matagorda Bay, which caused them to make their first settlement in Texas. This settlement was made in East Texas, near what is now the little town of Weches, in March 1690. Captain Alonzo de Leon marched from Coahuila with 110 soldiers. He was commissioned to destroy La Salle's fort, and to build a Mission in East Texas, with a presidio near the French Boundary. De Leon was accompanied by several priests among them being Father Damiean Manzanet. When this expedition reached Fort St. Louis, Father Manzanet destroyed the wooden buildings setting them afire, being only wooden buildings made from the wreckage of a vessel that had been wrecked on the coast. De Leon came with his soldiers into East Texas with mule trains loaded with wine and wax, powder and shot, and the arrival at the site where the Mission was established is thus recorded by Father Morfi in a *History of Texas,* which Professor Carlos F. Castañeda rescued from oblivion and, of Father Morfi's account of the founding of the first Mission, he gives the following account:

"The feast of Corpus Christi was celebrated May 25th, with the greatest solemnity. After the Mass was concluded, the ceremony of raising our standard was held, a formality which Provosti does not record as having been performed by La Salle, in the course of two years, as he declares was done at the Mis-

OLD SPANISH MISSIONS IN HOUSTON COUNTY

sissippi when La Salle temporarily stopped at its mouth before."

These two missions enjoyed but a brief existence, because after being maintained for a period of a little over three years the Spanish no longer feared the French and decided to abandon both missions. The location of these missions, after an elapse of more than 150 years, became lost, as there were no longer markers by which they could be located with certainty.

After the abandonment of the Missions, *San Francisco de los Tejas* and *Santissimo Nombre De Maria*, by the Spanish priests and soldiery, the Mission buildings in the course of time decayed and no trace of them was left. The Indian village in which the Missions were located also disappeared and no outward trace of it could be found. Sometime prior to the year 1934, an old cannon barrel was plowed up in the field of Mr. Moore, a short distance north of Weches. At the time nothing was thought of this relic being in any way connected with the old mission until it was called to the attention of Dr. Albert Woldert of Tyler. He recognized it as the barrel of an old cannon and had the matter investigated by sending information to Spain describing the old cannon barrel. From that source he became satisfied that it was a part of an old Spanish cannon that had been buried by the soldiers on leaving the old Mission. To Dr. Albert Woldert, of Tyler, is due the chief credit for having located the site of these old Spanish Missions. He spent years examining all the available records that bore upon this question and then came in person, more than once, and examined the ground in order to locate the site, according to the old Spanish authorities, and gave an able and scholarly review of his researches in his effort to locate the sister of these Missions.

"Of the co-operation and assistance of Miss Adina de Zavala what all shall I say, The people of Texas know what she did to save the Alamo from desecration. I was aware of that fact, and it was no surprise to me when she brought along her lady friends to go with us to see for herself where my locations of the two above-named missions were situated. The rain that came upon us one day and overtook us did not daunt her courageous spirit. She only laughed, and so did we. It is to her splendid courage and perseverance that you see standing out there' the beautiful granite marker for Mission San Francisco, and if you will drive over to the northeast, four and two-tenth miles you will see another granite marker of a similar kind, which was obtained and set up for the location of *Mission Santissimo Nombre de Maria*, on the banks of the river *Arcangel San*

Miguel. My sincere thanks are extended to her for her sincere good work in this matter of securing these markers."

After the locations of the two old missions had been made as told in the foregoing pages, the next step was to have them properly marked and designated. Fortunately, Miss Adina de Zavala was President of the Texas Historical & Landmarks Association, and realizing the importance of having some permanent markers made for the missions, at her insistence the Texas Historical & Landmarks Association provided two large granite markers, one for each of the missions, and had suitable bronze markers placed on them. These markers were received in Crockett in the fall of 1934, and on September 21st, 1934, the event was celebrated at the High School Auditorium in Crockett, where Governor Pat M. Neff was the principal speaker and a program of patriotic music was given to a large gathering of people, including the students of the Crockett High School. Following this celebration, Richard W. Knight, Secretary of the Crockett Chamber of Commerce, and the author of this history visited the locations and there conceived the idea that a park should be established at that site that would include the markers, and agreed upon a plan of raising the funds necessary to purchase this park. A price for the land that would constitute this park was obtained from Mrs. T. S. Cook, the owner, and the plan proposed was that one acre of land should be paid for by each subscriber for as much as $10.00, and in this way the full amount was readily subscribed and paid in. A deed was obtained for the property and it finally was conveyed to the Texas Forestry Commission for park purposes. It happened that a CCC Camp was located near the site of *Mission San Francisco de los Tejas,* and the management of this camp undertook to grade and gravel roads through the park and build a replica of the first old mission. After this had been done, plans were made for a great celebration to be held on July 4, 1935, at which the replica and park should be appropriately dedicated. This celebration was held on July 4, 1935, and was one of the most memorable and outstanding events that ever occurred in Houston County. The following is taken from *The Houston County Times* of July 11th, 1935:—

"A crowd estimated at 5,000, including many distinguished Texans and persons from all parts of the State, attended the Fourth of July Pre-Centennial Celebration held Thursday, at which time the beautiful 117-acre *San Francisco de los Tejas* Mission Park, twenty miles east of Crockett, near the community of Weches, was formally dedicated with impressive rites. The

OLD SPANISH MISSIONS IN HOUSTON COUNTY

dedication services were held at the replica of the *San Francisco Mission*, the first established in Texas, which was founded in 1690 on approximately the same spot where the recently constructed replica was erected. The site of Texas' second mission, *Santissimo Nombre de Maria*, is located only four miles to the northeast of the first mission site.

"The services were opened with high mass ceremonies under direction of Bishop Christopher E. Byrne, Catholic prelate of the Galveston diocese, in which Catholics from Galveston, Houston and Dallas participated. A vested Catholic choir of 50 voices also took part in the high mass, which carried out the dedication of the mission replica with the same ceremonies as were used when the mission was first founded by the Spaniards 245 years ago.

"Catholic rites, which were carried out in the native tongue, were impressive in every detail. Franciscan monks from Waco, who originally came from the same monastery in Spain which furnished many of the early Catholic priests to Texas in the days when the country was a wilderness inhabited only by Indians, participated in the ceremonies . . .

"R. W. Knight, secretary of the Crockett Chamber of Commerce presided at the opening of the services before introducing Representative Albert K. Daniel, who spoke briefly on the history of Texas and Houston County, stating that the mission park celebration will undoubtedly start a movement to revive interest in Texas history and create a greater interest in the Texas Centennial next year. Representative Daniel presented Judge A. A. Aldrich of Crockett, a grandson of Collin Aldrich, the first county judge of Houston County. Judge Aldrich acted as master of ceremonies for the program which followed the Catholic dedication services . . .

"Senator Gordon M. Burns of Huntsville delivered a patriotic address, recalling that 159 years ago America was engaged in a fight to establish independence . . .

"Miss Adina de Zavalla, whose grandfather was the first vice-president of the Republic of Texas, made a short address, recalling that De Soto and Coronado were among those who headed expeditions into Houston County. Miss Zavalla also introduced Father Edward J. Foik of St. Edwards University, Austin, a member of the Texas Centennial Historical Board, who dealt at length with the early history of Houston County.

"Miss Frances Donecker of San Antonio, a director of the Texas Historical and Landmarks Association, was also presented by Miss de Zavalla. Miss Donecker spoke briefly on the part Miss

De Zavalla has played in the location and marking of Texas' historical spots.

"Senator Gordon Burns presented State Senator Clay Cotton of Palestine, who complimented the citizens of Houston County upon their wonderful co-operation in establishing the mission park and stated that he always felt closely related to the people of Houston County. Dr. A. W. Birdwell, president of Stephen F. Austin State Teachers College at Nacogdoches, brought greetings from another pioneer East Texas county.

"Dr. Albert Woldert, Tyler historian, told how he and J. M. Lovell of Augusta, and G. A. Moore, Houston County farmer, had combined their efforts in establishing the approximate location of the mission sites. R. W. Knight, secretary of the Crockett Chamber of Commerce, sponsor of the July Fourth celebration, was also among the speakers."

Miss Frances Donecker, after returning home from the celebration, sent the author the following poem:—

"THE REPLICA IN THE PINE GROVE

(Mission San Francisco De Los Tejas—1690)

A little log chapel alone in the woods,
  Standing there in a forest of pines,
So modestly peeking through columns of trees
  As if watching for yesterday's signs.

Are you looking for brown-robed barefoot men
  Who walked here so long ago.
Or for Red-men to whom these forests were home,
  With secrets we never shall know.

They are gone, both Red-men and white,
  But their spirits still hallow this park,
And the trees join today in a hymn full of praise
  For the light kindled here by Faith's spark.

And the little log chapel alone in the woods
  Stands now, as it stood long before,
For the ideals and dreams of far-seeing men
  Who hold sacred their native land's lore.

—FRANCES DONECKER.

CHAPTER II

Houston County, Its Creation and Organization

More than a century after the abandonment of the old Spanish Mission, which has been treated in Chapter I, that part of Nacogdoches County which afterwards became Houston County, began to be settled by colonists in Vehlin's Colony. Many of these obtained titles from the Mexican Government before the creation of Houston County, and quite a number of them fought in the Battle of San Jacinto and are entitled to be numbered with the heroes of that great decisive battle in the history of Texas. Many of their names appear in the following document, which was a prelude to the creation of the county. This is a historic document and deserves a place in the history of the county. Many of the men whose names appear on this document were prominent citizens in the later development of the county. It is as follows:

"Mustang Prairie, April 22nd, 1837.

"To the Honorable the Senate and House of Representatives when in Congress Assembled:

"We, the undersigned, your petitioners, citizens of said republic do most respectfully pray that your honorable body make for us a county on the East side of Trinity River, beginning at Robbins Ferry on said Trinity; Thence running fifteen miles each side of the old San Antonio Road and East far enough to make a constitutional county, and we do further pray that your honorable body appoint three disinterested commissioners out of the bounds of said county to locate the seat of justice for said county in granting the aforesaid petition, we, your petitioners as duty bound will ever pray, etc.

Iredell Reding	Stephen Crist
John B. Reding	Reason Crist
Geo. W. Reding	William Anglin
James L. Gossett	Robin Brown
Wm. L. Gossett	Richard Eaton
Elisha Clapp	Thomas Denson
John Wortham	Nelson Box
John Hallmark	P. O. Lumpkin
William Dillard	John C. Moore
John V. D. Gossett	John Allbright
Jacob Masters	Jacob Allbright
John Box	Barton Clark

HISTORY OF HOUSTON COUNTY

James L. Gossett
E. Gossett
John L. Hall
Stephen White
Alfred Buge
Leon Pritchard
Thomas G. Box
Samuel C. Collison
R. A. Walker
Henry Masters
John Erwin
Chas. Erwin
H. C. Johnson
Williard Standley
William Cheairs
W. C. Standley
John Cheairs
John F. Cheairs
Elijah Cheairs
Frances Cheairs
John Denson
Joseph M. Masters
William Leagon
John H. Holder
Enaske Lapus
Albert Allbright
Ira C. Shute
Jas. Barns
William Johnson

Wm. H. Pate
Peter Gallahery
John C. Hayne
John B. (illegible)
James Neville
Stephen Dunston
Swanson Yarbrough
Stillwell Box
James M. Hallmark
Alfred M. Hallmark
George W. Hallmark
John B. Hallmark
George Hallmark
Thos. R. Townsend
Jowell Clapp
John E. Clapp
John Adams
Samuel Phillips
Joseph Cason
George Allbright
Joseph R. Yarbrough
Frances Bettict
Shedrick Denson
Wm. Riley
John Allbright
Solomon Allbright
Joseph Lapus
W. M. White
Martin Murchison.

Ballin Snelles
R. O. Lusk
Joseph Masterson
G. E. Dwight
Samuel Clerlosky
Stephen Bennett
Elish Anglin
Miles Bennett
Joseph Jorden

Stephen Box
Collin Aldrich
Henry P. Crowson
Isaac Parker
Thos. Garner
Dickerson Parker
J. Haley
Benjamin Parker

H. Barrett
Peterson Tate
J. D. Parker
Geo. W. Robinson
A. E. Gossett
Geo. Hallmark
Daniel Parker, Jr.
H. P. Walker

"The above petition contains the following endorsement:
"Petition of Eredel Reding and others, for a new county,

8

ITS CREATION AND ORGANIZATION

Presented by Mr. Arnold, May 16, 1837. Refd. to Com. on County Boundaries. County of Houston Co. No. 15, Box 38-H."

The Senate Journal of the First Congress of the Republic of Texas contains the following account of the proceedings on the above petition:

"Mr. Grimes, chairman of the Committee on County Boundaries, having obtained leave, introduced a bill to create a new county to be known as 'Houston'."

The rules being suspended, the bill passed a first and second reading and was ordered to be engrossed for a third reading.

On motion of Mr. Horton, the senate adjourned until "tomorrow morning, 10 o'clock."

The following action in the House of Representatives of the First Congress of the Republic, is taken from the House Journal:

" Wednesday, May 17, 1837

"On motion of Mr. Branch the house took up the bill creating the County of Houston; and

"On motion of Mr. Arnold, the bill was referred to the Committee on County Boundaries."

* * * * * *

"Tuesday, June 6, 1837

"On motion of Mr. Arnold it was

"Resolved, that the bill establishing the County of Houston, with the accompanying petition, referred to the committee on County Boundaries, be withdrawn from that committee and referred to a special committee of three, with instructions to report tomorrow morning.

"The speaker appointed Messrs. Arnold, Wharton and White the committee, and on motion, Mr. Gant was added to it."

"Wednesday, June 7, 1837.

"Mr. Arnold, from the select committee to which the subject had been referred, reported a bill establishing the County of Houston, which being read, on motion of Mr. Arnold the 51st rule was suspended and the bill read a second time. Mr. Gant offered an amendment in relation to the County of Washington, which was rejected.

"The rule was then further suspended, the bill read a third time and passed."

* * * * * *

HISTORY OF HOUSTON COUNTY

"June 7, 1837.

"A message was received from the house covering 'an Act to create the County of Houston.'

"On motion of Mr. Irion, the 'Act creating the County of Houston was called up, and the senate concurred in the amendments made by the house'."

The following represents the action of the Committee on Counties and County Boundaries:

"The Committee, to whom was referred the petition of sundry inhabitants of the County of Nacogdoches praying a division of said county and to form a new county of a part thereof, have had the same under consideration, and believe that the Western portion of said county is so remote from the seat of justice as to render it all together inconvenient for the citizens thereof to attend the seat of justice on business of a public nature.

"We therefore recommend the passage of the following bill.

"H. ARNOLD, Chm.

"Section I—

"Be it enacted by the Senate and House of Representatives of the Republic of Texas in Congress assembled.

"That all that portion of the County of Nacogdoches within the following limits, to-wit: Beginning on the East bank of Trinity River at a point two leagues above the mouth of Kickapoo Creek, from Thence in a Northwesterly direction to the Neches at the mouth of Big Pine Creek; Thence up the Neches to the 32nd degree of North latitude; Thence due West to the Trinity River; Thence down the said river to the place of beginning, form a county to be called and known by the name of Houston County.

"Section II—

"Be it further enacted that the citizens of said county be and are hereby authorized and required to elect seven commissioners who, a majority of them concurring, shall select a site for the seat of justice of said county.

"Section III—

"Be it further enacted that the President be and he is hereby authorized to order an election for one representative, and all the officers of the county to take place on the first Monday of

ITS CREATION AND ORGANIZATION

September next and also to appoint commissioners to hold said election.

"B. T. Archer,
"Speaker of the House of Representatives.

JESSE GRIMES.
"President Pro. Tem. of the Senate.

"APPROVED: June 12, 1837.
"SAM HOUSTON."

A careful examination of the foregoing Act of Congress of the Republic of Texas creating Houston County will show that it was, at the beginning, a very large county, and covered all of the territory now embraced within the bounds together with all of Trinity County and all of Anderson County and a large portion of Henderson County. The reader should refer to a map of the State of Texas as it existed in 1836, for a clearer understanding of the territory embraced within the original limits of the county. It might be a matter of interest to the people of Houston County to think of the exent of the jurisdiction exercised by the first officers of Houston County. The chief justices of the county courts of Houston County from 1838 when they were first chosen, to the creation of Anderson County in 1846, exercised jurisdiction over all that territory now embraced in Anderson County and the Southern part of Henderson County and in Trinity County. On March 24, 1846, Anderson County was created out of Houston County and it will be interesting to observe the boundaries as set out in the Acts of Congress creating that county which are as follows:

"Beginning at a place in the County of Houston, known as Houston Mound, about one mile North of Murchison's Prairie; Thence Westwardly by a direct line running through the old Ionie village, on the North Elkhart Creek to the Trinity River; Thence, beginning again at Houston's Mound, continuing said direct line Eastwardly to the Neches River; Thence, up said river with the meanders thereof to the Northeast corner of John Ferguson's League of land; Thence, by direct line parallel to the first above-named line, to the Trinity River; Thence down said river with the meanders thereof, to the intersection of said first named line with the Trinity River."

It will be noticed that one of the landmarks which must

have been well known in that early day, was known as Houston's Mound, and is located about a mile North of Murchison's Prairie. Both of these localities must have been well known in the very early stages of Texas History. Recently an oil well was drilled very near Houston's Mound, just across the line in Anderson County, and in reaching it the roadway led across the historic elevation known as Houston's Mound. Evidently Houston's Mound was so-called and named in honor of Sam Houston.

On the 17th day of April, 1846, the County of Henderson was created out of portions of Counties of Houston, and Nacogdoches and in the Act creating it is defined as follows:

"Commencing at the Northeast corner of Anderson County, on the Neches River; THENCE North with the Western Boundary lines of the counties of Cherokee and Smith, to the Sabine River; Thence down said river to the Southwest corner of Upshur County; Thence North with the Western Boundary line of said Upshur County to the Southern boundary line of Titus County; Thence, West with the Southern boundary of said county, to the county of Hopkins; and Thence, continuing West with the Southern boundary line of said Hopkins and Hunt counties, to the Northeast corner of said Dallas County; Thence South with the Eastern boundary line of said Dallas County, to its Southeast corner; Thence West with the Southern boundary line of said county to the Trinity River; Thence down said Trinity River to the Northwest corner of said Anderson County, and Thence East with the Northern boundary line of Anderson County, to the place of beginning."

After the creation of both Anderson and Henderson Counties in 1846, Houston County continued to exist, embracing all the territory known as Houston and Trinity Counties until February 11, 1850, when the County of Trinity was created including the following boundaries:

Beginning in the East bank of Trinity River, at the lower corner of Henry Golmon's survey of 980 acres; Thence North $21\frac{1}{2}$ degrees East to the Neches River; Thence down said river with its meanders to the present Southeast corner of Houston County; Thence Westwardly with the South boundary line of said county to the Trinity River; Thence up said river with its meanders to the place of beginning.

On January 26, 1850, by an Act of the Legislature of the State of Texas, the boundary line between Houston and Anderson Counties was more definitely defined as follows:

Beginning at a place in the County of Houston, known as Houston's Mound, about one mile North of Murchison's Prairie;

ITS CREATION AND ORGANIZATION

Thence Westwardly, by direct line running through the old Ionie Village on the North Elkhart Creek, to the East Boundary line of Samuel C. Boxe's Headright League; Thence South with said line to the South boundary line of said league to the Trinity River.

A curious freak of legislation should prove of interest to the people of Houston County. On the 6th day of December, 1841 the Congress of the Republic of Texas passed an act which proved to be an abortive effort to create a county known as Burnet out of Houston County, which Act in part is as follows:

Sec. 1. Be it enacted by the senate and house of representatives of the Republic of Texas in Congress assembled, That the boundary of Burnet be, and is hereby established within the following boundaries, to-wit:

Beginning at a place known by the name of Houston's Mound, North of Murchison's Prairie; Thence Westwardly, to the Iron-Eye village, on Elkhart Creek; Thence to the Trinity River; and from Houston's Mound (the place of beginning) to the Neches River, so as to make a straight line from the Trinity River to the Neches River; Thence up the main West form of the Neches River to Clarence A. Lovejoy's Survey, No. 177, on the West boundary line of the Cherokee lands; Thence due North to the Sabine River; Thence up the Sabine to the fork; Thence up the North fork, to E. W. Shultz Survey, continuing up the same to the Fannin County line; Thence West with said line to the Trinity River; Thence down said Trinity River to the above-named line running direct from the Neches to the Trinity.

Sec. 2. Be it further enacted, That Fort Houston is hereby permanently established as the seat of justice for said county.

So far as the record shows no effort was made to organize the county of Burnet under the foregoing Act, and later another county was created in Western Texas that is now known as the County of Burnet. The singular feature of the above Act of Congress is the fact that it designated Fort Houston as the county seat of the county, without giving the people residing in the county the opportunity to locate and designate the county seat. It is also a matter of interest to the people of Houston County that the Fort Houston mentioned in the foregoing Act is located at the home of Judge John H. Reagan, a few miles Southwest of Palestine, and was originally located in the County of Houston.

After the County of Houston was duly organized by the

selection of county officers and the selection of Crockett as the county seat, the town was incorporated by an Act of the Republic of Texas, December 29, 1837, as follows:

"AN ACT

"To Incorporate the City of Houston and other towns therein named:

"Be it enacted by the senate and house of representatives of the Republic of Texas, in congress assembled, That the citizens of the City of Houston, and the Towns of Washington, Crockett and Refugio, be incorporated under, and entitled to all the privileges and benefits of the Act granting a charter of incorporation to the Town of Brazoria, passed at the extra session of this Congress.

JOSEPH ROWE,
"Speaker of the House of Representatives

MARIBEAU B. LAMAR,
President of the Senate.

"Approved, Dec. 29, 1837,

"SAM HOUSTON."

In order to understand what powers and regulations were conferred upon the Town of Crockett as was incorporated, it will be necessary to refer to the Act incorporating the Town of Brazoria, which was enacted and approved November 16, 1837, just a little more than a month before the incorporation of Crockett.

Section three of the Act incorporating Brazoria, and which applies to the Town of Crockett, is as follows:

"Sec. 3. Be it further enacted, That an election shall be held in said town on the first Monday in January of every year for a mayor, a constable and eight aldermen; the election shall be conducted by the mayor and two aldermen, and the persons so elected shall continue in office for one year or until their successors are qualified. The mayor so elected shall be commissioned by the Chief justice of the County of Brazoria, and shall have all the powers of an ordinary justice of the peace, in all matters and cases arising under the criminal laws of the

ITS CREATION AND ORGANIZATION

country, and shall be authorized and empowered, to enforce and carry into effect such by-laws and ordinances as the corporation of said town shall from time to time ordain, for the better regulation of the police thereof."

Section 7, of said act is as follows:

"Sec. 7. Be it further enacted, That all free males between the ages of 18 and 45 years, and all male slaves over 16 and under 60 years of age, shall be liable to work on the streets; that such persons shall not be compelled to work more than ten days in any one year, and they shall be exempt from other road duty. The board shall impose such fines on defaulters as they may think necessary, in which they shall be governed generally by the laws of the land."

Section 12 of said Act is as follows:

"Sec. 12. Be it further enacted, That if the office of alderman of said town shall become vacant by death, resignation or removed from the town, the board shall have power to appoint a successor; and should the office of mayor become vacant from either of the above-mentioned causes or otherwise, the chief justice of the County of Brazoria, be, and he is hereby authorized to issue forth a writ for a new election to be held on a day mentioned in said writ, and if the election required to be held on the first Monday in January of every year, shall not be held on that day, it may be holden at any time, by giving five days notice, and all elections for mayor and aldermen shall commence at 10 o'clock a. m. and close at 2 p. m."

On account of the destruction, or loss, of the records of the Town of Crockett, we are not able to give the names of the first mayor and aldermen, selected for the Town of Crockett It had its periods of ups and downs, sometimes being allowed to lapse and again being revived, until about the year 1859 or 1860, when D. A. Nunn, was elected mayor, and it is a well known fact that he rigidly enforced the laws and brought order out of chaos. After that the corporation was allowed to lapse during the period of the Civil War and for some time afterwards, but was finally revived about the year 1890, and has continued to exercise its function as the City of Crockett from that day until the present time.

The original Act creating the County of Houston provided for an election to be held in September, 1837, and doubtless officers were elected at that time, as we know from old instruments still in existence, but no known record now exists of the names of said officers except some official instruments that bear their official signatures. We know from these instruments that at the original election held probably in September 1837, that Collin Aldrich was elected Chief Justice, Jacob Allbright, County Clerk and George Aldrich, county surveyor. The following official correspondence occurred while Collin Aldrich was chief justice."

"Mustang Prairie, April 7, 1839.

"Dear Sir:

"Yours of the 5th of March came to hand, and in answer I will state to you that so far as I can understand the law, that justices of the peace should be elected for two years from the time of their election, but that there shall be elected on the first Monday in February, 1837, and every two years after, one sheriff and also one coroner at the same time and in the same manner as sheriffs, but I cannot find any law saying the justices of the peace shall be elected at that time. The acting justices of the peace for the County of Houston are as follows:

"For Fort Houston, C. T. Minza and G. W. Browning in and for Capt. John Crists, militia district for Crockett and Mustang Prairie.

"Elijah Gossett and William Dillard in and for Capt. B. W. Davis, militia district, for San Pedro and Neches; S. E. Kennedy and Ruben R. Russell in and for Capt. William T. Sadlers, militia district. The county has been laid off in militia districts under the new organization, and elections for company officers will take place immediately and in answer to yours of the 9th of March, I will answer that three copies of abstracts of original titles upon record only have been received, one by the politeness of Mr. G. W. Henchett, and two by mail. Your letter states that ten copies were sent. The journals referred to in yours of the 7th February, came to hand and have been distributed.

I am, Gentlemen, very respectfully,

Your "Obedient Servant,

"Collin Aldrich,

Chief Justice, Houston County."

(Addressed:) Free—Mustang Prairie, April 7, 1839.
To, The Hon. Secretary of State, Houston.
(Endorsed:) Collin Aldrich, chief justice, Houston County, Ar'l 7, '39, Recorded Page 245.

ITS CREATION AND ORGANIZATION

(Source:) Domestic Correspondence Archives, Texas State Library.

Even before Houston County was created as a county and Crockett designated as its county seat, there was some post-offices and a mail service in the territory that is now known as Houston County. The first of these was known as Aldrich in 1836, before the organization of the county and the post-office records show that Collin Aldrich was postmaster. This post-office later became known as Mustang Prairie, for we find from the records that in 1840 Mustang Prairie was named as a post-office, but no name of the postmaster was given. However, in 1843, Mustang Prairie named as a post-office and George Hallmark as postmaster. This George Hallmark was the ancestor of all the Hallmarks in Houston County.

In 1843 Alabama is listed as a post-office in Houston County and James M. Caldwell was postmaster. In 1840 Crockett is named as a post-office but no one is named postmaster. In 1843 Thomas P. Collins appears on the record to have been the postmaster. In 1838 Randolph, in Houston County, is named as a post-office with Nathan as postmaster. If there were other post-offices in that early day the author is unable to find any record of them.

OFFICERS

The first county officers of Houston County, probably elected or chosen in September, 1837, were Collin Aldrich, Chief Justice; James Madden, sheriff; Stephen White, clerk of the district court; Jacob Allbright, county clerk; John Grigsby, John Gregg, Elijah Gossett and John Box were chosen as justices of the peace, but it is probable that they did not serve.

Later officers selected January 1, 1839, were S. E. Kennedy, William Dillard and R. W. Box, justices of the peace. Martin A. Walker was chosen as sheriff; John H. Kirchoffer was president of the Board of Land Commissioners of Houston County, and Elijah Gossett and John Wortham were associate land commissioners for the county. Samuel G. Wells was clerk of the Board of Land Commissioners and George Aldrich, County Surveyor. On January 23, 1839 P. O. Lumpkin was chosen chief justice for Houston County, and was commissioned on January 25, 1839, but promptly resigned. After his resignation, on

HISTORY OF HOUSTON COUNTY

March 12, 1839, John H. Kirchoffer was chosen and commissioned as chief justice of Houston County and resigned in June 1839. On February 4, 1839, G. W. Browning, C. T. McKenzie and R. R. Russell were chosen as justices of the peace. On June 28, 1839, John Collins was chosen and commissioned as chief justice of Houston County. On June 22, Mobley Rhone and Stephen White were chosen as justices of the peace on Beat No. 4, and were Commissioned on July 4, 1839. On June 22, 1839, A. T. Hallmark was constable for some unnamed precinct in Houston County.

On February 3, 1840, John Collins was chosen Chief Justice and resigned on January 24, 1841. On February 4, 1840, Andrew E. Gossett was commissioned as sheriff of Houston County, having been elected on September 14, 1839. On February 4, 1840, Waller Dickerson was commissioned as district clerk of Houston County, having been elected September 14, 1839. On February 4, 1839 Edley T. Powell and John Pettitt were chosen justices of the peace for Beat No. 9, and held the same until January 8, 1842. On February 12, 1842, Elijah Gossett was again elected chief justice of Houston County. On February 4, 1840 Stillwell Box was elected justice of the peace for the Crockett district. On February 3, 1840, Barton Clark and Leonard Williams were appointed commissioners to inspect the land office in Houston County. On April 18, 1840, John S. Martin was elected sheriff of Houston County, and Eli Meade at the same time was elected clerk of the district court. At the same election William S. McDonald was elected justice of the peace for the first precinct. On February 19, 1841, Jowell Clapp and W. D. Longstreet were commissioned justices of the peace for beat No. 3, having been elected on October 24, 1840. On February 13, 1841, T. D. Tompkins and G. G. Alford were commissioned justices of the peace for Beat No. 5, having been elected November 7, 1840. On February 13, 1841 Y. G. Dollahite and W. M. Johnson were commissioned justices of the peace of Beat No. 4 of Houston County, having been elected Nov. 7, 1840. On February 13, 1841, George Hallmark and W. Hallmark were commissioned justices of the peace for beat No. 2 of Houston County having been elected on November 14, 1840. On February 13, 1841, Cyrus H. Randolph was commissioned as justice of the peace of Beat No. 1, having been elected December 21, 1840. On April 26, 1841, George Aldrich was commissioned as county surveyor, having been elected on September 7, 1840.

On October 6, 1841, George H. Prewitt, was commissioned as justice of the peace, Beat No. 3, having been elected September

ITS CREATION AND ORGANIZATION

6, 1841. On October 27, 1841, Stephen H. Hatten and Nathaniel D. Acock were commissioned justices of the peace for Beat No. 10, having been elected September 18, 1841. On December 25, 1841 Lodovik E. Downs was elected district clerk of Houston County. On September 5, 1842, George Aldrich was elected County Surveyor of Houston County and was commissioned on April 11, 1843. On September 24, 1842, Samuel G. Wells was elected justice of the peace of Precinct No. 6, Houston County; He was commissioned April 11, 1843 and resigned March 18, 1844. On December 24, 1842 George W. Grant was elected justice of the peace of Precinct No. 3 of Houston County and was commissioned April 11, 1843. On December 24, 1842, David Barrett and G. G. Alford were elected justices of the peace, Precinct No. 5 of Houston County and were commissioned on April 11, 1843. On February 6, 1843, Joseph P. Burnett was elected sheriff of Houston County and was commissioned April 11, 1843. On February 6, 1843, Cyrus H. Randolph was elected coroner of Houston County and was commissioned April 11, 1843. On February 4, 1843 Turner S. Parker was elected justice of the peace, Precinct No. 7 of Houston County and was commissioned on April 11, 1843.

On February 18, 1843 George Luster was elected justice of the peace, Precinct No. 1, Houston County, and was commissioned April 11, 1843, and resigned February 7, 1844. On March 4, 1843 William M. Johnson was elected Justice of the Peace for Precinct No. 4 of Houston County; was commissioned on April 26, 1843 and resigned on January 13, 1844. On March 4, 1843 William Z. McLane was elected justice of the peace of Precinct No. 4, and was commissioned April 26, 1843. On March 18, 1943 Christopher Ellis was elected justice of the peace of Precinct No. 10, and was commissioned April 16, 1843. On April 8, 1843 S. E. Kennedy and James J. Thomas were elected justices of the peace, Precinct No. 8, Houston County, and were commissioned April 26, 1843. On April 8, 1843 James R. Bracken was elected justice of the peace for Precinct No. 9, and was commissioned April 26, 1843. On May 20, 1843, Jacob Allbright was elected justice of the peace, Precinct No. 3, and commissioned July 31, 1843. On November 13, 1843, Waller Dickerson was elected county surveyor of Houston County and commissioned on December 4, 1843.

On November 13, 1843, Cyrus H. Randolph was elected chief justice of Houston County and commissioned December 4, 1843. On December 23, 1843, William Lane was elected justice of the peace Precinct No. 1, commissioned December 29, 1843. His term expired and he was re-elected. On December 23, 1843,

HISTORY OF HOUSTON COUNTY

F. D. Bodenhamer was elected justice of the peace, Precinct No. 8, and commissiond on December 29, 1843. On January 1, 1844, George W. Grant and George G. Alford were elected as associate justices for Houston County. On January 20, 1844, H. W. Neville and Alexander C. Thornberg were elected justices of the peace, Precinct No. 10 and commissioned February 1, 1844. On February 17, 1844, Horatio Nelson was elected justice of the peace Precinct No. 1, and commissioned March 8, 1844. On March 18, 1844, Clinton A. Rice was elected justice of the peace, Precinct No. 4 and commissioned April 6, 1844. On March 30, 1844, Richard R. Powers was elected justice of the peace, Precinct No. 6, and commissioned April 6, 1844. On May 16, 1844, John Blair was commissioned as assessor of taxes and on May 14, was appointed county treasurer. On September 21, 1844, Samuel G. Well was appointed justice of the peace and commissioned October 31, 1844. On December 24, 1844, Albert G. Barnett and Henry W. Ward were elected justice of the peace for Precinct No. 5 and were commissioned February 17, 1845. On December 24, 1844, Robert W. Caldwell was elected justice of the peace for Precinct No. 3, and commissioned February 17, 1845. On December 30, 1844, R. G. Green was elected justice of the peace Precinct No. 1 and commissioned February 17, 1845. On January 6, 1845, Thomas P. Collins was elected county treasurer and commissioned on January 21, 1845. On February 3, 1845 Joseph P. Burnett was elected sheriff and commissioned November 22, 1845. On February 3, 1845, James R. Bracken was elected coroner and commissioned on November 22, 1845. On February 3, 1845, George Hallmark, Sr. was elected justice of the peace, Precinct No. 2, and commissioned February 27, 1845. On June 4, 1845, John Blair was elected justice of the peace, Precinct No. 10, and commissioned July 4, 1845. On June 4, 1845 George H. Prewitt was elected justice of the peace, Precinct No. 3 and commissioned July 4, 1845. On October 4, 1845, James H. Gillespie was elected County Clerk of Houston County and commissioned December 17, 1845. On November 13, 1845, Waller Dickerson was elected county surveyor of Houston County. On January 7, 1846, William Lane was elected justice of the peace, Precinct No. 1 and commissioned February 4, 1846.

REPRESENTATIVES IN CONGRESS

In the senate, Isaac W. Burton served in the Third and Fourth Congresses as senator; Isaac Parker of Houston County,

ITS CREATION AND ORGANIZATION

served as senator in the Eighth and Ninth Congresses.

In the House of Representatives, Isaac Parker served in the Third, Fourth and Sixth Congresses. G. H. Harrison served in the Fifth Congress as representative. S. L. B. Jasper of Houston County, served in the Eighth Congress and W. T. Sadler of Houston County served in the Ninth Congress. W. T. Sadler at that time lived in what is now a part of Anderson County, but then a part of Houston County.

After January 1846, Texas was admitted to the Union as a State, and early representatives in the Congress of the United States will be given later.

OFFICERS

STATE SENATORS

After the admission of Texas into the Union, Houston County was placed in a district composed of Nacogdoches, Rusk and Houston Counties, and elected two senators.

Isaac Parker of Houston County and Joseph L. Hogg of Rusk County represented the district in the First Legislature covering the years 1846 and 1847.

In the Second Legislature David Gage and Isaac Parker represented the same district.

In the Third Legislature the District consisted of Houston, Anderson and Cherokee Counties and was represented by Benjamin Selman in 1850 and 1851.

In the Fourth Legislature the senatorial district consisted of Houston, Nacogdoches and Angelina Counties and Adolphus Sterne of Nacogdoches was the senator in 1852 and 1853.

In the Fifth Legislature the district consisted of Anderson and Houston Counties and was represented by Senator W. G. Jowers in 1854 and 1855.

In the Sixth Legislature, consisting of Anderson and Houston Counties, and in the Seventh Legislature consisting of the same counties, Wm. M. Taylor of Houston County was senator from 1856 to 1859, covering two terms.

During the Ninth Legislature the senatorial district consisted of Houston, Anderson and Trinity Counties, and John H. Burnett of Houston County served as senator during 1862 and 1863.

During the Tenth Legislature the district, being the same,

HISTORY OF HOUSTON COUNTY

was represented by W. G. W. Jowers from Anderson County during 1864 and 1865.

During the Eleventh Legislature in the same senatorial district W. G. W. Jowers was senator during the years 1866 and 1867.

During the years 1874 and 1875, the senatorial district consisting of Houston, Cherokee, Trinity and Angelina Counties and J. P. Douglass was senator during the Fifteenth Legislature.

The Sixteenth Legislature was held during the years 1876 and 1877, the senatorial district consisting of Houston, Angelina, Nacogdoches, San Augustine and Sabine Counties, and Peyton F. Edwards was senator during the years 1876 and 1877.

The Seventeenth Legislature was held during the years 1878 and 1879, and the senatorial district consisted of the same counties and W. W. Weathered was senator.

The Eighteenth Legislature was held during the years 1880 and 1882, the senatorial district composed of Houston, Leon, Madison, Grimes and Angelina Counties, and was represented by Senator M. Y. Randolph of Madison County.

This brings us down to the period when our courthouse was destroyed by fire, in November 1882, and the records are preserved from that date to the present and can be consulted by those desiring later information.

HOUSE OF REPRESENTATIVES

In the First Legislature assembled in 1846, Houston County was entitled to two representatives under the Constitution of 1845 and was represented by Steward A. Miller and William T. Sadler, both of Houston County.

The Second Legislature, which assembled in 1847, had two representatives from Houston County, William T. Sadler and Steward A. Miller.

During the Third Legislature, which assembled in 1849, the representatives district consisting of Houston and Anderson Counties elected one representative, W. G. W. Jowers of Houston County, and Nacogdoches, Houston, Anderson, Angelina and Cherokee Counties composed the flotorial district and was represented by Adolphus Sterne of Nacogdoches County.

The representative district during the Fourth Legislature which assembled in 1851, consisting of Houston and Anderson Counties, elected two representatives, W. G. W. Jowers and

ITS CREATION AND ORGANIZATION

C. H. Randolph, both of Houston County at that time.

During the Fifth Legislature, which assembled in 1853, District 28 consisted of Houston County alone, and elected Cyrus H. Randolph representative.

During the Sixth Legislature which assembled in 1855, Houston County was a representative district and elected Cyrus H. Randolph as representative.

In 1857, Houston County elected John H. Burnett as representative to the Seventh Legislature.

In 1859, Houston County elected John W. Caddell as representative in the Eighth Legislature.

During the Ninth Legislature which assembled in 1861, Houston County was entitled to one representative and elected John T. Smith as representative and also was in a flotorial district consisting of Houston, Anderson and Trinity Counties, and George F. Alford of Anderson County was elected represenative.

During the Tenth Legislature which assembled in 1863, Houston County was entitled to two representatives and elected G. M. Brazier and James C. Wootters as representatives.

During the Eleventh Legislature which assembled in 1866, Houston County was entitled to one representative and elected John T. Smith as representative while George F. Alford was elected from the flotorial district, consisting of Houston, Anderson and Trinity Counties.

During the Twelfth Legislature which assembled in 1871, Houston County was placed with Cherokee County in the third district and elected three representatives, M. A. Gaston of Cherokee County, J. R. Burnett and L. W. Cooper of Houston County.

During the Thirteenth Legislature which assembled in 1873 Houston County was placed with Trinity and Angelina County and composed the Third District which elected three representatives, Frank Rainey and John T. Smith of Houston County and N. G. M. Walker of some county other than Houston.

During the Fourteenth Legislature which assembled in 1874 J. T. Smith was representative from Houston County and died while in office and was succeeded by W. W. Davis of Houston County on January 12, 1875. This district was also represented by Dr. Frank Rainey of Houston County who resigned from office on March 25, 1874, to accept the position of superintendent of the Blind Institute at Austin and was succeeded by Dr. J. H. Stuart of Houston County, who qualified on January 12, 1875. W. L. Denman of Angelina County was also one of the representatives in the Fourteenth Legislature from this district.

During the Fifteenth Legislature which assembled in 1876 Houston County composed district five and Wash Holly of Houston County was elected representative.

During the Sixteenth Legislature which assembled in 1879, W. A. Stewart was representative from Houston County.

During the Seventeenth Legislature which assembled in 1881, B. F. Frymier represented Houston County.

During the Eighteenth Legislature which assembled in 1883 B. F. Frymier represented Houston County, again.

This brings us down to 1882 when the courthouse was destroyed by fire and the records are now available for the public.

UNITED STATES SENATORS

While Houston County has never furnished a United States senator as they represent all Texas, including Houston County, it is proper to include them in a history of this county. The First United States senators served in the 29th Congress which covered the period from March 4, 1845, to March 3, 1847. The first senators for Texas were Sam Houston of Raven Hill, who took his seat March 30, 1846, his term to expire as determined by lot, March 3, 1847, and Thomas J. Rusk, then of Nacogdoches, who took his seat March 26, 1846, his term to expire as determined by lot March 3, 1851. Those same senators represented Texas in the 30th Congress, covering the period from March 4, 1847 to March 3, 1849.

In the 31st Congress covering the period from March 6, 1849 to March 3, 1851, these same senators represented Texas, the residence of Sam Houston being changed from Raven Hill to Huntsville. They continued to represent Texas in the 32nd Congress, the 33rd Congress, the 34th Congress, covering a period from March 4, 1851 to March 3, 1857.

In the 35th Congress, extending from March 4, 1857 to March 4, 1859, Sam Houston continued to represent Texas as senator during the entire term. Thomas J. Rusk died on July 29, 1857, and was succeeded by J. Pinckney Henderson, who was elected to fill the vacancy caused by the death of Thomas J. Rusk and took his seat March 1, 1858, and died June 4, 1858, when he was succeeded by Matthias Ward of Jefferson, Texas, who was

ITS CREATION AND ORGANIZATION

appointed to fill the vacancy caused by Henderson's death, and took his seat December 6, 1858.

In the 36th Congress, extending from March 4, 1859 to March 3, 1861, when Matthias Ward of Jefferson, Texas, was succeeded by Louis T. Wigfall, who was elected by the Legislature to fill the vacancy caused by the death of J. Pinckney Henderson, and took his seat January 4, 1860. The other senator who served with Wigfall was John Hemphill of Austin, Texas, who served during the entire term of the 36th Congress.

In the 37th Congress extending from March 4, 1861 to March 3, 1863, John Hemphill of Austin and Louis T. Wigfall of Marshall served until July 11, 1861, after the beginning of the Civil War, when they were both expelled by the resolution of Congress.

During the 38th, 39th and 40th Congresses, extending from March 4, 1863, to March 3, 1869, Texas had no representatives in the United States Senate as at that time the Civil War was being fought and Texas constituted a part of the Confederacy. In the 41st Congress, extending from March 4, 1869 to March 3rd, 1871, Texas was represented in the United States Senate by Morgan C. Hamilton of Austin, Texas, who took his seat March 31, 1870, his term to expire March 3, 1871, and James W. Flannagan of Wallings Ferry, who took his seat March 31, 1870, his term to expire on March 3, 1871. During the 42nd Congress, extending from March 4, 1871 to March 3, 1873, Morgan C. Hamilton of Austin, Texas, presented himself to take the oath of office on March 4, 1871, a certified copy of a joint resolution of the Texas Legislature, declaring his election by the preceding legislature illegal, was offered and he was not permitted to qualify. On March 15, 1871 credentials of Joseph H. Reynolds, claiming to be senator-elect were presented. On March 18, 1871, the senate agreed to a reported resolution declaring Morgan C. Hamilton duly elected and he took his seat March 20, 1871. During the entire 42nd session of Congress James W. Flannagan of Flannagan's Mills, continued to represent Texas in the United States Senate. During the 43rd Congress, extending from March 4, 1873 to March 3, 1875, Morgan C. Hamilton and James W. Flannagan served as United Senators from Texas.

During the 44th Congress, extending from March 4, 1875 to March 3, 1877, Morgan C. Hamilton of Austin and Samuel B. Maxey of Paris, Texas, represented Texas in the United States Senate.

During the 45th Congress, extending from March 4, 1877 to March 3, 1879, Samuel B. Maxey and Richard Coke of Waco represented Texas in the United States Senate. These same senators continued to represent Texas during the 46th, 48th and 49th Congresses covering a period until March 3, 1887.

In the 50th Congress, extending from March 4, 1887, to March 3, 1889, Richard Coke continued as one of the senators and Samuel B. Maxey was succeeded by John H. Reagan of Palestine. During the 50th and 51st Congresses, these same senators represented Texas in the United States Senate. During the 52nd Congress, extending from March 4, 1891 to March 3, 1893, Richard Coke was senator and on June 10, 1891, John H. Reagan resigned to accept a place on the United States Railroad Commission, and Horace Chilton of Tyler was appointed by Governor Hogg to fill his place and took his seat December 7, 1891. He was succeeded by Roger Q. Mills of Corsicana who was elected to fill the vacancy caused by the resignation of John H. Reagan, March 30, 1892.

In the 53rd Congress extending from March 4, 1893, to March 3, 1895 Richard Coke and Roger Q. Mills were United States Senators.

In the 54th Congress, extending from March 4, 1895 to March 3, 1897, Roger Q. Mills and Horace Chilton were United States senators from Texas. They also served during the 55th Congress from March 4, 1897 to March 3, 1899.

In the 56th Congress, extending from March 6, 1899 to March 3, 1901, Horace Chilton of Tyler, and Charles A. Culberson of Texas served as United States senators from Texas.

In the 57th Congress, extending from March 4, 1901, to March 3, 1903, Charles A. Culberson and Joseph W. Bailey were United States senators from Texas. These same senators continued to represent Texas until 1913, when Joseph W. Bailey resigned and Rienzi M. Johnston of Houston was appointed to fill the vacancy and took his seat January 7, 1913. He served until February 8, 1913, when Morris Sheppard of Texarkana was elected to fill the vacancy caused by the resignation of Senator Joseph W. Bailey. These senators continued to represent Texas until Earl B. Mayfield of Austin succeeded Charles A. Culberson.

Earl B. Mayfield was succeeded by Tom Connally of Marlin and Morris Sheppard by Andrew Jackson Houston and on his death by W. Lee O'Daniel.

REPRESENTATIVES TO UNITED STATES CONGRESS

After Texas was admitted to the Union in 1845, it was entitled to two senators and two representatives in the United

ITS CREATION AND ORGANIZATION

States Congress. A list of the senators has already been given. The representatives in the lower House of Congress, in which Houston County was represented are as follows:

In the 29th Congress which met on March 4, 1845, and continued to March 3, 1847, David S. Kaufman of Lowes Ferry and Timothy Pilsbury of Brazoria County represented the entire State of Texas.

These same representatives continued to represent all Texas in the 30th Congress extending from March 4, 1847 to March 3, 1849. The residence of David S. Kaufman was then recorded as Sabine County.

In the 31st Congress beginning March 4, 1849 and continuing until March 3, 1851, Texas continued to have two representatives only, David S. Kaufman and Volmey E. Howard of San Antonio.

In the 32nd Congress beginning March 4, 1851, and ending March 3, 1852, Texas was represented by Richard Scurry of Clarksville and Volmey E. Howard of San Antonio.

In the 33rd Congress beginning March 4, 1853, and ending March 3, 1855, Texas was represented by George W. Smyth of Jasper County and Peter H. Bell of Austin.

In the 34th Congress beginning March 4, 1855 and ending March 3, 1857, Texas was represented by Lemuel D. Evans of Marshall and Peter H. Bell of Austin.

In the 35th Congress beginning March 4, 1857 and ending March 3, 1859, Texas was represented by John H. Reagan of Palestine and Guy M. Bryan of Brazoria County.

In the 36th Congress beginning March 4, 1859, and continuing to March 3, 1861, Texas was represented by John H. Reagan of Palestine and Andrew J. Hamilton of Austin.

During the days of the Confederacy, Texas had no representatives in the United States Congress.

The first Congress after the Civil War in which Texas was represented was the 41st Congress, beginning March 4, 1861 and extending to March 3, 1871. The district of which Houston County was a part was represented by George W. Whitmore of Tyler, Texas, who took his seat March 31, 1870.

In the 42nd Congress beginning March 4, 1871, and continuing until March 3, 1873, the district which included Houston County was represented by William S. Herndon of Tyler. He continued to represent that district in the 43rd Congress.

In the 44th Congress the Houston County District was represented by John H. Reagan of Palestine, who continued to serve in the 45th, 46th, 47th, 48th and 49th Congresses and was elected to the 50th Congress but resigned after he had been elected United States Senator in 1887.

In the 50th Congress, beginning March 4, 1887 and lasting to March 3, 1889, the Houston County District was represented by William H. Martin of Athens, Texas, who was elected to fill the vacancy caused by the resignation of John H. Reagan, and took his seat December 5, 1887. He was known as "Howdy" Martin. He also represented the district in the 51st Congress lasting from March 4, 1889 to March 3, 1891.

In the 52nd Congress, March 4, 1881 to March 3, 1893, John B. Long of Rusk represented the district that included Houston County.

In the 53rd Congress, March 4, 1893 to March 3, 1895, Samuel B. Cooper of Woodville represented the district which included Houston County. He continued to represent the district in the 54th, 55th, 56th, 57th and 58th Congresses and was succeeded in 1905 by Alexander W. Gregg of Palestine. He continued to represent the district until 1919, and was succeeded by Clay Stone Briggs of Galveston, who continued to represent the district until his death, when he was succeeded by ———————— Thompson of Galveston, who served one term and was succeeded by Nat Patton, our present representative.

DISTRICT JUDGES

None of the earlier District Judges were from Houston County. In 1847, Amos Clark was district judge of the judicial district which included Houston County.

When courts were first established in 1837, practically all of Texas East of the Trinity River was included in the First District. In 1840, the Republic was re-districted and the counties of Houston, San Augustine and Nacogdoches were included in the 5th District, the earliest judges having been George W. Terrell, Wm. B. Ochiltree and Royall T. Wheeler, the latter having been one of the eminent judges of the Supreme Court.

In 1861, Judge Richard S. Walker of Nacogdoches was judge of the 5th District. He was the son-in-law of his predecessor, Judge Amos Clark. He was elected district judge in 1861, and served until 1864. Later Peyton F. Edwards of Nacogdoches was judge of the 5th District.

In 1880 W. D. Wood was district judge of the 4th Judicial

ITS CREATION AND ORGANIZATION

District which included Houston County. He was succeeded by J. R. Kennard of Navasota in 1881.

In 1884 the Third Judicial District, consisting of Houston, Anderson and Henderson Counties was created and the first judge of this district was Judge F. A. Williams of Crockett. Outside of Judge W. M. Taylor, he was the first district judge from Houston County. Judge W. M. Taylor was district judge prior to the creation of the Third Judicial District. Judge F. A. Williams served as district judge from 1884 until 1892, when he was elected associate justice of the First Court of Civil Appeals at Galveston. In 1893 W. Q. Reeves of Palestine was chosen district judge to succeed Judge F. A. Williams. In 1895, Judge J. R. Burnett of Palestine was elected judge of said district and held office for one term only. In 1897 Judge W. H. Gill of Palestine succeeded Judge J. R. Burnett, and held the office until he was appointed on the Court of Civil Appeals.

In 1900 Judge A. D. Lipscomb of Crockett was appointed to succeed Judge W. H. Gill and held office during the unexpired term.

In 1901 Judge John Young Gooch of Palestine was elected to succeed Judge A. D. Lipscomb.

Judge W. R. Bishop succeeded Judge John Young Gooch.

In 1906, Judge B. H. Gardner of Palestine was elected judge and held the office until 1912.

In 1912 Judge John S. Prince of Athens was elected district judge to succeed Judge B. H. Gardner.

Judge B. F. Dent of Crockett succeeded Judge Prince for district judge, and he in turn was succeeded by Judge Sam Holland, the present district judge.

CHAPTER III

Houston County Courthouses

Houston County has had five courthouses, including the present one, and their stories have a proper place in this history. Two of these were destroyed by fire and two were removed to make place for new ones. Much of Houston County's history clusters around these buildings.

It is not definitely known just when the first courthouse was erected, but there is good reason to believe that it was built as early as January or February 1838, for the county government was functioning then, and deeds and other legal documents were being recorded by Jacob Allbright, the first county clerk. The author has in his possession an original certificate of record showing that a certain instrument was recorded by Jacob Allbright in March, 1838, and that it was recorded in Book "A" of the Deed Records of Houston County. The author also has in his possession an old surveyor's record, containing the genuine signature of George Aldrich, the first county surveyor of Houston County, showing that surveys were made by him as early as February 26, 1838 and his official signature appears thereto as county surveyor of Houston County, and that Wm. S. McDonald was his deputy.

The first courthouse was constructed of logs and the author has a letter from Wm. Erwin, a son of John Erwin, a pioneer, who says that his father told him he worked upon the first courthouse when it was erected. Mrs. Bella Romain, who still lives in Crockett at the age of 94 years, is a daughter of L. E. Downes, who came to Houston County in 1839, and she says that when her father first came to Crockett that a log courthouse stood on the public square where the present courthouse now stands. Adolphus Sterne of Nacogdoches wrote a diary giving an account of a trip that he made through Crockett in 1850, and that he was in the courthouse at that time. That was prior to the erection of the courthouse in 1851, which was a brick structure.

The history of this second courthouse is an interesting and colorful one. The need for a new courthouse, and the inadequacy of the old log courthouse, became evident as early as 1850, and the citizens of Houston County petitioned the legislature for authority to levy a special tax in order to raise a fund for the erection of a new courthouse. As this old document contains the names of so many pioneers we believe that it has a proper place in this history and it is as follows:

HOUSTON COUNTY COURTHOUSES

"To the Senate and House of Representatives of the State of Texas:

"The undersigned citizens of Houston County respectfully petition your Honorable bodies for the passage of a special law authorizing the county court of said county to levy for the year 1851, and as often thereafter as may be necessary, an extra tax, not to exceed the county tax upon all property within the limits of said county subject to taxation, for the purpose of raising a fund for the construction of a courthouse of suitable plan and dimensions to be determined on by said court:

John Long	B. C. Vaughan	Wm. M. Peck
John McConnell	C. W. Bracken	A. T. Monroe
J. H. Collard	James R. Kimberly	Moses Warden
E. Collard	Clinton Allen	Geo. E. W. Bennick
M. McDonald	Thomas B. Henderson	Solomon Allbright
Chas. Wood		A. Morley
Cyrus H. Randolph	John P. Smith	O. C. Aldrich
S. R. Mayfield	John L. Hall	John G. Pettitt
Jno. A. Clark	S. A. Miller, whose name is followed by a rubric	James C. Dupree
William Vaughan		John Montgomery
John I. Burton		F. D. Bodenhamer
W. H. L. Burton	J. H. Gillespie	J. T. Heflin
D. L. Burton	C. Nevills	S. E. Kennedy
John Platt	John R. Hayes	Thos. P. Collins
John Wortham	Jos. F. Edmiston	Geo. F. Moore
Sam'l J. W. Long	B. B. Smith	Isaac Adair
J. H. Kirchoffer	A. C. King	D. L. Burton
Daniel Dailey	James English	W. M. James
J. W. Bodenhamer	Jesse David	Jacob H. Burton
W. F. Wall	George Ramsdale	Nathaniel W. Burton
John Lee	Maurice Townsend	J. R. Evans
Wm. Taylor	E. Pollard	John Smith
John Jones	L. E. Downes	Stilwell Box
F. H. Hill	Mat J. Edmiston	
	Benj. G. Hardwick	

This document is endorsed as follows: "Petition of Citizens of Houston Co. asking taxes to be levied to build a courthouse, ets. Referred to Committee on Finance, November 28, 1850."

The following proceedings were had in the Legislature upon the foregoing petition:

HISTORY OF HOUSTON COUNTY

"Thursday, November 28, 1850

"Mr. Parker presented the petition of the citizens of Houston County, asking tax to be levied to build a courthouse, etc. referred to Committee on Finance."

Journals of the Senate of the State of Texas, Third Legislature. Third Session, P. 50.

"Friday, November 29, 1850.

"Mr. Grimes, chairman of the Committee on Finance, to whom was referred the petitions of the citizens of Houston County reported a bill to authorize the County Court of Houston County to levy a special tax for county purposes. Read first time.

"On motion of Mr. Parker, the rule was suspended; bill read second time and ordered to be engrossed.

"On motion of Mr. Parker, the rule was further suspended; bill read third time and passed."

Journals of the Senate of the State of Texas, Third Legislature, Third session, p. 57.

"Austin, November 29, 1850

"A message was received from the senate, through their secretary, Mr. Raymond, informing the House that the Senate had passed a bill to be entitled an Act to Authorize the County Court of Houston County to levy a special tax for county purposes."

"Austin, November 30, 1850.

"Senate's bill to be entitled 'An Act to Authorize the County Court of Houston County to levy a Special Tax for County Taxes. Read first time."

"Austin, December 2, 1850

"Senate's bill to be entitled 'An Act to Authorize the County Court to levy a Special Tax for County Purposes,' read second time and passed to third reading."

As a result of the Act of the Legislature in 1850, authorizing the Commissioners Court of Houston County to levy a special tax for the year, 1851, a courthouse was erected during the year 1851, being a brick courthouse erected on the public square to replace the old log courthouse that had remained there ever

HOUSTON COUNTY COURTHOUSES

since 1837. The bricks for the courthouse were burned and made here in Crockett and the author is of the opinion that the brick yard was located about where the residence of Dr. W. C. Lipscomb stands, as he had seen at that place evidences of an old brick yard.

The courthouse was a substantial structure and sufficient to accommodate the various offices from the year 1851 until it was destroyed by fire on February 2, 1865. The cause of the fire that destroyed the courthouse was never solved, but a prominent citizen of Crockett was suspected of having caused the fire in order to destroy some records.

After the destruction of the brick courthouse in 1865, the county was without a courthouse for about four years. The courts were held in a building owned by L. E. Downes situated on the Southwest corner of the public square where the building erected by W. M. Patton and now owned by Mrs. O'Bannon, stands at this time. It is occupied by Morrow's Grocery Store, known as the Red & White. The various officers occupied temporary quarters until a new courthouse of lumber was erected about 1869. This was a large two-story, wooden building, the upper story being used for a courtroom, and was used as a courthouse until it was destroyed by fire in November, 1882.

The burning of this courthouse resulted in a great tragedy as a jail was located in said building when the fire originated in a room occupied by the jailor and near the only door giving entrance to the jail. The scene of that fire is a dreadful memory to the people who were awakened out of their sleep by the fire alarm. Every possible effort was made to break through the wall of the jail and release the prisoners but all in vain. At least two prisoners burned in the jail, and their charred bodies presented a horrible picture on the morning following the destructive fire. The wooden structure was built by John H. Burnett.

While this wooden structure was in course of construction a petition was presented to the legislature for a remission of the State Tax levied in Houston County, so that the citizens could raise funds for the erection of a new courthouse. We believe that this petition is a historic document and has a proper place in this history. It is signed by a large number of Crockett and Houston County citizens and their names will recall many prominent citizens of that day. The petition is as follows:

HISTORY OF HOUSTON COUNTY

"TO THE HONORABLE, THE TEXAS LEGISLATURE OF THE STATE OF TEXAS, NOW IN SESSION AT AUSTIN:

"Your petitioners, the citizens of the County of Houston, said State, would respectfully represent that in 1864 the town of Crockett was almost entirely consumed by fire, in 1865, the courthouse thereof was destroyed by fire; in April 1871, the jail and a large portion of the town was consumed by fire, on the first day of October the entire portion of the town remaining was destroyed.

"Before this last fire the county and police court had made provision for the erection of a new courthouse and jail, and the same is now in process of construction. In view of this series of untoward and calamitous misfortunes and the further fact that our crop for 1871 has been set off to less than one-half of a crop by the protracted drouth of last summer and the consequent prostration of our financial prosperity, and pecuniary embarrassment, and the great difficulty we experienced to raise the funds necessary to meet the demands of the government in the way of general and special taxes including the levies for building the courthouse and jail we would respectfully ask of the legislature a remission of the State Tax levied and collected in this county to the county to aid us in building the aforesaid public buildings:

H. W. McNeill	S. C. Haile	A. M. Race
C. W. Hall	James Burch	Thomas Harrison
Thos. J. Calhoun	S. A. Miller	Martin Reed
Wm. V. Tunstall	H. W. Moore	J. A. Janes
Jas. C. Wootters	W. H. B. Lacy	T. J. Stubblefield
W. P. Hayes	John Delong	J. H. Lee
Edw. Haupt	Frank E. Downes	Louis Loeske
F. H. Bayne	Jas. D. English	J. R. Simpson
D. M. Murchison	T. J. Cook	W. E. Burnett
F. H. Wagner	Clinton Allen	Isaac Zillig
S. C. Arledge	John De Long	E. L. Simpson
G. W. Leaverton	C. M. Monday	Robt. Furlow
William Johnson	D. A. Nunn	Geo. W. Roberts
Wm. B. Beavers	John H. Drake	W. H. Riggs
O. P. Millican	Sydney Dailey	Z. Stidham
J. H. Burnett	David Fryar	R. S. Pridgen
W. E. Hail	John Blair,	Joseph Beavers
S. J. Jones	J. P. Pre. 1.	Kenneth Murchison

HOUSTON COUNTY COURTHOUSES

W. H. Berry	H. G. Foot	A. E. Gossett
John I. Burton	B. W. Neal	John Rose
John B. Smith	M. M. Murchison	John Allen
James Collins	Wm. Worth	H. R. Jordan
John McConnell	Robert Flynn	J. T. Kent
A. P. Howel	J. F. Arledge	J. J. Woodson
John McGill	John Douglass	James Hyde
E. Curie	C. C. Guytor	S. V. Hyde"
J. E. Downes	J. C. Lacy	
W. H. Cundiff	E. M. Oliver	

Another petition was sent up to the legislature in connection with the building of the wooden courthouse in 1871, and will be found of interest to our citizens which is as follows (copy uncorrected):

"TO THE HONORABLE SENATE AND HOUSE OF REPRESENTATIVES OF TEXAS:

"The undersigned would most respectfully memorelize you honorable boddies & State that in the year 1864 the most of our Town, Crockett the county site of Houston County was consumed by fire that is to say 22-buildings business houses including the principal Hotell in the place, and again in the month of Sept. 1865 The Court House inc(l)uding the office of both the District Clerk & County Clerk and all the Books papers & records were consumed by fire and now on the 22nd day of April 1871, we are again visited with an other Severe fire consuming one entire Square including our county jail which was nearly new and one that we had build at great expense for a county so low in funds as we.

"We therefor— most respectfully state that today we are without either jail or courthouse. We are compelled to Hold our Dist. Courts in a Room over a Store House whis is of great inconvenienc, our courts of necessity holding fifteen weeks in the year. We wold futher state that over one-half of our voting population are of the newly infranshied & have no property, consequently no tax that the people can possible bear— (deleted) —will for years to come be sufficient to erect a court House & jail. In fact it will take all the Tax, raised for purposes of that character to pay for Rents, for court House Room, Jury Rooms &c & the expense of boarding prisoners in the jail of other counties and other expenses attending conveying prisoners to & from the county.

"We therefor most earnestly Memorialize & Pray You Honorable Boddies to pass a law permitting the County of Houston to retain the State taxes for Two years to enable her to erect the Public building we so much need & cannot erect without the relief here prayed for.

"John Blair, Presiding Justice.
"S. D. Sullivan, J. P. Prct. No. 3
"C. B. Keel, J. P. Pres. No. 4
"John Kirkpatrick, No. 5

"I do hope the Legislatur-- will grant the Relief here Sought. there is but one jail in my Judicial district & that a very inferior one— (delected) —but one Court House in the Dist & that a frame hall.

"Leroy W. Cooper, Judge 3rd Dist."

Another petition or memorial that was presented to the legislature in connection with the old wooden courthouse is of sufficient interest to deserve a place here. It is as follows (copy uncorrected):

"TO THE HONORABLE LEGISLATURE OF THE STATE OF TEXAS:

"We the under signer Members of the County Court of Houston County would respectfully represent to your Honorable body that we are Justly indepted (sic) to John H. Burnett in the Sume of about five thousand dollars in Money ballance due to him for building & completing according to the Contract & specifications formerly Entered into by the County Court of said County with the said Jno H. Burnett a Court House & jail in the town of Crockett for the use & benefit of the state & county and that the same was done in due time and according to the Contract & specifications and was received by us about one year ago which building was to have been paid for by us according to contract & specifications when completed in cash at that time and Ever since there was & has not been any money in the treasury of said county to pay said dept, we therefore respectfully ask the passage of a bill— (Deleted) —authoriseing

HOUSTON COUNTY COURTHOUSES

said Court to levey a special Tax to pay the said ballance due on the said Court House & jail to be collected as soon as practiable. Very Respectfully Your obt. Servants.

"We further respectfully represent that the amount due said Burnett is drawing interest at the rate of twelve per centum per annum, which is gradually augmenting the amount of our county indebtedness.

Very Respectfully,

"John Blair, Presiding Justice Prec. No. 1, H. Co.
"C. D. Skidmore, J. P. Prec. No. 2
"C. G. Oliver, J. P. prec. No. 3, H. Co.
"C. B. Keel, J. P. prec. 4
"Sam H. Sharp, J. P. Prec. No. 5, H. Co."

Immediately after the destruction of the wooden courthouse in 1882, the Commissioners Court began preparations for the erection of another courthouse. A contract was made to build a brick courthouse and the brick were burned at a place immediately south of the present residence of Congressman Nat Patton. The courthouse was finished during the year 1883, and its erection was supervised by O. Peterson, who came to Crockett from Jefferson, Texas, for that purpose. Judge W. B. Wall was the county judge at that time and a bond issue of $20,000.00 was ordered by the Commissioners Court to provide funds to cover both the costs of the building and furnishing the same. Col. Thos. H. Nelms of Pennington purchased all or a greater part of the bonds. This was the fourth courthouse and was used as such until the contract was made for the present splendid building that constitutes the chief ornament of our City.

The campaign that was made in favor of a bond issue for the erection of this courthouse is familiar to our people today. In addition to a bond issue, a PWA grant of $90,000.00 was first obtained and later an additional amount was added to this. The people of Crockett will remember the dedication exercises when this building was completed. It will probably last for almost another century.

CHAPTER IV

Houston County Newspapers

"THE CROCKETT PRINTER"

The first newspaper published in Houston County was owned and published by Oscar Dalton, who probably began the publication soon after coming to Crockett. The author did not know him personally but knew his family quite well. He married a widow by the name of Hall, who had two children, Mary Hall and Frank Hall, at the time of her marriage to Dalton. The first issue of The Crockett Printer was dated December 6, 1853, and it contained the following statement:

"THE CROCKETT PRINTER

Edited By the Publisher

Vol 1.

The Crockett Printer

Issued every Wednesday by Oscar Dalton, Proprietor.

At $2.00 per Annum, invariably in Advance

Rates of Advertising:

One Square (10) lines 1 year $15; 1 Square, 1 insertion $1.00. Each Additional insertion, 50c. Announcing candidates for State or District offices, $10.00; Announcing for County Offices, $5.00.

All transient advertisements must be paid for at the time their insertion is ordered. A liberal discount will be made to yearly advertisers."

* * * * * *

In the first issue of the paper a contributor, writing under the name, "The Oldest Inhabitant," undertook to give a brief sketch of Crockett, up to that date. This contribution contains so much information about the beginning of Crockett, that it deserves a place here. It is as follows:

HOUSTON COUNTY NEWSPAPERS

"A SKETCH OF CROCKETT.

"Unlike most historians, who depend upon preceding writers for their materials, the Oldest Inhabitant himself contemporary with Crockett, is enabled to note its rise and progress, free from the melancholy task of recording its decline and fall.

"Crockett was located at the county site of Houston County, in the winter of 1837, owing to its position to its being the only point within a reasonable distance of the San Antonio Road, and the center of the county, where running water could be found.

"It was emphatically a frontier village, but three hours ride from the buffalo range; for several years Indian outrages were committed in its vicinity. The Coshattas hunted on the South, the Cherokees joined the county on the East, while North and West the wild or Prairie Indians penetrated the sparse settlements almost unperceived, and too generally unpunished.

"A very narrow chain of settlements along the San Antonio road, formed the connection with the white population of Texas. This road, as is well known, passes through the poorest and worst watered portion of Houston County, giving no promise of a better country to the passing stranger.

"Distance from market (Trinity not being then navigated) danger from Indians and the usual inconvenience of a frontier country, long retarded the settlement of the county and the growth of the village.

"Although a log courthouse and jail were erected and the liberality of the legislature had granted a charter providing for the election of a mayor, eight aldermen, a town clerk, etc. yet for some months the solitary citizen, who kept a store in a 16-foot lot cabin, was daily asked, 'How far to Crockett?'

" 'You are right in the public square of Crockett now, Stranger,' was the answer.

"In 1839 there were two resident families, and the danger from Indians was so urgent that the neighbors fortified the courthouse lot with pickets and took shelter with their families until immediate danger had passed over.

"For two years the sittings of the district court were suspended, during which time cases of assault and battery were so multiplied that succeeding grand juries declined to notice them.

"Card playing (not then prohibited) and quarter racing, were the favorite amusements on public days. The eastern and western mails arrived on an average of twice a month. The northern mail for Fort Houston was sent whenever there was a chance, and then generally in the crown of a hat. The Galveston mail was once suspended for five months, and at last arrived in coffee sacks on an ox wagon.

"Sassafras tea, rye coffee, milk and whiskey, were the only beverages that could be depended on, as coffee frequently could not be had at any price. In the way of diet, steel mill bread and jerked beef were the great staples.

"Indian hardships and it is to be hoped, dissipation, have passed away forever from Crockett, and there is every indication that its course is onward and upward. The telegraph has entered our town, a substantial brick courthouse has just been completed, the Masonic Hall, Temple of Honor, and free church are well attended; six stores, two taverns, a boot and shoemaker, four smith shops, a wagon and three cabinet shops, a tanyard and saddler's shop accommodate the public; professional gentlemen offer their services to clients and patients, our bricklayers are busy and all the usual means and appliances of civilized life may be found in our village.

"Of the future of Crockett there can be but one opinion. With the increase of population of the county and the cultivation of its fine cotton lands, the wealth and the population of the village must increase.

"The very institution of a newspaper indicates the progress of Crockett, and there can be no doubt that its future pages will record a state of things, that will throw into the shade and almost render incredible these scanty reminiscences of the Oldest Inhabitant."

Mr. Dalton launched his enterprise under unusual difficulties and note the following from his first issue.

"OUR TROUBLES—We deem it a duty to our patrons to give the causes why the 'Printer' has been so long in showing himself to their admiring eyes; first, then, we failed in getting our materials up before the yellow fever broke out in Houston, after which it was impossible to get a wagon at any price here, we are compelled to acknowledge our indebtedness to Messrs. F. D. Bodenhamer, J. H. Gillespie, Steward, Dr. Corley, and last, though not least, Col. J. Long for their exertions in endeavoring to procure wagons for us; they succeeded in engaging four or five, but, from some unknown cause, they all declined, afterward, in this extremity Messrs. Inman, Johnson & Co., came to the rescue and placed our press, etc. upon one of their wagons, and here it is. Next came a demand on the merchants

HOUSTON COUNTY NEWSPAPERS

for freight, and they paid up like princes, without a single exception.

"But the end is not yet, for some 'Blaggard' on the road near Houston stole our keg of ink, and placed us under the necessity of borrowing from our neighbors of the Trinity Advocate, may their sheet never be pale for the want of ink."

NEWSPAPERS

(Items From the Crockett Printer)

"We were pleased to see Dr. Kirchoffer enter our office last Monday, after an absence of some weeks. The doctor confirms the report that cholera is in New Orleans and also that several died at the wharf in Galveston. We fear that Galveston and Houston may witness another epidemic as dreadful as that just past."

"It would be well for us here to notice that Dr. Kirchoffer has brought us a lot of cards. We can now accommodate those of our friends who may desire a neat business card, circular or other job work."

"We are authorized to say that Bishop Andrews of the Methodist Episcopal Church will preach in Crockett the 18th inst. Sermon will commence at half past ten o'clock a. m."

"The Trinity Presbytery of the Cumberland Presbyterian Church convened on the 2nd inst. We could learn nothing more of their proceedings than that the Rev. D. W. Braughton was ordained. Eight congregations were represented and six ordained ministers were present. We understand that some arrangements were made for the establishment of a Presbyterian school in the bounds of the Presbytery."

(Note by Author: The Presbyterian school above referred to was later established at Tenhuacana, and was known as Trinity University. It is the same institution now located at Waxahachie in Ellis County.)

"Our thanks are tendered to our representative, Judge Randolph and Senator Jowers for public documents. We thought the judge would not forget us."

The following ad in the first issue of the Crockett Printer has sufficient historic value to justify including it here:

"NOTICE TO TRAVELERS—Travellers and emigrants going West are informed that the best and most direct road from

Shreveport and other points on Red River to Austin and San Antonio is through the Town of Rusk in Cherokee County. From the latter point an excellent road of twelve miles leads to Stinson's Ferry at which place ferry boats cross the Neches River constantly, causing no detention at any stage of water. Wagons, carriages, etc. are landed on high and dry roads, without any mud or river bottom to pass through.

"This is on the (mail route) main and principal road leading to Crockett, Hall's Bluff, Robbin's Ferry, Cincinnatti, Huntsville, Washington and from thence to Austin and San Antonio.

"From Grand Encore to Waco Village, the route lies through Sabine Town, San Augustine, Nacogdoches, Douglas, Linwood and Alto, on the San Antonio Road, from thence to Stinson's Ferry, from which place there is excellent road to Palestine, Magnolia and Parker's Bluff on to Springfield and Waco Village, from thence a fine road to San Antonio and Austin. There is at all times a plentiful supply of provender and forage on the route. No detention. Boats run at all stages of water.—Wm. N. Bonner.

"There is a House of Entertainment kept at the ferry. Every attention given to make man and beast comfortable, and there are various other food houses kept in the road.—W. N. B."

Another advertisement contains enough historic information about business conditions in Crockett at that time as to deserve mention here. It is as follows:

"DRY GOODS, GROCERIES, HARDWARE, ETC.
"COLLINS & BROTHER

"Are receiving a stock of goods purchased last month by their senior in New York, to which they request the attention of their customers, and the citizens of Houston County generally. It is by far the largest they have ever brought to this place, and embraces almost every article usually kept in stores in this country, viz:

WOOLEN, COTTON, SILK AND LINEN GOODS
"A large assortment of
"LADIES' FANCY GOODS, JEWELRY

"Their Assortment of YANKEE NOTIONS Is Unusually Large.

"Their stock of shoes, boots, ladies garters, slippers, boots,

HOUSTON COUNTY NEWSPAPERS

is very large, having cost over $2700 in New York. They also purchased large amount of clothing!

"Chinaware, Queensware and Glass, Saddlery, Books and Stationery, Groceries, Medicines, Ladies' Bonnets of the latest styles and trimmings to match. Men's and Boys' Hats and Caps in great variety.

"HARDWARE, CUTLERY, ETC., ETC.

"N. B.—They bought a large number of John Moore's Celebrated Ploughs, so well known and much approved in this country. Also extra points, landslides and mouldboards, which will be brought out as soon as the Trinity admits of navigation. Also a large stock of iron and steel, wagon boxes, etc. Crockett, Dec. 6-ly."

The firm of Collins & Brother above mentioned, conducted business where the Crockett Hotel now stands, and was composed of Thos. P. Collins and his younger brother, Dr. John Collins, who had previously been the second Chief Justice of Houston County in 1840.

Other leading merchants advertising in this copy of the Crockett Printer were A. T. Monroe, a pioneer merchant and citizen, and W. F. Wall whose store was located where the Crockett State Bank now stands.

The firm of Long & Downes, also had an ad in this issue of the paper, and was composed of Col. John Long, a pioneer citizen and L. E. Downes, who was district clerk of Houston County as early as 1852. Both of these pioneers spent the balance of their lives in Crockett and are both buried in the old Crockett Cemetery in Crockett.

Andrew Butts, a blacksmith, was also an advertiser in this issue of the paper, and stated that his shop was located at the fork of Rusk and Nacogdoches Road. That location was evidently where R. L. Shivers now has his store.

That first issue of the paper gave a list of the officers of Houston County as follows:

"The following is a list of officers for Houston County and also the time of holding court in said county, to-wit:

"John H. Reagan, Judge of the 9th Judicial District.

"James H. Gillespie, County Clerk.

"James M. Hall, District clerk.

"F. D. Bodenhamer, Sheriff.

"Mat J. Edmiston, Chief Justice.

HISTORY OF HOUSTON COUNTY

"John Blair, A. E. Gossett, A. H. English, R. Matthews, county commissioners.

"A. C. King, coroner.

"The District Court for said county meets the first Mondays in March and September.

"The County Court for Roads and Revenues meets the third Monday in February, May, August and November.

"The County Court pertaining to Estates of deceased persons, etc. meets the last Monday in each month."

Other ads in this paper are as follows:

"HALL'S HOTEL, CROCKETT, TEXAS

"The proprietor of the above establishment is now prepared to entertain TRAVELLERS IN THE BEST MANNER the country affords. He has just completed a LARGE and COMMODIOUS STABLE which is contiguous to the house, and has a good and careful hostler, always in attendance.

"A well of good water in the horse lot."

Hall's Hotel was located at the Southwest corner of the public square where the K. of P. Lodge now stands.

* * * * * *

"YOAKUM & TAYLOR, Attorneys at Law

Henderson, Yoakum, Huntsville——Wm. M. Taylor, Crockett.

"Crockett, Dec. 6, 1853-ly."

"S. A. MILLER, Attorney and Counsellor at Law

"Crockett, Texas.

"Will continue to attend promptly to such professional business as may be entrusted to his care in the District Courts of the 9th Judicial District and of the Counties of Cherokee and Trinity, also in the Supreme Court of the State at Tyler."

"Business Communication (pre-paid) will be punctually answered and attended to. Office at his old stand opposite the N. W. corner of the Public Square."

HOUSTON COUNTY NEWSPAPERS

"DR. J. W. MEREDITH

"Having determined to make Crockett his home, offers his services to the public in various branches of his professions. Office over drug store upstairs."

The Crockett Printer in November, 1857, gave a description of Hon. John H. Reagan, who had but recently been elected to Congress and which description was published later in the Clarksville Standard under date of November 21, 1857, and is as follows:

"Hon. John H. Reagan came to Texas eighteen years ago, a poor, friendless stranger, wearing buckskin breeches and hickory shirts. He educated himself; he labored Saturdays, at night and the hours usually devoted to rest were spent in toil to pay for his schooling and the purchase of books. He split rails, drove oxen, toiled in farm fields, surveyed in a wild, unsettled country until he became inured to hardships; strict integrity and honesty marked his course and met its reward. He gradually rose from constable, higher and higher; admitted to the bar; was selected as the ablest man for the legislature, where he served faithfully; came back to the people and they made him judge of the Superior Court, he studied how to fill (sic) and administer the law; how well he succeeded is evident by his re-election to the same office; and almost immediately after to a higher post, the highest in the gift of the people of Eastern Texas—representative in the Congress of the United States—and is spoken of as having fair prospects before the Legislature for United States senator. Will he pause there? No. His energy and decision of character may yet place him in the presidential chair of these United States. John H. Reagan was nobody, no wealth, or influential friends to help him on—no wars to give him military fame—no crisis in affairs threw him to the surface—but, slowly he rose, by his own industry. Here, boys of Texas, is an example for you—. The Standard Clarksville, November 21, 1857, p. 2, c. 6."

* * * * * *

The Author is fortunate enough to have a second copy of The Crockett Printer, published under date of Wednesday,

HISTORY OF HOUSTON COUNTY

November 11, 1860. It might be well to remember that this date was exactly 58 years before the Armistice of November 11, 1918.

Under the head of "The Election" the editor says:

"We condense from our different exchanges the returns of the election on last Tuesday into as small a space as possible. We are by no means disappointed at the results. We are indebted to Mr. Aldrich, County Clerk for this (Houston) County, and also the different postmasters for information of various precincts that we could not otherwise obtain. Houston County: Breckenridge 446, Bell and Everett 128. Precincts not received came in too late. Bennetts, Randolph and Antrem Church."

Then follows the return from a large number of Texas counties, giving the vote for President.

The following appears under the head of "Mail Arrivals and Departures."

"For the benefit of our readers we shall keep the following schedule of mail arrivals, and departures standing as a reference:

"The Nacogdoches four-horse stage bringing the 'States' mail arrives Sundays, Wednesdays and Fridays; leaves at midnight of the same days.

"The Huntsville four-horse arrives Sundays, Wednesdays and Fridays, bringing the Houston, Austin, San Antonio and Galveston mails, leaves next mornings at 4 o'clock.

"The Liberty stage arrives at midnight on Saturday, Monday and Thursday, leaves at 5 o'clock a. m. Friday, Sunday and Wednesday. This line brings the Galveston, Coast and New Orleans mail, supplies Sumpter, Livingston, Woodville, and in fact, the whole section of country between Liberty and Crockett.

"The last two mails, it will be seen, arriving on intermediate days affords us a daily mail with Galveston.

"The Shreveport four-horse stage arrives Sunday, Wednesday and Friday nights at 10 o'clock, leaves next days at 5 o'clock a. m. This stage brings the Rusk, Henderson, Marshall, Shreveport and intermediate places, as well as much of Louisiana and Arkansas mail.

"The Tyler mail arrives Sunday, Wednesday and Friday, leaves next day at 5 o'clock a. m. This line brings the mail from Palestine, Waco, Dallas and all northern Texas.

"The Keechi mail arrives on Sunday and leaves on Friday at 6 o'clock. This is a horseback mail and supplies Telegraph Mills, Navarro, Keechi, Ringgold and intermediate ports.

"The Anderson mail, horseback, arrives Tuesday at 12 Noon and leaves at 1 p. m. same day. This mail supplies Madisonville,

HOUSTON COUNTY NEWSPAPERS

Elwood, Bedi, Midway, Troy and Anderson and Grimes Counties, with intermediate posts.

"The Nacogdoches horseback mail arrives on Tuesday at 12 M. and leaves at 1 p. m. same day. This mail supplies Randolph, Coltharps, Glenco, Shooks P. O. and intermediate posts.

"The Centerville mail, horseback, arrives Tuesday at 6 P. M. and leaves next day at 6 A. M. This mail supplies Centerville, Clapp's Creek, Leona, Kidd's Mills and Alto Springs, with intermediate posts.

"These are not the schedule days for the arrival and departure of several of the above mails, but the actual days they do arrive and depart; the connections are correct as they stand and we give them for the benefit of our readers.

"The Galveston mail, via Huntsville, reaches Houston on the second day after its departure from Crockett.

"The Galveston mail, via Sumpter, reaches Liberty on the second day after its departure from Crockett."

The following unusual and interesting item appears in this copy of the Crockett Printer:

"STOP THE MURDERERS !!

"My son, Miles Robinson, was, on the 21st day of May, 1860 waylaid and most brutally murdered by James L. Landrum and John W. Mathes. And at the same time and place, the same parties did with a club inflict great bodily violence upon my grandchild, Isham Tolbot, so that his life is despaired of. Now, any person arresting and delivering the above-named murderers to the Sheriff of Houston County, State of Texas, shall receive the above reward.

"Description: James L. Landrum is about 24 years of age, about 6 feet high, dark complexion and black hair, weighs about 175 pounds, has generally very weak eyes. John W. Mathes is about 23 or 24 years of age, about 6 feet 1 inch high, light complexion and light hair, weighs about 165 pounds, a great talker, and boaster, and a gambler—Elizabeth Robinson, Crockett, Texas, May 25, 1860."

The following item also has some historic value:

"TEMPLE OF HONOR

"The old stockholders of the Temple of Honor will find a cash purchaser for their entire stock in the Temple Building by applying to the subscribers.—W. F. and J. A. Corley."

HISTORY OF HOUSTON COUNTY

The following appearing in said issue of The Crockett Printer, deserves a place in Ancient History:

"NEGROES TO HIRE.—Two or three likely negroes to hire. Apply to Jas. A. Corley." (This ad is accompanied by pictures of two negroes with hoes in their hands.)

The officers and teachers in our public schools will find considerable interest in the following, which appears in this issue of The Crockett Printer:

"NOTICE TO SCHOOL TEACHERS

"Attention is directed to the following order of the county court, under the late school law. Teachers in the county who expect a benefit from the school fund, must come forward and receive a certificate, from the school board appointed by the court, to entitle them to receive from said fund.

"The State of Texas, Houston County: County Court pertaining to roads, revenues, etc. May term. May 18, '58.

"Ordered by the Court, that L. W. Cooper, William M. Taylor and Oscar Dalton be, and they are hereby appointed school examiners for Houston County to examine all persons proposing to teach public schools within the limits thereof, and upon examination, if finding them qualified to discharge the duties as such, shall grant him or her a certificate stating the branches he or she is qualified to teach.

"A true copy of the minutes.

"Given under my hand and seal of office at Crockett, this 22nd day of May, A. D. 1858.

" (L. S.)   O. C. Aldrich, Clerk"

"Our Methodist bretheren will be interested in the following item:

"The last Methodist Episcopal (Eastern) Conference, which was held at Jefferson, Cass County, appointed upon the Crockett Circuit, the Rev. J. A. Scruggs and the Rev. W. C. Collins. The late pastor on this circuit, the Rev. Samuel Lynch, has been assigned to the Mount Enterprise Circuit. It will be seen that we are to have a double 'parson power' the coming year to plough up the hardened sinners in these dry diggens of the Lord's great cotton patch."

In this issue of The Crockett Printer, of date November 11, 1860, Dawson Moore & Chapman advertise that they have made "extensive arrangements for the manufacture of brick, and are

HOUSTON COUNTY NEWSPAPERS

prepared to take contracts to do brick-laying, plastering and mason work."

E. Currie advertises that "the partnership theretofore existing between him and C. E. Ford, under the name of Currie & Ford, in the mill business is dissolved." Under date of April 4, 1860.

W. D. Hicks, professor of vocal and instrumental music advertises that he will "re-open his singing school for the winter at the Baptist Church."

In said issue of the Crockett Printer, William E. Moore advertises as attorney-at-law and land agent, office upstairs in the courthouse.

Groves M. Brazier advertises as attorney-at-law, office in the courthouse, in Col. Cooper's room.

Dr. A. J. Dawson advertises as an eclectic physician, having permanently located in Wigfall, Houston County, office at Mrs. Kennedy's.

Dr. W. H. Edwards announces that he has permanently located in Crockett and solicits a share of the public patronage, with office in the City Hotel.

Dr. J. W. Meredith announces that he has determined to make Crockett his home and offers his services to the public in the various branches of his profession, office upstairs in the house opposite Hall's Hotel.

Dr. W. L. McNeill, surgeon dentist, advertises that he has extended his regular circuit so as to embrace Crockett and will remain in Crockett during the September term of court. Office at Col. Long's Hotel.

The following advertisement may prove of interest to the many friends of early days of Judge R. N. Read:

"THE CROCKETT HOUSE

"The undersigned having recently become the proprietor of this well-known hotel, beg leave to say to the traveling public and everyone else that he intends to use every effort in his power to make it a first class No. 1 hotel.

"The table will always be furnished with the best the country affords.

"At the stable will always be found attentive hostlers to take charge of horses.

"As this will continue to be the State House, travelers will find it to their interest to put up at it.

"In addition the proprietor will keep a good supply of hacks.

"Horses and buggies to hire at all times, for the accommodation of those going off the stage route, in the country.

"Trusting that the old friends of the House will not forsake it and new ones give it a trial.—R. N. Read."

Dr. W. T. Taylor advertises as physician and practical dentist, office in Long's Hotel.

F. T. Sawyer advertises four-horse mail stages from Galveston to Crockett, and that Col. John Long is his agent at Crockett.

W. R. Smith advertises that he is the proprietor of the new stage route from Crockett to Palestine with fine four-horse coaches and careful drivers, leaves Crockett every Monday, Thursday and Saturday, and that Col. John Long is his agent at Crockett.

H. F. Craddock advertises Steam Mills, five miles East of Crockett, on Conner's Ferry road. Price of lumber $1 per 100 feet cash; $1.25 per 100 feet on credit, and will grind Wednesdays. He also advertises that he will grind wheat into the highest grade flour for one-sixth toll. He states his mill will saw 32-foot lumber if necessary.

Another advertisement is of Wortham's Steam Sawmill, five and a half miles Northwest of Crockett, near the Navarro Road. His prices are for cash: select $1.25 per 100, sheeting 50 cents per 100. He also advertises that he has a grist mill for grinding corn, and that he will grind every Saturday.

W. J. Foster & Brother advertise their cabinet shop where they keep on hand a good assortment of furniture, consisting in part of wardrobes, bedsteads, lounges, safes, cribs and tables and state: "the ladies are particularly invited to call and examine our work."

"Coffins are made at shortest notice in any style desired."

John McConnell, general blacksmithing says: "Mac considers himself too well known to praise his own work or promptness."

S. Box & Brother advertising a blacksmithing business "East of Wright's ten-pin alley, on the Nacogdoches Road," and have set "Old Claiborne to work. Claib's work is too well known to need further commendation from us."

L. C. Richardson advertises that he is prepared to execute all orders for wagon making, repairing and all kinds of cabinet work. His shop is on the corner of Rusk and Nacogdoches streets.

HOUSTON COUNTY NEWSPAPERS

J. M. Wingfield and J. F. Butts advertise a blacksmith business at Augusta.

T. W. Craddock announces to the public that he is prepared for carriage-making in all its branches. Also blacksmithing, harness-making, painting and trimming, and says that his shop is well known as "Craddock's Wheelright Shop."

The following personal item of the editor of the Crockett Printer, Oscar Dalton, sheds some light upon the controversy that resulted in his tragic death:—

"ATTACK NO. FIVE:—Another Champion in the Field: My attention has been called by a friend to an article published last week in a sheet I seldom notice, signed by one B. F. Davis. The object of the writer seems to be to impeach my evidence given at Palestine, in the case of the State against Hepperla, as well as to abuse me individually and generally for divers things I might do, as postmaster, or that I could do, would or should do in some past, present or future time.

"As far as my evidence as a witness at Palestine is concerned, the verdict of the jury is sufficient to show how twelve honest men regarded me. Then my conduct and management of the post-office has been represented and mis-represented as the department of my friends and foes, with a result quite satisfactory to me. I took and keep charge of the post-office at the request of two hundred and eighty-seven persons who signed a paper to that effect. It is well known that the profit or pay of the office is a mere nothing—at most, not equal to the expense.

"I have never been guilty of, or charged with a breach of trust or confidence reposed in me, and I do not believe that my character in this community, or any other in which I have lived can be injured by every waif that the tide of chance may drift in our midst. Therefore, I shall decline any further notice of those who wantonly, and without cause, make an attack upon me, unless I have reason to think they have some other object than mere notoriety in view.—Oscar Dalton."

The second newspaper to be published in Houston County was:

THE CROCKETT ARGUS

which began publication about the year 1857. The author has never seen a copy of this paper, and after diligent search has failed to locate a copy of same. Having information that there was a newspaper published in Crockett in 1860, by a rival editor to The Crockett Printer, an extensive search was begun to learn the name of the paper, which has been completely lost so far as the author knows.

The first information we received was from the diary of J. M. Hall, in which he mentioned the fact that the proprietor of the Argus was indebted to him for office rent. With that simple clue, search was begun for further information about the paper, and it was learned that items from the Argus had been quoted in the Clarksville Standard. After much effort, some of these were obtained and will be of sufficient historic interest to be included here. The following reference to a unique method of advertising in The Crockett Argus is taken from the Clarksville Standard under date of October 30, 1858:—

"There are people who unwisely imagine that advertisements in a newspaper, are either not read at all, or only carelessly glanced at. Our experience gives us an impression exactly the opposite of this. In agricultural communities especially, the advertisements are all carefully conned (sic).

"This brings us to the point—that the Crockett Argus, are the best papers in the State, has an advantage over most of its confreres in possessing an advertising contributor, who adds interest to its columns and pays for the privilege. We append some of his emanations—such advertisers would be valuable to any country journal, if to be found generally.

"Nole me (or my property), Tangere, I implore you!

"THE STATE OF TEXAS

"County of Houston

"Be it known to all men (and the petticoats also) by these presents, that whereas certain persons, at the instigation of— I will not name the old rascal—are not having the fear of anything good before their eyes, have, in place of saying their prayers like good boys, concocted and put in circulation reports to this effect, viz: That I have been selling, alienating, enfoeffing and otherwise conveying my lands and hereditaments, and my colored bipeds, vulgarly yclept 'niggers.' Now, although I am a shade over twenty-one years of age; think I have a pretty good modicum or hard horse-sense; consider myself strictly compos mentis, as there has not been a writ of 'de lunatico inquirendo' instituted in the premises, yet I will acknowledge their authority and plead guilty. 'I have done the deed,' but will promise not to do so pro temporat forturo, unless it suits me! Lest there should be any misconceptions, anxieties, tribulations or other bad feelings, impress on the minds of my good friends and self-constituted guardians, on my behalf, I conceive it my duty to apprize them that I have in my noddle for some time past some crude notions of perigrinations by 'flood and field,' and it is highly probable that I shall carry some of them into execution.

"Imprimis: I think of taking my daughter to Live Oak Seminary, in Washington County—a first rate school—and the principal is a genuine Presbyterian. But hush! not a word about the pig, for some of my hard-shell or methodist friends may be taxing me with sectarianism!—Again: In my cogitations and ratiocinations, I have concluded it to be my duty to accompany my wife on a visit to her mother (very old and infirm) in Tuscumbia, North Alabama in November proximo, but fully calculate on achieving the trip within twenty-five days, as business matters will imperiously demand my presence at home, for I am importing a bully stock of goods—you'd better believe it— and, as for prices, I will astonish the 'natives.'

"As I have made clean breast of it, I beg you will not, during my absence, be harpies snort usis, fiery faces, or coram boguses issued against me—nor yet be taken out letters of administration on my estate, as has been done in our vicinity, for if my life and health be spared, I will come back to you like a bad six-pence! As one of my neighbors is reported to have said 'I will stay with you until a certain hot place (which shall be nameless) will freeze over four feet thick! Like poor old Joel D. I was here first, and it will not be my fault if I am not here last.

"THOMAS P. COLLINS.

"N. B.—I was one of the 'vagrants' who voted for James H. Bell, for associate judge to the captain's office and settle, or at least make a good showing. 'Necessitus legem nullam habet.'

"THO. P. COLLINS.

"Crockett, Texas, April 17, 1858."
"Request—Special and earnest.

All persons writing to me, would confer a superlative favor by addressing their letters thus, 'General Collins,' and this stretch of courtesy would cost them nothing, at least in a pecuniary point of view. I have never really ranked as high as a corporal yet the title, or prefix, of General is a very pleasing handle to a man's name, particularly when traveling and it costs the donor nihil; my reasons for this request is there is a person named J. P. Collins residing in Crockett, and frequently newspapers and letters, although intended for me, but not plainly superscribed, fall into his hands and are opened.

"Now, although I am a married man, and nearly up to the notch of three score years, and do not of course, look for any love letters, billet-dous, or other such morceaux, nor is there anything treasonable in my correspondence, but it is somewhat unpleasant to have the cream taken off my papers and letters before they reach my hands, and I feel under a Himalaya of gratitude to all those acceding to my request.

THO. P. COLLINS."

"Crockett, Texas, May 1, 1858."

These are only a part of the writer's contributions, to be found in the Argus of the 16th.—Journalists sometimes go back to papers issued in revolutionary, or anti-revolutionary times, for quaint advertisements, tending to show the peculiarities of the people of those days. These are quite as amusing as any of the old researches that we have seen.

Under date of July 10, 1858, the Clarksville Standard has this to say about The Crockett Argus:

"We find on our table, the Crockett Argus, and the Indianola Courier, both but a few weeks old, and both journals of creditable appearance and well edited. We wish them success in the not unusually very profitable path of journalism."

During the year 1859 there was a warm political contest between Sam Houston and H. R. Runnels for the governorship of Texas. The Texas Republican, a paper published at Marshall, Texas, under date of September 10, 1859, published a list of Texas newspapers showing their support for the respective candidates. The Crockett Argus is listed as supporting Runnels for governor, and as surprising as it may seem, the Huntsville Item is also listed in the Runnels column. The Trinity Advocate and Tyler Reporter are also placed in the Runnels column while the Centerville Herald, the Nacogdoches Chronicle, the Henderson Era, the Rusk Enquirer, are placed in the Houston column. As a matter of history in that campaign, Sam Houston was successful, after having been defeated by Runnels in a former campaign.

Succeeding the Crocket Printer and the Crockett Argus, the next paper published in Crockett was

HOUSTON COUNTY NEWSPAPERS

THE CROCKETT SENTINEL

This paper began publication about September, 1865. The following appears in an issue, under date of March 3, 1868:

"The Crockett Sentinel, A. D. Elam, editor; Leaverton & Hall, publishers. New series. Crockett, Houston County, Texas, March 3, 1868. Vol. III, No. 21."

The editor, A. D. Elam, married the oldest daughter of A. T. Monroe, Sara Jane Monroe, and later was elected a member of the Texas Legislature. He was an ardent Democrat while his father-in-law, A. T. Monroe, was a prominent member of the Republican party.

The publishers, Leaverton & Hall, were G. W. Leaverton, or Wash Leaverton, as he was generally known, and Charlie Hall, a brother of Mrs. John Shivers. The proprietors were A. D. Elam & Company. We do not know who constituted the members of the firm, except A. D. Elam. The terms of subscription were one copy, 12 months, $2.50; one copy 6 months, $1.50; one copy 4 months, $1; single copies, 10c.

The rates for announcements of candidates were $10 for State and district offices, and $5 for county offices. U. S. currency taken at market rates.

The agents of the Sentinel were Z. B. John, Cochino Bayou; C. H. Davis, Shiloh; Kyle & Aldrich, Augusta; and Col. C. C. Taliaferro was requested to act as agent at Sumpter, in Trinity County.

The following significant statement is made in this issue of the Sentinel:

"To meet the stringency of the times and to extend the circulation of The Sentinel we will in future receive corn, pork, bacon, potatoes, eggs, chickens, or butter for subscription."

The following item reflects the labor situation at that time:

"In the State of Mississippi the best hands hire for from five to seven dollars currency per month, with three and a half pounds of meat and a peck of meal per week, the laborers furnishing their own families. This is quite as much as they are worth, although our farmers pay from twelve to fifteen dollars specie. This is ruinous, as has been clearly proven by the experience of the last three years. Notwithstanding the proofs the high prices for labor are maintained, and unless soon corrected the planting community will be universally bankrupted."

The following personal item relating to one of Crockett's most prominent citizens and his family, will be of interest not only to the family of that citizen, but also to all the people of Crockett:

"PERSONAL—After an absence protracted over three months, of Capt. D. A. Nunn, lady and child, on a visit to friends in the State of Mississippi, they reached Crockett on Saturday last, all much improved in health by the trip. They met a warm greeting from their many friends on their return. The Captain will be on hand at our district court to attend to the interests of his clients. He represents affairs in a most unsatisfactory state in Mississippi. The people are despondent, taking no interest in politics, and of money, there is none. On the route home he noticed some improvements on farms going on, with an apparent desire on the part of freedmen to make a living. He thinks Texas far better off than any part of the country that he has seen."

When it is remembered that so many Crockett citizens and citizens of Houston County were members of Hood's Texas Brigade, including W. D. Pritchard, W. B. Wall, Gus Aldrich, Col. Aldrich, G. B. Lundy, W. J. Foster and many others, and that also included in this brigade was Russell Crawford Mitchell, the grandfather of Margaret Mitchell, who enlisted at Alto, Texas, the following item from this issue of the Crockett Sentinel will be a matter of interest to the present generation:

"PERSONAL—General John B. Hood was in town the past week. His health seemed quite good. On political subjects the general has but little to say,—but exhibits an evident feeling of despondency. And well may be, for never has the political horizon of any nation been so overspersed with lowering clouds of destruction as ours. The old ship of State has got among the breakers and if she does not go to pieces and become a complete wreck, the multitudes have not judgment."

The following advertisement will furnish news to the majority of the people of Crockett, who never knew that the dissolved firm ever existed:

"DISSOLUTION

"From and after this date the co-partnership heretofore existing between Murchison and Rainey, is this day by mutual consent dissolved and will be continued by Murchison & Arledge who will settle all claims with the late firm. Please call and settle up. We will pay the gold for cotton and hides. Crockett, Texas, Jan. 1, '68."

The Crockett Sentinel was fearless in dealing with violations

HOUSTON COUNTY NEWSPAPERS

of the law. A killing had occurred in Crockett and the Sentinel gave the following straight-forward opinion of the matter:

"COLD-BLOODED HOMICIDE.

"On yesterday (Monday), about 4-1/2 o'clock p. m. our community was shocked by one of the most unmitigated and cold-blooded murders ever perpetrated in our midst. The life of Henry T. Driskill, an honest, whole-souled, hardworking clever gentleman was foully taken by a reckless wretch, named Ed. Wingate, a son of old Ned Wingate.

"Some three months since, Frank Wingate, a brother of the murderer was arrested on a charge of killing a negro by Maj. Reinhard the bureau agent of this county. On the representation of some of our citizens, Reinhard was induced to release Frank Wingate on bail. Old Ned Wingate becoming one of the sureties on the bond. This release was secured only that Frank Wingate might make an escape, which he did. Reinhard took summary action to recover the bond. An order was issued to Marshall McDaniel to seize upon the effects of old Ned Wingate, which, after calling to his aid proper assistance, Driskill being one of the party, the marshall proceeded to execute the order. And from that time he was spotted by the Wingate clan. Old Ned Wingate had threatened the lives of Maj. Reinhard, bureau agent; U. S. Marshall H. G. McDaniel, H. T. Driskill and E. L. Dorsett and there is no question but what with the third party, they came to town yesterday to execute that threat, and as the sequel proves too well, have accomplished their hellish purpose.

"Henry Driskill sleeps that last long sleep of death, while the foul fiend who ended his existence breathes in health and gloats over the blood he shed. His presence alone is a curse to our land and the honest indignation of the people should terminate his worthless existence and, if necessary, exterminate the party and thus vindicate itself from our rage and wrong.

"Mr. Driskill had been to the post-office and on returning, when about the saloon of M. Helms, some words passed between him and the murderer, he being on the opposite side of the street, and Driskill started across the street towards Wingate who threatened if he did not stop he would shoot him. Driskill, catching hold of both sides of his coat collar and opened it, told Wingate to shoot, that he had nothing. He was entirely unarmed and offered no resistance to Wingate, who as Driskill continued to walk toward him, drew his revolver and shot poor Driskill, the first ball taking effect in the collarbone and lodging, perhaps in the shoulder, and the other struck about the right temple, and passed through the body.

"After being shot Mr. Driskill turned back across the street, entered Mr. Helms barber shop, remarked that his arm was broken, and it being observed that he was about to fall he was caught by friends and eased to the floor, and expired in about two minutes. Thus ended the career of a brave and good man.

"Life after life has been taken by this party, yet not one has been punished. It is time that something was done, that something must be done by the united action of the community, for there is no law in this land to punish such reprobates. The sooner it is done, the better for the safety of the community.

"Mr. Driskill has been married a little over two months, his wife was one of the most estimable ladies of our town, who is now a weeping and desolate widow."

The Sentinel evidently reflected upon the plainness and bluntness of the preceding account of the killing of Henry T. Driskill, for in the next issue of the paper we find the following:

"We have been reminded by those who listened to the testimony in the examining trial of Edward Wingate for the murder of Henry T. Driskill that our animadversions in our last issue, on the affair were entirely too severe and that circumstances did not warrant the expression of "cold-blooded" murder that we used. We are even told by an attorney that interested himself in the defense that it was a case of justifiable homicide, but from what we know of the evidence we can not see it in that light. We are free to admit that Mr. Driskill acted rashly, but as he did not make an attack on the man Wingate, was unarmed, had not even touched the hem of a garment, how, we ask, could the killing be justifiable? Driskill had said in the hearing of young Wingate that he had intended to drive the party from town, but there is no evidence that he knew the party, who courting an opportunity to wreak his vengeance, proclaims that he was a son of old man Wingate and that he could not be driven away. But it is needless to say more, for 24 hours after any murder in Texas, the popular voice proclaims for the innocence of the offender. This is a sad but true commentary."

Because the name of the outstanding citizen, who contituted

HOUSTON COUNTY NEWSPAPERS

the jury inquest, on the death of Henry T. Driskill, we here include the same in full, as follows:

"COUNTY OF HOUSTON.

"The undersigned, a jury of inquest to examine the causes of the death of Henry T. Driskill, having the testimony of the witnesses and examined the body of said Driskill, do pronounce the following verdict, to-wit: That Henry T. Driskill came to his death on the evening of the second day of March, A. D. 1868 in the Town of Crockett, Houston County, State of Texas, by pistol shots fired by one Edward Wingate, he having fired a six-shooter twice at the said Driskill, both shots taking effect in the breast of the said Driskill which was the cause of his death.

"IN TESTIMONY whereof the coroner and jurors have hereunto set our hands this 3rd day of March, A. D. 1868.

"J. H. Stuart, John T. Cook, B. F. Frymier,
"K. Murchison, J. P. Acting Coroner.
"T. W. Craddock, W. D. Bryan, J. W. McGill, Jury."

In the same issue of the Sentinel appeared the following notice:

"MARRIED—Driskill-Milling. Tuesday evening, March 3rd, 1868, at the residence of the bride's father, Mr. Robert Milling, by Judge James M. Odell, Mr. R. C. Driskill of Leon County and Miss Mary Milling of Houston County."

Another issue of the Crockett Sentinel published under date of Nov. 17, 1868, being Vol. IV, No. 6, contains very little local news, or items of general interest. Attention is called to a few items, however:

It is stated that Mr. Murchison, we do not know which one, supplied Crockett merchants with spun yarn from his factory in Mound Prairie. Our opinion is that this Mr. Murchison resided in the Northern part of Houston County, and that the Mound Prairie spoken of is the prairie adjoining Houston's Mound.

An editorial expressed an opinion on Grant's unfitness as a presidential candidate, which opinion was based on the remark

HISTORY OF HOUSTON COUNTY

of Horace Greely, that Grant was neither a general nor a Statesman.

On page 2, of this issue, there appears an advertisement of the U. S. Mail State Line between Bryan and Crockett, containing the statement that there would be no night travel.

This issue also contains a reconstruction joke, as follows: "The coming men—Grant and the tax collector."

There is also an advertisement of "THE BURNETT HOUSE, Mrs. M. J. Brown, proprietress."

THE QUIDNUNC.

Contemporary with the Crockett Sentinel, or perhaps just a little later, a paper was published in Crockett called "The Quidnunc" by Judge James R. Burnett. As no copy of this paper is available, we must content ourselves with the simple statement that such a paper was published soon after the Civil War.

THE HOUSTON COUNTY HERALD

Sometime between 1870 and 1880, a paper was published in Crockett, called The Houston County Herald, but no copy is available, and we can do nothing more than mention the bare facts that such a paper was published, and that it was distinctly democratic. It was ably edited and some of our most prominent citizens contributed both to its editorial matter and financial support.

THE CROCKETT PATRON

A paper by the name of The Crockett Patron was published in Crockett about 1880, and our recollection is that it was founded by E. A. Gause, and carried on later by Dr. P. W. Archer. No copy of this paper is available.

THE ECONOMIST

A paper by the name of The Economist was published in Crockett from about 1880 to 1890. It was probably established

HOUSTON COUNTY NEWSPAPERS

by Professor G. J. Nunn, and later was published successively by Judge A. D. Lipscomb, Gause & Aldrich, Dabney White and by Albert Wortham, and discontinued publication while in his hands.

THE CROCKETT COURIER

The Crockett Courier was established by Honorable W. B. Page in January 1890. Giles M. Haltom being the publisher. It was first published under the name of The Crockett Weekly Courier. In an issue of this paper published under date of January 29, 1892, the Church Directory showed the following: Methodist, J. T. Dawson, pastor; Baptist, W. M. Gaddy, pastor; Presbyterian, S. F. Tenny, pastor. The Court Directory showed: Hon. F. A. Williams, district judge; W. H. McGill, district attorney; W. A. Champion, district clerk; W. A. Davis, county judge; John I. Moore, county attorney; A. J. C. Dunnam, county clerk; F. H. Bayne, sheriff; M. M. Baker, county treasurer; Charles Stokes, tax assessor; Charles Long, tax collector; Enoch Broxson, county surveyor. This issue contains an obituary of Captain John H. Wootters, and also one of W. P. Collins. As the Courier is now being published every week by its enterprising editor and proprietor, W. W. Aiken, and our readers are familiar with it, it needs no further mention here.

THE CROCKETT ENTERPRISE

The Crockett Enterprise was established in Crockett in 1896, by Tom M. Bowers, who had his office in the Stokes building, northwest corner of the public square. It was published for only a short time, when Col. Bowers returned to his former home in Henderson, Texas.

THE HOUSTON COUNTY TIMES

The Houston County Times was established February 16, 1906, by Gus Goolsby, who was owner and publisher until his death and was later carried on by his widow, until she married Thomas J. Welch, who published the paper until his death, and is now being published by his son, T. J. Welch, Jr.

HISTORY OF HOUSTON COUNTY

THE GRAPELAND MESSENGER

A splendid paper has been published for many years under the able management of A. H. Luker, who still carries on with one of the best county papers in Texas. Mr. Luker also published from his Grapeland office the Lovelady Enterprise, which is a creditable paper, and disclosed the fact that Editor Luker is a real newspaperman.

THE CROCKETT DEMOCRAT

The most recent publication established in Crockett is the Crockett Democrat, published by Henry J. Paul, and is a worthy competitor of other papers now being published in Houston County

All together Houston County has contributed her share of able newspapers and deserves high rank among all the counties of the State.

CHAPTER V

Schools in Houston County

No authentic information can be found about the earliest school in Houston County. All schools taught in Houston County prior to and during the Civil War were private schools. No public school system had been established prior to the close of the Civil War.

TRINITY COLLEGE

There probably were a few scattered schools in the county prior to 1841, but no record exists of any such schools. On January 30, 1841, the Congress of the Republic of Texas passed an act entitled "An Act to Establish and Incorporate Trinity College" which reads in part as follows:

"Sec. 1. Be it enacted by the Senate and House of Representatives of the Republic of Texas, in Congress assembled, that a seminary of learning be, and the same is hereby established at Alabama, in Houston County, to be denominated the 'Trinity College.'

"Sec. 2. Be it further enacted, That there shall be eleven trustees, who are hereby authorized to take charge of the interests of the college; and a majority of the whole number shall constitute a quorum to do business.

"Sec. 3. Be it further enacted, That the following persons have been duly chosen trustees of the college, and are recognized as such, viz: G. W. Grant, Jacob Allbright, George Pruitt, Collin Aldrich, Elisha Clapp, John Wortham, Isaac Parker, Ralph Nelson, Elijah Gossett, William Clark and James Carr.

"Sec. 4. Be it further enacted, That the trustees aforesaid be, and they are hereby constituted a body politic and corporate, in deed and in law, by the name of 'The President and Trustees of Trinity College,' and by that name they and their successors shall and may have succession, and exercise the privileges granted herein, for the term of twenty years, and no longer; and be able and capable in law to have, receive and enjoy, to them and their successors, land, tenements, hereditaments of any kind whatsoever; and also all sums of money which may be given, granted or bequeathed to them, for the purpose of promoting the interests of the said college; provided, that the property owned by the body corporate under the provisions of this act, shall at no time exceed in value the amount of one hundred thousand dollars, over and above the buildings, apparatus, and library."

The Act establishing the above-mentioned college, contains seventeen sections, which relate to the government of the college and to the powers of the trustees. These all indicate that the framers of this charter were educated men and had a clear conception of what an ideal college should be.

It is not certainly known that Trinity College was ever really organized as an institution of learning. It is reasonable to believe that some kind of educational institution existed at Alabama, in Houston County ,at the time this charter was enacted. The Act was signed as follows: "David S. Kaufman, speaker of the House of Representatives; Anson Jones, President pro tem. of the Senate. Approved January 30th, 1841. David G. Burnet."

It should be a matter of interest to the people of Houston County that among the names of the trustees originally selected appear the names of Collin Aldrich, first chief justice of Houston County; Jacob Allbright, first county clerk of Houston County; Elijah Gossett, another chief justice of Houston County, in an early day; Elisha Clapp, a most distinguished pioneer and Indian fighter; and John Wortham, who had a distinguished share in the development of Houston County, having rendered distinguished service in the military department, and Isaac Parker, who was a congressman from Houston County during almost the entire period of the Republic, and later a prominent representative in the Legislature of the State of Texas. These men were all worthy pioneers, who came to Texas imbued with the idea of securing the independence of the Republic, and whose memories deserve to be perpetuated. Some of them had a high degree of education and were educationally-minded during the very infancy of the Republic. It should be remembered that this charter was granted less than five years after the Declaration of Independence was signed at old Washington.

OTHER SCHOOLS

It is not certain where the next school was taught in Houston County. It is probable that there were several private schools in different portions of the county during the last days of the Republic and the early days of the State after annexation.

SCHOOLS IN HOUSTON COUNTY

C. H. DAVIS

C. H. Davis was one of the early teachers of the county and was living in Houston County as early as 1851, as shown by the account book of Thomas P. Collins. The purchases he made, at that time, indicate that he was teaching school, either in Crockett or at some other point in the county. He taught at Old Pleasant Grove and at Shiloh, during the days of the stage coaches. It is difficult to designate the exact time when these schools were taught, but C. H. Davis was one of the early educators of the county.

MRS. H. B. DILLINGHAM

About 1858 to 1860, Mrs. H. B. Dillingham, a sister of Collin Aldrich, a pioneer of the county, taught school in Crockett at an old school house, either on the southwest corner of the town of Crockett, or at a point near by, South of that point. There are indications that there was a log school house near where the Jim Smith Memorial Hospital now stands, and that school was taught in this building by Mrs. H. B. Dillingham and perhaps, earlier, by L. E. Downes.

OLD RANDOLPH SCHOOL

It may be that school was taught at Old Randolph prior to the year 1855, as there was a school house there prior to that time. However, the first school of which we have any authentic information was taught at Old Randolph by Judge Samuel M. Thompson, during the years 1855 and 1856. Judge Thompson moved to Old Randolph in 1855 and was furnished a house for himself and family and the old log schoolhouse in which he taught school during the years 1855 and 1856. The next teacher for Old Randolph School was a man by the name of Wiley who taught there in 1857. Among the well-known citizens of Houston County who were students under Judge Thompson in 1855 and 1856 were Gus Aldrich and Tom Vaughn. They both entered the Confederate Army in 1861 and went to Virginia as a part of Hood's Brigade. We do not know who taught school at Old Randolph subsequent to 1857, although it is probable that others taught school there.

HISTORY OF HOUSTON COUNTY

COCHINO SCHOOL

In 1864 there was a settlement on Cochino Bayou consisting of farmers with slaves, who constituted the backbone of the community. Among these were Dr. W. W. Adair, Rough Kennedy, James McLemore and a man by the name of Kitchens. These men engaged Judge S. M. Thompson to teach their school in 1864, paying him in corn. The school house was a small log cabin, with puncheon floor, situated just South of where Kennard State Bank now stands, on the old Dodson Road. The log cabin school house was so shabby and disreputable looking, that many of the pupils belonging to aristocratic families, rebelled against the school house and resolved to burn it down. Judge Thompson received a tip from one of the students and knew of their plan to set fire to the building and hid himself in the school building. When the young conspirators appeared to carry out their scheme, they were suddenly confronted by Judge Thompson, who had them brought before the trustees of the school. They were tried by a kangaroo court and convicted, but their energetic protest resulted in the trustees agreeing to build a new schoolhouse, which they promptly proceeded to do, erecting a house of sawed lumber, situated near the old Cicero Dupuy home. It will be interesting to know who these young students were who made their bold protest against the schoolhouse. Some of them were: Porter Thompson, son of Judge Thompson; George Adair, Billy Adair, Columbus West, Dump McLemore and George Dodson. There may have been others.

OLD PLEASANT GROVE SCHOOL

Prior to 1857, there was an old log schoolhouse at Pleasant Grove made of round pine logs. It is not known who taught school in this old log house, but sometime prior to 1857, a new two-story schoolhouse was erected, the school being taught in the lower story and the upper story was used as a Masonic Lodge. C. H. Davis taught school in this schoolhouse in 1857, and school was taught there in 1858, by James Moore, at which time T. W. Thompson, his brother, Porter Thompson and Sally Thompson, later Mrs. G. B. Lundy attended school under James Moore. Later, the school was taught by a Mr. Wilkerson when the children of John F. Arledge, Captain John English, Arch English and R. B. S. Owens attended the same.

SCHOOLS IN HOUSTON COUNTY

OWENS SCHOOL

A little schoolhouse was built on the farm of R. B. S. Owens about eight miles East of Crockett, and situated a short distance South of the old Owens home. It is not known how many people taught school in that schoolhouse, but a school was taught there in the fall and winter of 1865 by Mark Miller, afterwards county surveyor of Houston County, and also postmaster, and T. W. Thompson, his brother, Porter Thompson, Mrs. Sally Lundy and at least one of the children of Uncle Billy Stanton, Miss Kate Stanton, afterwards the wife of Billy Beavers, attended the school.

OLD SHILOH SCHOOL

Old Shiloh is principally noted for the camp meetings that were held there in the early days. Old families would go there and camp out for a week at a time, and preaching would be held day and night. Many big revivals were held at that place. As early as 1868 a school was taught there, but as the school was close to the mail route between Crockett and Huntsville, some traveling was done on the stagecoach by pupils of C. H. Davis. Miss Florence Johnson, now Mrs. Florence J. Arledge, attended this school in her girlhood and traveled on the stagecoach to Crockett. For many years school was taught at Old Shiloh but we will not undertake to give a list of the teachers since the days of C. H. Davis.

CROCKETT SCHOOLS

It is not known by the writer who taught the first school in Crockett, but evidently some schools were taught long prior to the Civil War. Mention has already been made of a school taught by L. E. Downes near his old home on the Southwest corner of the pubic square, and later by Mrs. H. B. Dillingham, probably in the same old schoolhouse. It is not known who taught school at that place last.

A substantial school building was erected one-half mile East of the courthouse about 1855, which was known for many years as the Crockett Academy. Some schools were taught in that building, but the names of the early teachers are not known.

One maiden schoolteacher from the North taught school there and during the time she was there, something was said or published by General Thomas P. Collins about her which resulted in a suit for damages, in which she recovered a substantial sum. About the beginning of the Civil War, Mrs. Helen Nunn, wife of Col. D. A. Nunn, taught school there and some of our oldest citizens were her pupils, including Mrs. Nan Hail and Mrs. Bella Romain. It was in this building that in January 1871, Major John Spence began the first well organized and equipped school that Crockett ever had. He taught until June, 1873, when he entered the practice of law and was succeeded by Hon. W. B. Page, who taught a very successful school for many years. He was later elected State Senator and then in 1890 began the publication of the Crockett Courier. He was succeeded in this school by a Professor G. J. Nunn, who presided over the schools for a number of years. The Crockett Academy continued to be used as a school building until the corporation of the City of Crockett was revived about 1890, and a new school building was erected on the campus where our present grammar school now stands. In this school a number of distinguished educators presided as superintendent, including: Walker King, E. A. Pace, C. E. Godbey, Donald McDonald, I. J. Deck, and is now presided over by W. L. Jordan. No attempt is made to give a full list of the superintendents and distinguished teachers who had a share in making this an outstanding school. Among those who taught there were Mrs. A. R. Spence and Mrs. Lucy Collins, who both had a large share in the educational program of Crockett.

PROFESSOR J. W. BARROW

As early as January 1868, a school was taught in the old Baptist Church building, where Miss Lena Woodson's home now stands, and the following advertisement appears in the Crockett Sentinel in its issue of March 3rd, 1868:

"CROCKETT HIGH SCHOOL

(For Both Sexes)

"J. W. Barrow, A. M., principal and professor of Latin and Greek, French, Algebra, Geometry, etc.

SCHOOLS IN HOUSTON COUNTY

"Prof. C. W. Edmiston has charge of the Intermediate Department.

"Mrs. Allie Barrow, the Primary Department.

"_____, professor of vocal and instrumental music.

"This institution will be open for the reception of students on the 6th of January. The location is healthy; the community highly moral.

"There is a flourishing Sabbath School;

"Preaching regular and often; as a centrality, Crockett has few, if any equals, in the State. As to enlightment, it has vast advantage. Sectarianism discarded. Students received at any time and charged from date of entrance to close of session. A deduction will be made for protracted sickness. Good board easily obtained at from $9.00 to $15.00 per month.

"Patrons, visit us.

"Rates of tuition in specie or its equivalent per session of five months.

"Orthography, Reading, $10.00; Spelling and reading, primary arithmetic, and geography, $12.50; Advanced Arithmetic, grammar, history, natural philosophy, rhetoric, logic, etc., $15.00; Astronomy, botany, chemistry, geology, geometry, surveying, Latin, Greek or French, $10.00; Music on piano or guitar, $30.00; Patrons and friends of education, visit our school. Crockett, Texas. January 7th."

Among the early teachers in the old Crockett Academy were Mr. Edward A. Gause, and his sister, Mrs. Mary E. McColl. They taught there in 1866, and later. Prior to that time it was a difficult matter for teachers to control their older students. There were a number of unruly boys nearly grown who took pride in disobeying the rules established by teachers and breaking up schools. Mr. Gause had heard of these pranks on the part of the older boys and determined upon what course he would pursue. He had been forewarned what to expect. On a certain day one of the unruly students, Oscar Burnett, decided he would purposely disobey the rules and defy Mr. Gause to inflict the proper punishment. As a result, when Mr. Gause and his sister came to the old academy on that morning he brought his pistol and laid it on the desk. The boys also came prepared for the difficulty, but had such simple weapons as sticks and stones. At the proper time Mr. Gause called the refractory Oscar Burnett to take his punishment which was to be a severe whipping with a switch. He refused to respond so Mr. Gause seized him and took him into the smaller room of the school building and was inflicting the usual punishment on him, when some of the other boys said, "Boys are we going to let him kill him?" Then it was that Mrs. McColl with the pistol that had been lying on the desk commanded the boys to remain where they were. They read determination in her looks and refrained from taking part in the matter. The result of this experience was that Mr. Gause had no more trouble in controlling his school.

This incident may seem frivolous for a place in history, but the author believes that it marks an epoch in the history of Houston County schools.

Mrs. McColl later taught school about five miles North of Crockett, probably at the old Bethel Church, near Murdock Murchison's home, and boarded in the Murdock Murchison home.

Mr. Gause later founded the East Texas Patron, which he published for some years, and later sold to Dr. F. W. Archer, who conducted the same until he disposed of it to Professor G. J. Nunn. Mr. Gause was born in Alabama on May 8, 1819 and came to Crockett in 1866, when he purchased the home where he lived and died, which is now known as the home of Mrs. H. J. Phillips.

PENNINGTON SCHOOL

Another school that was located in what is now the town of Pennington, in Trinity County, Texas, in territory that was originally included in Houston County, was being taught as early as January 7, 1867, as will appear from the following advertisement in the Crockett Sentinel published on March 3, 1868:

"PENNINGTON MALE AND FEMALE INSTITUTION

"The exercises of this institution will commence Monday, January 13, 1868.

"RATES OF TUITION PER SESSION OF SIX MONTHS

"Orthography, reading and writing, $12.00; English grammar, geography and arithmetic, $18.00; philosophy, chemistry, rhetoric, &c. Latin & Greek languages and advanced mathematics, $24.00; music on piano with use of instrument, $36.00; incidental expenses per pupil $1.00.

"The above rates payable in specie. Pupils charged from the time of entrance to close of session. No deduction made

SCHOOLS IN HOUSTON COUNTY

for the time of entrance to close of session. No deductions made for absence, except in cases of protracted sickness. This institution is located in a healthy section of the country, surrounded by an intelligent population and no pains will be spared by Teachers and Trustees to make this one of the First Institutions of the State. Board can be obtained at reasonable rates. John J. A. Patton, principal; Mrs. M. E. Patton, associate. Pennington, Texas. Jan. 7, 1867."

Mention has been made of the Cochino school, taught by Judge S. M. Thompson. This school was later taught by a daughter of Judge Thompson, Dolly Thompson, who is now Mrs. W. B. Worthington. Later, the community formerly known as Cochino became the site of the present Town of Kennard, and the school has been maintained there ever since.

KENNARD SCHOOL

About the year 1898 or 1899, Miss Ernestine Myricks was called to teach the Kennard School. While teaching there she married A. J. McLemore, a son of James McLemore, one of the original patrons of the school taught at Cochino by Judge Thompson. Mrs. Dump McLemore, after the death of her husband, moved to Crockett and taught in the city schools of Crockett. The Kennard School has grown into one of the large outstanding schools of the county. Several adjacent country-schools have consolidated with the Kennard school until it has developed into a large educational institution, employing a large number of teachers and is now under the management of Professor Earle Bland.

THE HEFLIN SCHOOL

About the year 1870 or 1871, a school was taught about two miles Southwest of Crockett by a teacher by the name of Andrew Hassell. He was a brother of our well-known townsman, and former city marshall, Charles Hassell. He was a young, unmarried man when teaching the Heflin school and attracted the attention of Dr. S. F. Tenney, at that time pastor of the First Presbyterian Church of Crockett. Dr. Tenney, taking quite an interest in the young man, persuaded him to study for the ministry, and fortunately, knowing a benevolent friend who wanted to aid a ministerial student, obtained for Mr. Hassell some financial help which enabled him to attend a theological seminary and fit himself for the ministry. He became a very useful and able minister of the Southern Presbyterian Church, and was the father of two sons who also became ministers of the gospel. One of these, J. W. Hassell, commonly known as Woodrow Hassell, spent many years as a missionary in the East, and later came to Texas, and was stationed at McAllen in the Rio Grande Valley. He is still engaged in ministerial work in some other State. The other son was Rev. A. P. Hassell, who has been for many years a missionary in China and is still laboring there, and underwent some trying experiences during the war between Japan and China. He is one of the brave missionaries who refused to desert his post, even in the face of great dangers and the risk of his own life.

THE OAKLAND SCHOOL

It is not certainly known who was the first teacher at the Oakland school, but Miss Bunnie Arrington taught the school for a number of years and some of our best-known citizens were pupils under her teaching. This school is situated about eight miles West from Crockett on the Porter Springs road. Other teachers followed Miss Arrington at this school, but now the old building in which school was taught, no longer exists.

PORTER SPRINGS SCHOOL

A school has been maintained at Porter Springs from very early times. The first teacher of that school is not known, but among the early teachers was the widow of John H. Potts, Mrs. Graves, who later married Captain T. J. Pridgen, and who died while making her home in the Porter Springs community. Her husband, Captain T. J. Pridgen, was for many years justice of the peace at Porter Springs. One of the outstanding teachers of the Porter Springs school was Professor Thompson, a highly educated man and an able teacher, and his reputation as a teacher was very high, and he will long be remembered by the older citizens of the Porter Springs community. He died while engaged in his work as teacher of that school. During the time of the above-named teachers, the building in which the school

SCHOOLS IN HOUSTON COUNTY

was conducted was a simple wooden building, but now a splendid brick building has been erected there and a high grade school is being conducted by a succession of able teachers. This school is one of the best in the county.

OLD CORINTH SCHOOL

This school was situated near what is known now as the Center Hill Community near Kennard, composed largely of the Morgan, Julian, Maples, Harrison and West families. In 1857 this school was taught by Miss Dollie Thompson, now Mrs. W. B. Worthington, who made trips back and forth from her school to her home on horseback. Either her father or brother would ride horseback to the school, leading another horse for her to ride on her return journey. On one occasion a heavy downpour of rain compelled her and her pupils to remain in the school building for the entire night. Mr. Dan Morgan, an oldtimer, now dead, remained at the schoolhouse also, as protector. Old Corinth has now disappeared and was succeeded by the Center Hill School, and that in turn was consolidated with the Kennard school.

JONES SCHOOL HOUSE

This school was originally taught in a one-room, log schoolhouse, about ten miles northeast of Crockett on the old Rusk road. The school building was situated directly across the road from the home of Jim Monroe, a son of Col. A. T. Monroe. This school was first taught by John Ed Smith, who later resided in Crockett and then moved to Groveton. About 1875 or 1876 this school was taught by John Howard for several years. He later moved to Crockett and became cashier of the G. W. Roberts Bank, and in 1877 married a Crockett lady, and a few days afterwards absconded to Canada or elsewhere, with the funds of the bank. This school was later taught by Miss Mollie Moore, a member of a well-known Crockett family. A number of years ago the site of the schoolhouse was changed and now there stands a substantial school building and equipment known as the Jones School House, about nine miles northeast of Crockett, where a successful school has been maintained for many years.

HISTORY OF HOUSTON COUNTY

AUGUSTA SCHOOL

We have no record of the earliest school taught at Augusta but in the Crockett Printer of November 14, 1860, it is shown that W. M. Waddell taught a school at Augusta and had the following advertisements in the Crockett Printer:

"AUGUSTA MALE AND FEMALE ACADEMY

"This second session of this academy will commence on the first Monday of October, 1860. Under the supervision of Mr. and Mrs. Waddell.

"Rates of Tuition:

"Orthography, Reading, Writing, Primary Geography, Higher Arithmetic, English, Grammar, History, Chemistry, Philosophy, Composition, Etc. $30.00.
"Higher branches Latin and French, $40.00.
"Incidental expenses, $50.00.
"Students will be charged from the time of entrance until the close of the session, and no deduction except in cases of protracted sickness.
"Board can be had in the town and in families in the vicinity —the principal will take some twelve students as boarders, if applications be made early. At the end of the first five months a vacation of four weeks will be given. To parents and guardians who wish the advantage of a retired locality, and who are desirous of securing to their children the advantages of a sound, moral discipline and practical education, Augusta affords many advantages.

"W. M. WADDELL, Principal.

"Argus please copy."

It is not known that school was taught at Augusta during the Civil War, but probably some effort was made to carry on a school there during that period. Sometime after the Civil War, the Rev. Kilpatrick was superintendent of the school at Augusta. He was the grandfather of our recently nominated State senator, Honorable Clem Fain, and Mr. Fain's mother attended school at Augusta when her father taught there. Dr. W. C. Miller taught school at Augusta for a number of years and built up one of the best schools in Houston County there. He numbered among his students some who became prominent

SCHOOLS IN HOUSTON COUNTY

in Houston County and elsewhere in Texas.

T. H. Stout and wife, Callie Stout, also taught school at Augusta.

John B. Zimmerman, who later became a distinguished lawyer at Bryan, Texas, a partner of Judge Henderson, also taught school at Augusta. He was the son of J. C. Zimmerman, who came to Crockett in an early day and was one of the best bootmakers and shoemakers who ever lived in Crockett.

Some additional teachers of the Augusta School were a Mr. Humphrey and a teacher by the name of Dennis. Vergil Long also taught at Augusta. Some time ago, this school was consolidated with the Glover school, over which Professor Euclid Smith presides as superintendent. No school is now being taught at Augusta.

ALABAMA SCHOOL

The following item appearing in the Crockett Printer in its issue of November 14, 1860, has a historic interest, and deserves a place in this chapter:

"ALABAMA SCHOOLHOUSE

"This academy is located near Alabama, and will commence the fifth session the third Monday in March, 1860, and continue five months on the following terms, viz:

"Spelling, Reading, Writing, Arithmetic, Grammar, Geography and Philosophy, $10.00 per scholar.

"No deduction made for absence of scholars except in case of serious and protracted sickness, or at the discretion of the teacher, S. M. Stovall."

The following notice also appears in the same issue of the Crockett Printer:

"NOTICE TO SCHOOLTEACHERS

"Attention is directed to the following order of the county court, under the late school law. Teachers in the county, who expect to benefit from the school fund, must come forward and receive certificate from the Board appointed by the court, to entitle them to receive from said fund.

HISTORY OF HOUSTON COUNTY

"STATE OF TEXAS, HOUSTON COUNTY
"County Court, pertaining to Roads, Revenues, Etc.
"May Term, May 18, '58.

"Ordered by the Court that L. W. Cooper, William M. Taylor, and Oscar Dalton be, and they are hereby appointed school examiners for Houston County to examine all persons proposing to teach public schools within the limits thereof, and upon such examination, if finding them qualified to discharge the duties as such, shall grant him or her a certificate stating the branches he or she is qualified to teach.
"A true copy of the minutes.
"Given under my hand and seal of office at Crockett, this 22nd day of May, A. D., 1858.

"O. C. ALDRICH, Clerk."

(SEAL)

LOVELADY SCHOOL

The town of Lovelady had its beginning when the Houston & Great Northern Railroad reached that point in 1872. At that time a townsite was laid off and a plan made of the town. The first school taught there was located in a little schoolhouse Southeast of the Station House and according to the best information was taught by Mrs. Sarah J. Elam, afterwards, Sarah J. Holmes, a daughter of Col. A. T. Monroe. C. H. Barbee, who still resides in Lovelady, was a pupil of Mrs. Elam, when he was only five years of age. He remembers distinctly her son, Roland Elam, who was a pupil at the school at the same time. Since that time there have been a large number of teachers and it will be difficult to name them in the order of their service. After Mrs. Elam, the school was taught by a Mrs. Hannah. Another teacher during the early days was named Watt Patterson. He was a Presbyterian Preacher and taught only one year, and returned to the state from which he came. Thereafter, the school was taught by a Professor Humphreys, who was a peculiar character and was noted for the marvelous stories he could tell of his various experiences, particularly as a hunter. This same Professor Humphreys also taught at the old Read School House on Nevills Prairie. After Professor

SCHOOLS IN HOUSTON COUNTY

Humphreys, the school was taught by Virgil Long, who was a son of John Long of Augusta. Another teacher was named Cannon. Another teacher of the school was Professor Christian, an old bachelor, who taught about 1889 or 1890, and taught for five or six years. The school was also taught by Mr. A. J. Rape, who was also a surveyor. One of the ablest teachers that the Lovelady school ever had was Professor Thompson, who was a highly educated man, and an able teacher. He had already taught at Porter Springs and died at Lovelady, while engaged in teaching there.

One of the most eminent teachers that Houston County ever had was Professor F. M. Martin, who began to teach at Lovelady, about the year 1894, and taught for several years. He left his impress on the community and had as his students Judge B. F. Dent, who later became our District Judge and J. F. Mangum, who later became Houston County's School Superintendent. Both of these men in turn taught the Lovelady school.

One of the most acceptable teachers and superintendents that Lovelady ever had was Rev. T. N. Mainer, the scion of an old family, who taught the school successfully for fourteen years. He trained many young people who went out from the Lovelady school to become teachers and leaders elsewhere.

Mr. Mainer was succeeded by E. O. Eason, who after teaching a successful school for several years, is now the able superintendent of the Grapeland schools.

The present superintendent of the Lovelady school is Professor F. H. Burton, who also belongs to one of the old Houston County families.

For a number of years the business affairs of the Lovelady school district have been successfully managed by a competent board of trustees, who first built a substantial brick school building, and the school now has an attractive and well-equipped school plant, and this school has a bright future for the education of the Lovelady community.

One of the things to which the Lovelady school can point with pride is the fact that it was there that Dr. Homer P. Rainey received a part of his education, that sent him on his way to be President of the University of Texas, one of the greatest educational institutions in all the nation.

GRAPELAND SCHOOLS

The situation in Grapeland is very similar to that in Lovelady. There was no town of Grapeland until the railroad reached that point during the year 1872. No school had existed at that place until the Railroad Company laid out a town and sold off lots for residence and business purposes. The first school taught there was taught in an old log schoolhouse where the Baptist Church now stands. It was a one-room, one teacher school. As far as information has been obtained N. A. Hickey was one of the earliest teachers of the Grapeland School. He taught in the little schoolhouse above mentioned.

Miss Molly Moore of Crockett also taught the school following Professor Hickey. No record has been furnished as to how long she taught the school.

Professor Waltrip also taught the school for a short time.

The old log schoolhouse in which the school was conducted up to this time, was located on the west side of the railroad. Later ,a two-story school building was erected on the east side of the railroad, southeast of the railroad station. It was in this new building that Professor A. W. Cain, who married a daughter of Dr. F. C. Woodard, taught for seven or eight years beginning in about 1904. A Mr. Price taught the school later, and about the year 1909 Professor Wade L. Smith was chosen as superintendent, and taught the school for two years, and then was absent for about two years, after which he returned and taught for another two years.

Another teacher of the school was Albert Moore, who later was elected county clerk. He taught the school for about five years.

In more recent times Professor C. V. Reed taught the school several years in the new school building which was erected on the west side of the railroad, and is the present school building. He was succeeded by Professor T. B. Blackstone, who was the immediate predecessor of Supt. E. A. Eason, the present efficient superintendent.

The present High School at Grapeland is one of the best in Houston County. The school reflects the enterprising spirit of the Grapeland people. The Grapeland Independent School District now controls its own school system, and is a strictly up-to-date school enterprise. It has turned out some of the most prominent and outstanding citizens of Houston County and many have gone abroad, with the inspiration received from this school, to have a large part in the affairs of the State. It is difficult to estimate the influence radiating from this up-to-date school.

SCHOOLS IN HOUSTON COUNTY

CREEK SCHOOL

The Creek Community is situated about 15 miles southwest of Crockett, and derived its name from its vicinity to Big Creek, formerly known as Caney Creek. This community has numbered among its citizens quite a number of pioneers, among them being Washington Taylor, commonly known as Uncle Wash; R. H. Furlough, commonly known as Bob Furlough; A. P. Hester, commonly known as Addison Hester; J. W. Goodwin, commonly known as Jim Goodwin; J. W. Thompson, commonly known as Turkey Thompson; Wm. C. Hallmark, commonly known as Uncle Billy Hallmark, and S. B. Hallmark, commonly known as Steve Hallmark. There were others who could be numbered among the pioneers, and whose descendants still live in that community.

According to information received the first school taught at Creek was taught by A. J. Cary, who taught the school in 1885, for one year.

The next teacher was Hugh Hatton, who taught from 1886 to 1890.

He was followed by Miss Jennie Bever, who taught the school for three years, beginning in 1890.

Miss Bever was followed by C. G. Lansford, commonly known as Gershom Lansford, who taught the school for two years.

Lansford was followed by a teacher by the name of Hollis from Midway, who taught the school for two years.

Mr. Hollis was followed by A. J. Wood, who taught the school one year only, in 1895.

Mr. Wood was followed by Joe Bob Oliphint, an eminent educator, who taught the school for three years.

Oliphint was followed by C. W. Butler, in his younger day, who has now become quite famous as Dr. C. W. Butler, the owner of Butler's Hospital, who taught the school for one year.

Dr. Butler was followed by Fred Smith, who taught the school for two terms and at the end of his teaching the school was merged with the Austonio School. It was about this time that the Creek School House was destroyed by fire.

AUSTONIO SCHOOL

After the Creek School was merged with the school at Austonio, the Ash School was also consolidated with it, and the

HISTORY OF HOUSTON COUNTY

school had a prosperous outlook from the beginning.

The Austonio Community is located on the Kings Highway, or old San Antonio Road, about 14 miles southwest of Crockett, and was first known by the nickname of "Pearville." The significance of this name is derived from the fact that pears were used by some of the people in either distilling or brewing a kind of intoxicating liquor. The good people of the community, becoming tired of the name, the matter was brought before the Crockett Chamber of Commerce which offered a prize of $10.00 for a new name for the little town. The price was won by Miss Isbell, who lived east of Crockett, and the name was chosen from many proposed names. It is a blend of the two Texas cities, Austin and San Antonio.

The first superintendent of the Austonio School, was J. B. Daniel, a well-known teacher of Houston County, commonly known as Buford Daniel. He is a member of one of the pioneer families of Houston County, and is still engaged in teaching a Houston County school.

Mr. Daniel was followed by Professor G. H. Brooks, who taught the school for eight years and up until the present year.

The present superintendent, who succeeded Professor Brooks is L. J. Lowery. This school has developed into one of the most efficient and outstanding schools of the county, and has accomplished a great work, not only for the Austonio Community, but for Houston County. Its influence has reached out very far in the educational circles of Houston County, and it is destined yet to carry forward a great work, and exercise a fine influence, for years to come.

ANTRIM SCHOOL

One of the early schools of Houston County was located about 8 or 10 miles northwest of Grapeland, and was first known as the Antrim School. The first teacher of the school of whom we have any information was a man by the name of Rowe. He was followed by Mr. Russell Wilson, the father-in-law of Colonel W. N. Sheridan. He lived for a while in the home of Col. Sheridan and taught the school about the year 1865 or 1866. He was the father of Zach Wilson, who married Mary, the daughter of Thomas P. Collins and died about the year 1869.

The next teacher of the Antrim School was a Dr. Turner. The school at Antrim was taught in a large, one room, log

SCHOOLS IN HOUSTON COUNTY

schoolhouse, about 24 feet square. It had no glass windows, but one log was sawed out to make an opening for a window.

The Antrim School was later moved to a new community known as Pleasant Hill. A little town grew up around Pleasant Hill, consisting of two stores, one blacksmith shop, one saloon and a schoolhouse, which was also used as a churchhouse. Among those who preached there were the Rev. Matt J. Edmiston, the Rev. Barbour and the Rev. Richards, all Presbyterian preachers. Among the old time citizens who supported the Antrim School were John A. Davis, a son of Bradford Davis, Reuben Matthews and John A. Williams. Other prominent citizens of the community were: John McElroy, Jim Grey, J. H. B. Kyle and John Little. B. F. Edens also was a merchant at Pleasant Hill and afterwards moved to Grapeland and became one of the most successful merchants and business men of Grapeland, accumulating quite a little fortune. The old Antrim and Pleasant Hill schools deserve a place in Houston County history.

WELDON SCHOOL

The history of the Weldon School contains much matter of historic interest, but the author has been unable to obtain complete information about this school, as the first school taught in that locality was taught in a very early day. As early as 1880, a school was taught in the old schoolhouse by Rev. John Sullivan, the schoolhouse then being on the Burton Goodrum Place, near where the dipping vat is now located. Other teachers at this old schoolhouse were G. G. Alexander, James Reynolds, Miss Nora Goodgoin, and John A. Long. A new school building was later erected nearer the town and was burned. About the year 1930 the present commodious school building was erected and the following Superintendents have conducted the school there: Ben Lawrence, Prof. Forrester, J. P. O'Keefe, Louis Farris, Charles Heath, Clifton Crowson and the present Superintendent is Prof. J. B. Daniels.

CHAPTER VI

Lodges, Fraternities and Civic Clubs in Houston County

The first lodge of any secret order to be organized in Crockett was a Masonic Lodge, organized in 1845. The inception of this lodge has behind it a most interesting and historical background. The following matters of record bring to light many names that have been forgotten in Houston County's colorful history. The following is certainly worthy of being preserved as history of local interest and importance.

"TO THE WORSHIPFUL GRAND MASTER, WARDENS AND BRETHERN OF THE GRAND LODGE OF THE REPUBLIC OF TEXAS:

"The undersigned Ancient York Masons of the County of Houston most respectfully represent that they, Ancient and Accepted Master Masons, that they have been members of a regular Lodge, that having the prosperity of the fraternity at heart, they are willing to exert their best endeavoring to promote and diffuse the genuine true copies of Masonry that for the convenience of their respective dwellings and for other good reasons they are desirous of forming a new Lodge in the Town of Crockett, in the County of Houston to be called or named Trinity Lodge. That in consequence of their desire they pray for a Charter to empower them to assemble as a legal Lodge to discharge the duties of Masonry in a regular and constitutional manner according to the original forms of the order and the regulations of the Grand Lodge; that they have nominated and do recommend Selden B. Jasper to be the first Master; George G. Alford, Senior Warden; John Shomaker, Junior Warden; Wm. T. Miller, Sen. Deacon; John Blair, Junior Deacon; Wm. Y. Lacey, Sec.; and E. W. McCracken, Treasurer of said Lodge. If the prayer of a petition should be granted they promise a strict conformity to all the constitutional regulations and laws of the Grand Lodge, December 2nd, 1844, A. L. 5844.

" (Signed)   S. L. B. Jasper, G. G. Alford, John Shomaker, Wm. T. Miller, John Blair, Wm. Y. Lacy and E. A. McCracken.

"I certify that the Brethern, who have signed the above, and foregoing Petition are all worthy Master Masons. Furthermore certify that the nearest Lodge to Crockett (to-wit) Milam

LODGES, FRATERNITIES AND CIVIC CLUBS

No. 2 does not work at present for want of a proper room and that McFarland No. 3 has surrendered for Charter, which is the reason the Brethren of Crockett did not send the Petition to said Lodge for recommendation.

"Washington, December 5th, 1844.
"A Stern, D. D. G. M., 3rd Masonic Dist.

"Dispensation granted 12-7-1844. John M. Wisher, Grand Secretary. Grand Lodge. (Signed) Thomas G. Western, Dep. G. Master."

The above information is furnished from the Grand Secretary.

Extracts from reprint Vol. 1:

"The Eighth Grand Annual Communication of the Right Worshipful Grand Lodge of Ancient Free and Accepted Masons, of the Republic of Texas, was convened at the town of Washington, on the 2nd Monday, 13th of January, A. D. 1845, A. L. 1845."

Page 151.

"A Lodge has been established at Crockett, in Houston County, working under a Dispensation of the Right Worshipful Deputy Grand Master of the Republic. Said Brethren have but recently (since the 27th of last month) commenced their labors, I would recommend a Charter to be granted said Brethren, on their paying the requisite fees.

"Yours very respectfully and fraternally
Adolphus Sterne, D. D. G. M. 3d M. D. R. T."

Page 165: "Saturday, January 18, A. D. 1845, A. L. 1845, 7-1/2 o'clock P. M. On motion of Bro. Sterne.

"Resolved, That Trinity Lodge, No. 21, receive a Charter on application for the same, by paying the balance of the fees as specified in the Constitution of the Grand Lodge of the Republic of Texas.

"Tuesday, June 24, 1845, at 1 P. M. Page 180:

"On Motion of Bro. Alford, the following resolution was adopted:

"Resolved, That the name of Trinity, Lodge No. 21, be changed to Lothrop Lodge, No. 21."

Page 187: "Since the meeting of the last Annual Communication there have been Charters sent to Graham Lodge, No. 20; Trinity No. 21; Marshall No. 22; Clinton No. 23; Red Land No. 24; and Paris No. 27; and Dispensations to Montgomery Lodge at Montgomery; Olive Branch Lodge at Cincinnati; and Frontier Lodge at Corpus Christi."

LOTHROP LODGE NO. 21

The Lodge at Crockett, when first organized, bore the name of Trinity Lodge, No. 21. The following letter from the Grand Secretary of the Grand Lodge of Texas will throw some light upon why the name was changed from Trinity Lodge to Lothrop Lodge.

"THE GRAND LODGE OF TEXAS
Office Of
George H. Belew, Grand Secretary

Waco, Texas, May 22, 1939.

Mr. Houston Wade,
2314 Morse St.
Houston, Texas.

"Dear Brother Wade:

"At the request of Brother Sam B. Cantey I am giving you herewith such information as I have been able to assemble regarding the name of Lothrop Lodge No. 21 of Crockett, Texas; the Charter members of said lodge: The Masonic Record of Brothers Selden L. B. Jasper and J. K. T. Lothrop.

"The dispensation to form this Lodge was issued by Brother Adolphus Sterne, D. G. G. M. of the third Masonic District of Texas on December 5, 1844. The Lodge was set to work on December 27, 1844 and operated as Trinity Lodge No. 21, Crockett, Texas.

"I do not know and cannot find from the records in this office, the reason for the changing of the name of the Lodge from Trinity No. 21 to Lothrop No. 21. I find the following record in the Minutes of the Grand Lodge at the June 24th session in 1845:—"On motion of Brother Alford the following

LODGES, FRATERNITIES AND CIVIC CLUBS

resolution was adopted. That the name of Trinity Lodge No. 21 be changed to Lothrop Lodge No. 21."

"There existed at this time (1844-45) Trinity Lodge No. 14, Livingston, Texas, chartered in 1840.

"There are seven names signed to the original petition for a Lodge or rather for a Dispensation to organize a Lodge at Crockett to be known as Trinity Lodge. These seven Brothers were the first officers of that Lodge, they are: S. L. B. Jasper, W. M.; John Shoemaker, J. W.; John Blair, J. D.; E. A. McCracken, Treas.; G. G. Alford, S. W.; Wm. T Miller, S. D.; Wm. Y. Lacy, Sec'y.

"I have very little information concerning the Masonic Records of Brothers Jasper and Lothrop. All the record that I have of Brother S. L. B. Jasper is that he was at one time a member of Temple Lodge No. 2, Houston, Texas, and a Charter member of Lothrop Lodge No. 21.

"I have no record of Brother J. K. T. Lothrop under that name. One J. L. Lothrop was reported by Holland Lodge No. 1 as receiving the degrees on the following dates: Initiated 12-3-1838. Passed 6-5-1839. Raised in 1839. He is shown to have demitted in 1842 and to have died in 1844. Because of the dates involved, I believe this to be one and the same person.

"Trusting that the above information will be of some value to you, I am.

Sincerely and Fraternally,

George H. Belew, Grand Secretary."

The following information has been furnished the author by Mr. J. S. Sturgis of Trinity, Texas. In this connection the author desires to say that Mr. Sturgis deserves great credit for his untiring efforts in gathering and peserving the history of Masonry in Texas.

"The Grand Lodge of Ancient, Free and Accepted Masons, of Texas, at the Masonic Hall of Lothrop Lodge, No. 21, in the Town of Crockett in the County of Houston, on Monday the 13th day of June, A. D. 1859, at 10 o'clock A. M., being the Twenty-Third Annual Communication."
Page 145: "On motion the Grand Secretary was ordered to strike out in the Charter Of Lothrop Lodge, No. 21, the word 'Trinity' and insert the word 'Lothrop.'"

"The thirty-fifth Annual Communication of the Most Worshipful Grand Lodge of Texas convened in the City of

HISTORY OF HOUSTON COUNTY

Houston, at the Masonic Temple, on Monday, June 12th, A. L. 5871, A. D. 1871, at 10 o'clock A. M."

Page: 99: "Having been informed by P. G. M. Richard Duglass that the hall of Lothrop Lodge, No. 21, has been consumed by fire, together with their charter, jewels, and furniture, on the 4th day of May, 1871, I granted a dispensation permitting this Lodge to assemble and work until the present time. I recommend that a Charter issue to this Lodge, with the original number, and without fee."

Page 76: "The following resolution was read and adopted:

"Resolved, That Past G. Master Brother Wm. M. Taylor be and is hereby authorized to insert the original names of W. Master, S. and J. Wardens, in the duplicate Charter to Lothrop Lodge No. 21."

Below is a list of the W. M.'s who were elected and installed to preside over the Lodge:

Year	No.	Name	Year	No.	Name
1845	No. 1	L. S. B. Jasper			Taylor
1846	No. 2	D. C. Neville	1867	No. 7	Wm. M. Taylor
1847	No. 3	Andrew C. Love	1855	No. 8	C. H. Randolph
1848	No. 3	Andrew C. Love	1857	No. 9	T. B. Henderson
1850	No. 4	James M. Hall			
1850	"	" "	1861	No. 10	J. C. Wootters
1851	No. 5	James H. Collard	1862	No. 10	J. C. Wootters
1852	No. 6	James R. Bracken	1865		
			1868		
1858	No. 6	James R. Bracken	1869		
			1970		
			1871		
1853	No. 7	Wm. M. Taylor	1872		
			1873		
1854	No. 7	Wm. M. Taylor	1875		
			1893		
1856	No. 7	Wm. M. Taylor	1894		
			1898	No .10	J. C. Wootters
1859	No. 7	Wm. M. Taylor	1863	No. 11	John McConnell
1860	No. 7	Wm. M. Taylor	1876	No. 11	John McConnell
1864	No. 7	Wm. M. Taylor	1874	No. 12	B. F. Frymier
			1877		
1866	No. 7	Wm. M.	1878		

LODGES, FRATERNITIES AND CIVIC CLUBS

Year	No.	Name	Year	No.	Name
1879	No. 12	B. F. Frymier	1910	No. 38	D. C. Scott
1880	No. 13	J. L. Lipscomb	1911	No. 39	M. P. Jensen
1881	No. 14	T. H. Jones	1912	No. 40	Arch Baker
1882	No. 15	W. B. Page	1913	No. 41	C. W. LeGory
1883	No. 15	W. B. Page	1914	No. 42	J. S. Wootters
1884	No. 16	E. Winfree	1915	No. 43	R. H. Wootters
1885	No. 17	C. O. Webb			
1886	No. 18	W. C. Lipscomb	1916	No. 44	J. H. Smith
			1917	No. 45	J. G. Beasley
1887	No. 19	J. L. Williams	1919	No. 45	J. G. Beasley
1888	No. 20	J. H. Wootters	1918	No. 46	A. C. Collins
1889	No. 21	J. M. Campbell	1920	No. 47	W. P. Bishop
			1921	No. 48	B. F. Thomas
1890	No. 22	A. H. Wootters	1922	No. 49	Nat Patton
			1923	No. 50	C. H. Callaway
1891	No. 23	E. A. Pace			
1892	No. 24	John A. McConnell	1924	No. 51	H. J. Trube
			1925	No. 52	R. D. Allen
1895	No. 25	Joe Adams	1926	No. 53	G. L. Cook
1896	No. 26	R. Cassidy	1927	No. 54	H. L. Ellis
1897	No. 27	H. F. Moore	1928	No. 55	T. J. Welch
1899	No. 28	Hyman Harrison	1929	No. 56	John W. Markam
1900	No. 29	Jim Brown	1930	No. 57	B. O. Perdue
1901	No. 30	Earle Adams, Jr.	1931	No. 58	Jack Barbee
			1932	No. 59	H. O. McCarty
1902	No. 31	M. Bromberg, Jr.			
			1933	No. 60	J. C. Shotwell
1903	No. 32	J. W. Young	1934	No. 61	T. B. Goolsbee
1904	No. 32	J. W. Young	1935	No. 62	A. B. Brown
1905	No. 33	T. R. Deupree	1936	No. 63	W. A. Spain
1906	No. 34	J. W. Shivers	1937	No. 64	T. E. Walden
1907	No. 35	F. F. Schupak	1938	No. 65	W. H. Schmidt
1908	No. 36	John LeGory			
1909	No. 37	George W. Crook	1939	No. 66	J. H. Reinicke

After a long lapse of time, the reason for giving the name, Lothrop Lodge, to the Masonic Lodge at Crockett, became lost to its membership, and there seemed to be no one living in Crockett who knew just why it was called Lothrop Lodge. That fact has been explained to some extent in the foregoing part of this chapter. It seems that in this connection some facts relating to the life of J. T. K. Lothrop should be included, and we include the following, which was published in the La-Grange Intelligencer, under date of August 22, 1844:

"Departed this life, on Wednesday the 14th inst, at twenty minutes past nine o'clock P. M. at this place, of billious fever, commander J. T. K. Lothrop of the Navy of Texas.

"Capt. Lothrop was a native of the State of Massachusetts. His parents whilst he was an infant moved to Utilda, the State of New York where the subject of this obituary was reared and educated. In the death of this inestimable young man (he was but 30 years of age) our beloved country has lost one of her noblest defenders, and society one of her brightest and richest ornaments. He was a direct descendant, on the maternal line, from Kirkland, one of the early pilgrim fathers, who, flying from the storms and persecutions of their country, sought an asylum, and planted the standard of freedom upon the Western shores of the Atlantic.

"Capt. Lothrop in 1836 joined the Naval service of this country, under Com. Hawkins, and drew his sword in the cause of Texas Liberty proving him a worthy descendant of his illustrious ancestry. He continued in the service of his country, without intermission, save upon a short leave of absence to visit his aged mother, until July 1843, when our Navy was laid up in ordinary. In 1837 he was 2nd Lieutenant on board of the Independence, captured by two Mexican brigs, after an action of four hours. His coolness and officer-like conduct on that occasion won him the admiration of his country. The schooner was taken to Matamoros, and this gallant officer was thrown in prison, where he was confined for six months, during which time neither his manly spirit cowered, nor his love of country diminished. When released, he again flew to its standard, buckled on his sword, and with a high resolvent went forth to establish the character of the Naval flag of Texas and most nobly and gloriously did he lend his arm and the energies of his mighty soul to its accomplishments.

"In 1840-1 he commanded the Steamer Zavalla upon her cruize of ten months off the Mexican Coast, and at the time the City of Tobasco was surrounded. He commanded the Brig Wharton off the coast of Campeche, and sustained with iron nerve his gallant leader, Commodore Moore, who for fifty seven days confronted the overwhelming force of the foe, consisting of two powerful iron steam frigates, carrying Paixhan guns, and five sail vessels. The flag of Texas with her single star, which was so proudly thrown to the battles breeze, was supported only by the ship Austin and Brig Wharton on the 30th of April and the

LODGES, FRATERNITIES AND CIVIC CLUBS

16th of May, 1843, a day ever memorable in naval history, for its daring and success, thus engaged the fleet of the for-the-enemy were repulsed, Yucatan disenthralled, and the name of Lothrop was added to the list of naval heroes.

"In private life he was one who cultivated all the social virtues —his hand was ever active and prompt to the appeals of charity, or to give help to the calls of suffering humanity. As a friend his devotion was untiring—his counsels were those of wisdom— every pulsation of his heart was responsive to live and kindness. His life was one of elevated thought, in all that exalted the soldier, christian, patriot and friend. In death he resigned himself with christian fortitude to his fate. The people of this place and its vicinity, with whom he had passed two months of social intercourse, gave full and ample testimony of the estimation in which they held his private virtues, his patriotic zeal and indefatigable ardour in the service of his country, by the kind of officers and deep solicitude manifested towards him in his last illness and the mourning multitude that followed his remains to the grave. Such was Lothrop. That sword which he had so gallantly borne in defense of his country's right, he carried with him folded to his bosom, to his sepulchre, as if even in death, he would save his bright blade from blot or blemish. And thus passed from life to the cold grave of death one

> "Who never to tyranny's vile domain,
> Could his generous neck ignobly bend,
> Nor see Texas drag the odious servile chain,
> And mourn her virgin glories at an end.
> In the kind bosom of his adopted land,
> Ended are his toils and peaceful is his grave.

Washington, August 16th, 1844. J. S. M."

From the list of Worshipful Masters of Lothrop Lodge No. 21, of the Masonic Fraternity, it can be seen what a large share this Lodge had in the past history of Crockett and Houston County. The long list of names represents the leading citizens of Crockett and Houston County for nearly 100 years. The following items taken from the Crockett Printer published by Oscar Dalton under date of November 14, 1860, will bring to light the names of other prominent citizens who ranked high in Masonic circles and have passed on to their reward. Among the list of lodges of different orders appearing in the above named issue of the Crockett Printer, appeared the following:

HISTORY OF HOUSTON COUNTY

"Lothrop Lodge No. 21, of A. F. A. M."

"The stated communications of this Lodge are held at the Masonic Hall, in the Town of Crockett, on the last Saturday in each month, at 3 o'clock P. M.

OFFICERS

Wm. Taylor, Worshipful Master
John McConnell, Sen. Warden
J. C. Wootters, Jr., Warden
J. T. Heflin, Treasurer
R. Douglass, Secretary
R. J. Johnson, S. D.
J. H. Saxon, J. D.
Wm. H. Edwards, Sr. Deacon
Wm. Wortham, Jr. Steward
J. D. Richardson, Tyler."

The ROYAL ARCH MASONS also had a chapter in Crockett, known as Trinity Chapter No. 4 and in the above mentioned issue of the Crockett Printer, under the date of November 14, 1860, the following appeared:

"TRINITY CHAPTER NO. 4, OF R. A. M.

"The stated convocations of this chapter are held at the Masonic Hall in the Town of Crockett, on the first Monday in each month at 3 o'clock P. M.

M. E. John McConnell, High Priest
E. T. B. Henderson, King
E. Moses Warden, Scribe
Comp. Wm. W. Davis, Ca. of the host
James L. Lipscomb, P. Sojourner
J. R. Bracken, R. A. Captain
A. T. Monroe, Treasurer
R. Douglass, Secretary
J. T. Heflin, M 3rd Veil
Wm. M'Lain, M. 2nd Veil
James Cartwright, M. 1st Veil
W. F. Wall, A. E. Gossett, Stewards
James B. Dawson, Chaplain
J. C. Zimmerman, Sentinel

There was also a Council of Royal and Select Master Masons, which held its convocations in the Masonic Hall of Crockett. The following notice of its meetings appeared in the Crockett Printer, of November 14, 1860.

"TRINITY COUNCIL, NO. 8, OF ROYAL AND SELECT MASTER MASONS.

"The stated convocations of this council are held at the

LODGES, FRATERNITIES AND CIVIC CLUBS

Masonic Hall in Crockett, on the third Monday in each month, at 3 o'clock P. M.

OFFICERS: William M. Taylor, The Ill. Master
John McConnell, P. C. of the work
Moses Warden, Treasurer
Richard Douglass, Recorder
Wm. A. Stewart, Capt. of the Guard
Wm. R. Matlock, Conductor
Wm. McLain, Marshall
J. C. Zimmerman, Sentinel"

In 1860, the Town of Randolph, located 12 miles east of Crockett, on the Corltharp road was of sufficient importance to have a Masonic Lodge and the following notice of its meetings were advertised in the Crockett Printer, under the date of November 14, 1860 as follows:

"RANDOLPH LODGE NO. 229, F. A. M.

"The Stated convocations of this lodge are held at their hall, in the town of Randolph, on the 3rd Saturday in each month at 3 o'clock P. M.

OFFICERS: James L. Richards, W. Master
Samuel O. Foster, S. Warden
Wm. Denny, J. Warden
John H. Burnett, Treasurer
Richard Douglass, Secretary
J. A. Stubblefield, S. Deacon
J. S. Carleton, J. Deacon
D. M. Brown, Morgan Rye, Stewards
Wm. Wood, Tyler.

Students of local history should be interested in considering the names of prominent Crockett and Houston County citizens that appear in the foregoing list.

* * * * * *

INDEPENDENT ORDER OF ODD FELLOWS

The next oldest fraternity to be organized in Crockett or Houston County, was the Independent Order of Odd Fellows.

HISTORY OF HOUSTON COUNTY

We have no data to show just when the first Lodge of this order was organized, but we have some information about the existence of more than one lodge on November 14, 1860. In the issue of the Crockett Printer, under the date of November 14, 1860, the following notices of Lodges of this Fraternity appeared:

"FRIENDSHIP LODGE NO. 41, I. O. O. F. meets every Saturday evening at 7 o'clock P. M. at its hall in Crockett.

E. H. Bibo, N. G.   S. A. Hough, V. G.
Chas. Stokes, Secretary   R. J. Johnson, Treas.
Wm. H. Moore, Warden   Oscar Dalton, Cond.
                                 Wm. H. Moore, R. S. N. G.

"SAN PEDRO LODGE NO. 86, I. O. O. F. meets at its hall in Augusta every Saturday night.

Robert Acree, N. G.   J W. Bradshaw, R. S V G.
L. H. Winfield, Sec.   W. M. Waddell, V. G.
L. W. White, Warden   John F. Butts, Treas.
C. W. Butler, I. G. and O. G.   T. N. Cutler, Cond.
J. S. Cartwright, R. S. N. G   Jas. McDowell, L. S. F. G.

"ELLA LODGE NO. 81, I. O. O. F. meets at its hall in Randolph, every Thursday night.

Jos. Blakey, N. G.   J. L. Richards, V. G.
A. H. Casteel, Sec.   R. Cox, Treasurer
J. Odell, I. G.   W. E. Vaughn, L. S. N. G.
C. E. Ford, R. S. V. G.   A. J. Connor, L. S. V. G.
           T. C. Hicks, R. S. N. G.

KNIGHTS OF PYTHIAS, DAVY CROCKETT LODGE NO. 193

The next oldest lodge of any order in Crockett, was the Knights of Pythias, Davy Crockett Lodge No. 193. The Charter of this lodge bears date of April 18, 1894, and the signatures of

LODGES, FRATERNITIES AND CIVIC CLUBS

the Charter Members affixed to the same are the following:

John R. Sheridan	C. W. Moore	T. D. Craddock
Jim Brown	Walker King	J. F. Downes
Richard Cassidy	A. H. Murchison	John F. Baker
W. A. R. French	B. F. Chamberlain	Joe Adams
John G. Harring	F. F. Fifer	Allen Newton

The above are the only names appearing on the charter, although there were a few more who attended the first meeting of the lodge, when it was originally organizd. Of the above charter members, only two are now living, viz: C. W. Moore and B. F. Chamberlain. This indicates the fleeting nature of human life, that after 46 years only two out of fifteen should be still alive.

This lodge has kept up an unbroken existence and has held regular meetings ever since it was organized. It still has an active membership of nearly, or quite 200, and has had a prosperous existence. It has acquired a valuable piece of property situated on the southwest corner of the public square in Crockett, in which is located its castle haus, the ground floor being used as a place of business, from which a substantial revenue is derived. New members are being added at nearly every meeting. Among the above named charter members are some who have left an undying impression on the history of Crockett.

THE CROCKETT LIONS CLUB

The Crockett Lions Club was organized on September 15th, 1923 with the following charter members:

Earl Porter Adams	L. H. Arnold	C. D. Towery
J. W. Young	Mose Bromberg	A. S. Lee
W. W. Aiken	F. A. Smith	S. L. Murchison
E. C. Arledge	M. L. Shapira	H. L. Ellis
B. L. Satterwhite	C. H. Callaway	A. A. Aldrich
J. S. Cook	E. B. Stokes	J. R. Herrin
W. G. Cartwright	W. D. Julian	D. C. Kennedy
J. G. Beasley	J. H. Smith	W. P. Bishop
C. L. Edmiston	W. A. Beaty	H. J. Berry
Jas. S. Shivers	W. A. Mize	G. Q. King
D. O. Kiessling	F. M. Posey	C. W. LeGory
W. C. Wells	Harry J. Trube	

HISTORY OF HOUSTON COUNTY

At the first meeting of the Lions Club the following officers were elected:

C. L. Edmiston, President
W. P. Bishop, First Vice-President
Jas. S. Shivers, Second Vice-President
H. J. Berry, Third Vice-President
D. O. Kiessling, Treasurer
F. M. Posey, Lion Tamer
W. C. Wells, Tail Twister
H. J. Trube, Jr., Secretary

DIRECTORS: F. A. Smith, Chairman; C. D. Towery and M. L. Shapira.

Charter night was celebrated at the Green Parrot Tea Room on January 23, 1924, with the following program:
Toastmaster: Lion-Judge A. A. Aldrich
America
Invocation, Lion-Rev. A. S. Lee
Solo, Mrs. Robert Allen
Feeding the Lions:
Introduction of Toastmaster, Lion-President, C. L. Edmiston
Welcome to Guests and Members, Lion-Rev. A. S. Lee
Response, Earl Porter Adams
Quartette, Mesdams John LeGory, Johnson Arledge, Jas. S. Shivers and D. O. Kiessling
Reading, Miss Otis McConnell
Address, Lion Louis C. Perry, District Governor of Texas, Terrell, Texas
Saxaphone Solo, Miss C. C. Stokes, accompanied by Mrs. D. O. Kiessling
Presentation of Charter, Lion Louis C. Perry
Acceptance of Charter, C. L. Edmiston, President Crockett Lions Club
Solo, Cecil Haughton. Auld Lange Syne, Entire Jungle
LIONS ROAR.

ACCOMPLISHMENTS:—No civic organization in Houston County ever justified its existence better than the Crockett Lions Club. It began its program of improvement at once. On November 13th, 1923 the City Council of Crockett accepted a proposition to deed it the Shakespeare lot for the erection of an auditorium, library and restroom and this deal was consumated. On March 5th, 1924, Mr. Moffatt of Palestine was retained as architect to supervise the erection of the auditorium.

Later under the sponsorship of the Lions Club the street to Glenwood Cemetery was paved largely through the efforts of

LODGES, FRATERNITIES AND CIVIC CLUBS

Mrs. Hortense Sweet acting in conjunction with the Lions Club.

Later still the Lions Club sponsored the improvement of the Pickwick Hotel and it was transformed from a two-story into the present three-story Crockett Hotel.

It was sponsored many minor projects. Including the Big Brothers, which still lives and annually brings joy to many homes which might not otherwise have a Santa Claus.

But the crowning achievement of the Lions Club was the sponsorship of the new Courthouse. This project was born in a meeting of the Directors of the Lions Club and was carried to a splendid conclusion through the untiring efforts of the club, through the unrivaled guardianship of Lion C. W. Kennedy.

THE CROCKETT ROTARY CLUB

This Club was organized on February 28th, 1937 with the following charter members:

C. L. Edmiston	Dr. R. S. Traylor	J. G. Arledge
R. L. King	B. L. Satterwhite, Jr.	S. L. Murchison
J. G. Beasley	Guy Blandenship	C. H. Callaway
Dr. Paul B. Stokes	J. G. LeGory	Terry Van Pelt
W. G. Cartwright	Earl Bryan	J. C. Millar
H. J. Berry	Harvey G. McCarty	M. L. Berry
Sam F. Arledge	Loch Cook	
J. W. Young	W. H. Denny, Jr.	

The first officers elected were:

Dr. Paul B. Stokes, President
Loch Cook, Vice-President
J. G. LeGory, Secretary &Treasurer
W. H. Denny, Jr., Sergeant at Arms

The Board of Directors were:

Dr. Paul B. Stokes, Loch Cook, J. G. Beasley, J. G. LeGory, C. L. Edmiston, J. H. Berry, and J. W. Young.

The Club meets regularly every Thursday at the Crockett Hotel.

HISTORY OF HOUSTON COUNTY

THE CROCKETT CHAMBER OF COMMERCE

Among the institutions that deserve a high place in this history of civic organizations that have contributed to the development of Crockett is "THE CROCKETT CHAMBER OF COMMERCE." It had its birth in a mass meeting held on February 11th, 1926, and the following is taken from the minutes of said meeting.

"Crockett, Texas, Feb. 11, 1926.

"Pursuant to call—A mass meeting of the Citizens of Crockett was held at the rooms of The Crockett Shrine Club on Thursday, February 11th, 1926, for the purpose of organizing a Chamber of Commerce.

"Approximately 100 citizens were present, and—On Motion made and carried C. L. Edmiston was nominated and elected Chairman of the Meeting, and on motion made and carried E. C. Arledge was nominated and elected Secretary of the Meeting.

"Meeting called to order by Chairman Edmiston and purpose of meeting stated.

"After open discussion—On motion duly made and carried, the following committees were named (said Committees having been instructed to report back to a called meeting to be held Feb. 19th, 1926):

"Committee on By-Laws and Constitution: A. A. Aldrich, W. C. Wells, and E. J. Callahan.

"NOMINATING COMMITTEE: J. C. Millar, D. O. Kiessling and M. L. Shapira.

"Much enthusiasm prevailed; and after Committees were named they set about plans for their work."

The next meeting of the members was held on February 19th, 1926 and the following is taken from the proceedings of that meeting:

"Crockett, Texas, Feb. 19, 1926.

"Pursuant to call—A Meeting of the subscribing members of the proposed Crockett Chamber of Commerce was held at the Shrine Club Rooms in Crockett, Texas, on this the 19th day of February, 1926; said meeting having been called by the Chairman of a mass meeting held at Crockett on February 11th, 1926.

"Meeting called to order, and on motion made and carried C. L. Edmiston was elected Chairman of the meeting, and Geo. W. McLean, Secretary of the meeting.

LODGES, FRATERNITIES AND CIVIC CLUBS

"On motion made and carried, the name adopted for the organization was "THE CROCKETT CHAMBER OF COMMERCE."

"The Committee on Nominations reported names of 25 citizens (subscribing members) and recommended their election as Directors of the Chamber, and further recommended that the number of Directors be 25—on motion made and carried the 25 were duly elected directors to serve the Chamber for the ensuing year, their names being as follows: A. A. Aldrich; D. O. Kiessling; F. A. Smith; C. L. Edmiston; E. J. Callahan; H. L. Ellis; M. L. Shapira; B. L. Satterwhite; D. C. Kennedy; E. C. Arledge; T. J. Welch; D. G. Moore; W. G. Cartwright; A. M. Rogers; F. M. Posey; Loch Cook; D. A. Nunn; J. W. Shivers; L. H. Arnold; Claude Brown; E. P. Adams; M. Bromberg; C. D. Towery; W. C. Wells and Dr. J. S. Wootters."

The first meeting of the Board of Directors was held on February 26th, 1926, and the following was taken from the minutes of said meeting:

"FIRST MEETING (Called) of the Directors of the Crockett Chamber of Commerce held at the Crockett Shrine Club Rooms in Crockett, Texas, following meeting of the full membership of the Chamber, this the 26th day of February, 1926.

"Meeting called to order by A. A. Aldrich—On motion made and carried Judge Aldrich was nominated and elected Temporary Chairman of the meeting and E. C. Arledge was nominated and elected Temporary Secretary of the meeting.

"Full attendance of the 25 directors were present as shown by the Directors' Attendance Record in front of this Minute Book.

"On motion duly made and carried, the following officers of the Chamber were elected to serve for the ensuing year—the said Officers to be the "Executive Committee" of this Chamber and Board of Directors:

President	M. Bromberg
1st Vice-President	W. C. Wells
Sec'y of the Board	E. C. Arledge
Treasurer	D. O. Kiessling

"The fifth member of the Executive Committee to be named by the President at next meeting."

On March 9th, 1926 the following appears on the minutes of the Meeting:

"A. A. Aldrich, Chairman of The David Crockett Memorial

Association made statement—On motion made and carried (unanimously) this Chamber went on record as fully approving "The David Crockett Memorial Association."

CHAPTER VII

Crockett Churches

The churches of Crockett and Houston County have had such an important part in the development of the town and county, that a history of these churches is almost synonymous with a history of the county. The pioneer of these churches is the Crockett Methodist Episcopal Church.

So far reaching has been the influence of this church on the lives of the people and on the progress of our city and county that it constitutes an indispensable part of their history. independence of the Republic of Texas, the first Methodist Church of Crockett was founded. Crockett was one of the fifteen Methodist charges in the Republic of Texas. At the session of

The author is indebted to Rev. F. D. Dawson for the greater part of the information of this article and takes pleasure in giving full credit for the same.

The following is his statement:

A HISTORY OF THE
CROCKETT METHODIST CHURCH

In the latter end of the year 1839, just one hundred years after the founding of the first Methodist Society in London, and three years after the decisive battle of San Jacinto and the the Mississippi Conference held at Natches, Mississippi, December 4, 1839, the Republic of Texas was divided in two vast districts and the following appointments were made:

East Texas District—Littleton Fowler, presiding elder
San Augustine, S. A. Williams
Jasper, Daniel Carl
Nacogdoches, Francis Wilson
Crockett, Henderson D. Palmer
Montgomery, Moses Spear and Robert Crawford
Harrison Circuit, to be supplied
Rutersville District—Robert Alexander, presiding elder
Rutersville, C. Richardson and President of Rutersville College.
Austin, John Haynie.
Matagorda, Robert Hill
Brazoria, Abel Stevens
Victoria, to be supplied

HISTORY OF HOUSTON COUNTY

Houston, Edward Fontaine
Galveston, Thos. O. Summers
Washington, Jesse Hord and J. Lewis
Nashville, Joseph P. Sneed

PASTORS OF THE CROCKETT METHODIST CHURCH

1839—Henderson D. Palmer
1840—Daniel C. Carl
1841—Nathan Shook &
　　　James H. Collard
1842—Nathan Shook &
　　　James H. Collard
1843—James H. Collard
1844—M. H. Jones &
　　　Wm. K. Wilson
1845—M. H. Jones &
　　　Wm. K. Wilson
1846—Jacob Crawford
1847—John C. Woolam
1848—Jefferson Shook
1849—C. Box
1850—John Powell
1851—William E. George
1852—Samuel C. Box
1853—Alfred Leroy
　　　Kavannaugh
1854—Alfred Leroy
　　　Kavanaugh
1855—William P. Simpson
1856—William P. Sampson
1857—William P. Sampson
1858—Samuel D. Sampson
1859—Samuel Lynch
1860—Samuel Lynch
1861—James A. Scruggs &
　　　W. C. Collins
1862—Harvin W. Moore
1863—Harvey W. Moore
1864—George S. Gatewood
1865—Samuel Lynch
1866—H. B. Phillips
1867—Francis M. Stovall
1868—Francis M. Stovall
1869—Francis M. Stovall

1870—W. C. Collins
1871—W. C. Collins
1872—A. M. Box
1873—John C. Woolam
1874—John C. Woolam
1875—D. M. Stovall
1876—D. M. Stovall
1877—D. P. Cullen
1878—J. B. Hall
1879—D. P. Cullen
1880—N. T. Burks
1881—J. W. Johnson
1882—J. W. Johnson
1883—J. R. Wages
1884—J. R. Wages
1885—W. A. Sampey
1886—B. R. Bolton
1887—B. R. Bolton
1888—B. R. Bolton
1889—B. R. Bolton
1890—J. T. Smith
1891—J. L. Dawson
1892—J. L. Dawson
1893—L. M. Fowler
1894—John S. Mathis
1895—John S. Mathis
1896—John S. Mathis
1897—A. S. Whitehurst
1898—A. S. Whitehurst
1899—J. A. Beagle
1900—Ellis Smith
1901—Ellis Smith
1902—E. L. Crawford
1903—Geo. A. LaClere
1904—H. A. Hodge &
　　　Moreland Whaling
1905—C. E. Smith
1906—Irvin B. Manly

CROCKETT CHURCHES

1907—James W. Downs
1908—F. M. Boyles
1909—Geo. W. Davis
1910—Geo. W. Davis
1911—Geo. W. Davis
1912—D. H. Hotchkiss
1913—D. H. Hotchkiss
1914—D. H. Hotchkiss
1915—C. U. McLarty
1916 C. U. McLarty
1917—C. U. McLarty
1918—C. B. Garrett
1919—C. B. Garrett
1920—
1921—E. A. Maness
1922—E. A. Maness
1923—E. A. Maness

1924—C. W. Hughes
1925—C. A. Lehmberg
1926—C. A. Lehmberg
1927—C. A. Lehmberg
1928—C. A. Lehmberg
1929—C. A. Lehmberg
1930—P. T. Ramsey
1931—Terry W. Wilson
1932—Terry W. Wilson
1933—John V. Berglund
1934—Bob L. Pool
1935—F. D. Dawson
1936—F. D. Dawson
1937—O. W. Hooper
1938—H. L. Munger
1940—H. V. Rankin

SECOND DECADE (1849-1858)

The second decade opens under the ministry of C. Box. This appointment was made by Bishop Paine at the session of the East Texas Conference held in Paris, Texas, November 14, 1849. This is likely Samuel C. Box, who was admitted on trial at the session of the conference held at Henderson in December, 1848. Little is known of his history except the fact that he was pastor at Marion, in the Nacogdoches District in 1850, again at Crockett in 1852 and at Cherokee in the Rusk District in 1852. During the year of his ministry the membership of the church increased from 150 white members and no colored members to 234 white members and 8 colored. Though the records are very scant for this period, it is easy to infer that his year at Crockett was one of intense evangelism.

At the session of the East Texas Conference at Palestine, November 27, 1850, John Powell was appointed to succeed Samuel C. Box. The only thing that is known of this pastor is that he was transferred from the Louisiana Conference this same year and was appointed to the Crockett Charge. The Statistical reports of this year are not available and it is not, therefore, possible to compare the work of this year with that of the preceding year. The records of the East Texas Conference indicate that at the close of this year he was "located at his own request."

At the next session of the East Texas Conference held at Henderson, Texas, opening on November 26, 1851, William E. George was appointed to take the place of John Powell. William

HISTORY OF HOUSTON COUNTY

E. George was admitted on trial into the East Texas Conference at the session held at Palestine in November 1850, and was appointed to the Athens Mission. After serving this charge one year he was appointed to Crockett. After this his name appears in the records for years later, 1858, when he transferred to the Texas Conference and was appointed to have charge of the Trinity African Mission in the Springfield District.

The next session of the Conference was held at Rusk, Texas, opening on December 2, 1852. At this session of the Conference, Samuel C. Box was appointed to Crockett for his second pastorate. During the ninety-seven years of its history only four pastors have been reappointed to Crockett after having served another charge. The name of Samuel C. Box heads the list. The other three who have been reappointed are: Samuel Lynch, John C. Woolam and D. P. Cullen. There are no statistical records for this year. At the beginning of this year the Crockett Charge was shifted from Palestine District to the newly created Woodville District, and William K. Wilson was the Presiding Elder.

On November 30, 1853, Bishop Andrew presided over the session of the East Texas Conference held at Marshall, Texas. When the appointments were read William K Wilson was reappointed Presiding Elder of the Woodville District, and Alfred Leroy Kavanaugh and J. McMillen were appointed to the Crockett Charge to follow Samuel C. Box. A. L. Kavanaugh was a brother of Bishop H. H. Kavanaugh who was elected Bishop at the General Conference of 1854. Phelan's History of Texas Methodism gives this information concerning A. L. Kavanaugh.

"Alfred Leroy Kavanaugh had died during the year. He was born in Davidson County, Tenn. June 12, 1819. Removed to Randolph County, Ark. 1829. In 1840 or 1841, converted and joined the Methodist Church. Licensed to preach May 12, 1842, immediately employed by the P. E. on Little Red River Mission. Admitted Arkansas Conference 1842. At close of first year discontinued at own request. In 1844 came to Texas and engaged in teaching and surveying. In 1845 married Miss Martha Frazier of Tyler County. In 1851 admitted into East Texas Conference. He served Livingston one year. His name disappears from the minutes of 1856. He died May 31, 1857, of pneumonia. He was described as a man of feeble constitution, yet of much energy, and of a sanguine temperament. He was possessed of a good mind and fine social qualities."

Likely the J. McMillen who was appointed with A. L. Kavanaugh was John McMillen who was admitted on trial at the session of the East Texas Conference held at Henderson in 1851. There was another McMillan, Joseph, who was admitted into the East Texas Conference at Palestine in 1850 and appointed to Kaufman Charge along with E. P. Chisolm. The reason for concluding that John McMillan was the one appointed along with Kavanaugh is the fact that the list of appointments for the year 1854 indicate that A. L. Kavanaugh was returned to the Crockett Charge with a co-pastor to be supplied, and John McMillan was appointed to Kaufman as indicated above. No other information concerning him is available.

Bishop Early presided over the session of the East Texas Conference held at Tyler, November 29, 1854; William K. Wilson was returned as Presiding Elder of the Woodville District, and A. L. Kavanaugh as the pastor of the Crockett Charge. The records indicate that another preacher was to be supplied to take the place of J. McMillan. For the first time report is made in the records of the Annual Conference of the local preachers in each charge. The report indicates that there were six local preachers in the Crockett Charge this year. There was reported a decrease in membership. The report at the close of 1853 was 274 white membes and 43 colored; in 1854, the report was 271 white members and 23 colored and 6 local preachers.

The Crockett Charge was transferred back to the Palestine District by the Conference which was held at Marshall in November of 1855. Bishop Pierce presided over this conference and Napoleon W. Burkes was appointed Presiding Elder of the Palestine District and William P. Sansom was appointed to follow A. L. Kavanaugh as pastor. From Phelen's *History of Texas* we get this brief sketch of the life of William P. Sansom:

"William P. Sansom was born in Tennessee in March 1812. Married in 1832. Emigrated to Texas in 1837; licensed to preach in 1842, and in 1846 joined the East Texas Conference, of which he remained a useful and zealous member up to the time of his death."

He died in 1858. There is no record of the last two years of the ministry of William P. Sansom. The East Texas Conference which met in Paris, Texas, November 5, 1856, and presided over by Bishop Paine, reappointed Napoleon W. Burkes as Presiding Elder of the Palestine District and William P. Sansom as pastor of the Crockett Charge.

Samuel D. Sansom was appointed to succeed William P. Sansom. This appointment was made by Bishop Kavanaugh at the session of the East Texas Conference held in Rusk in 1857.

So far as the records go, there is no indication as to whether or not William P. and Samuel D. Sansom were related. Samuel D. was admitted on trial into the East Texas Conference at Henderson, Texas, in 1851. In 1854 he was pastor of the Athens Charge. At the close of this year the membership report for Crockett Charge was 252 white members, 46 colored members and 5 local preachers.

In the last year of this decade, 1858, the session of the East Texas Conference was held at Tyler, Texas, and Bishop Pierce was the presiding bishop. The Crockett Charge was transferred to Rusk District, and Samuel A. Williams was made Presiding Elder and Samuel Lynch pastor of the Crockett Charge. Samuel Lynch was born in Norfolk County, Virginia, November 3, 1824. He was licensed to preach in 1848 by the man who is now his Presiding Elder, Samuel A. Williams. He was admitted to the East Texas Conference at Paris, Texas in 1849. He died in Cherokee County, Texas, October 8, 1867. Though the records are not very clear he seems to have been pastor at Mount Pleasant from 1851 to 1855.

* * * * * *

BAPTIST CHURCH

We do not know who was the first minister who served this church, but there must have been a Sunday School as early as December, 1853, for we find in the Crockett Printer, in the first issue of that paper, a speech made by J. T. Heflin as follows:

"Teachers, Students, Parents and Friends:

"At the close of the privileges of this Sabbath School for the present year, permit me to make a few remarks on the past, and speak a word in reference to what would be the future prospects of a Sabbath School, provided an interest of parents could be engaged in this blessed and holy cause, the Sabbath School. You have seen some of the fruits of a few young ladies' and gentlemen's labors of love this day, dropping from these young and tender plants.

"At the commencement of this school in the spring, when I was made the choice of this Sabbath School, as their Superintendent, I was put by my studies what to do, whether to refuse their request or accept the blessed position I now occupy, so kindly

CROCKETT CHURCHES

offered to me by the voice of those then present, most of whom I am now surrounded with on this occasion.

"Between that time and the next Sabbath, I came to a final conclusion. I had an interview with some who promised to assist as teachers, some of whom are now present which greatly encouraged me in my undertaking, and they, I assure you, will always have the warmest feeling in my heart; and today I can from my heart, thank God and take courage, for that He has inclined our hearts together in the blessed labors of this school and present year, until we have been able to bring it to a close with marked increased interest, both for a spirit to excell among the students, and increased number of teachers and students.

"And now parents, you have already seen some of the rapid advancement some of your children have made, and only some for the want of time, you can only have a part shown you, of what has been done these ten weeks, without reference to the first term or quarter. You hear them answering questions that many of you could not, and only listen to them recite the blessed words of life and think how many verses they have all read every Sabbath morning. Their teachers were deeply interested for them, and on Sunday morning while going up to sanctuary of the Lord, they wonder who of their class will excel this morning and with intense interest here, and instruct them with all the ability they have and encourage them for the next lesson, but think you this is all the interest for them, no thank God, it is only a small part, the Blessed spirit is engaged in impressing the truths upon the young and tender minds of the students of his or her class, and Angels who excel in their strength, wisdom and power are every Sabbath morning with intense interest, beholding what rapid progress these young ladies, gentlemen, girls and boys are making in the knowledge of the things that pertain to eternity and a blessed immortality beyond this mode of existence.

"And to you young Ladies, Gentlemen, Girls and Boys, I return to you, to you I return my most sincere thanks for the kind attention you have given to me both in carrying out my instructions and giving yourselves up most studiously to your studies, to try to accept your classmates for which you have all been rewarded accordingly as I promised you. I have served you as your superintendent the best I could, and have put up and passed over my imperfection far beyond my expectations and I assure you today I feel under lasting obligations to you all and hope that the good Lord will enable you at the next organization of the Sunday School to select one that will far surpass me, as I feel assured such a one can be had.

"In closing this Sabbath School today, it brings solemn impressions upon my mind, my teachers, students and friends, that is this, shall we all meet here again next year? Will I or you be here? In all probability we will not, and before we will have the privilege of convening together again, as we have been for those many weeks past, Death! Death may intervene and separate us forever, as far as meeting in our Sunday School here is concerned; but here arises another solemn thought—should you or I be the victims death should claim, we are prepared to meet in that Sabbath School above, where nights and days will not separate us, but where one glorious day shall shed forth its enlightening rays upon our happy souls; who of us have been faithful to labor to obtain that rest, that remains for the faithful in the Lord, and this be your ever happy lot in my prayer.

"A word to you that have been so faithful as teachers, and I am done. Your labors have been tedious and your sacrifices many I know, to keep up an interest in this school, but I feel assured, you are happy today when you see your labors and sacrifices have not been in vain and we can thank God that our lives have been spared to see this blessed day, since you commenced your labors as teachers here; your motto has been onward and upward, you all have manifested a *perseverence* disposition to advance your classes, and I think I can say to you with Safety, you have the best wishes and warmest feelings of the parents of the children of your classes, for the interest given to them in their studies. And now as an evidence to you young ladies, that have manifested so deep an interest for the prosperity of this school, as teachers, I present to each of you a Bible with my prayer, that it may ever be a light to your feet, a lamp to your way and the guide to you in instructing the tender minds committed to your care as Sabbath School teachers, until your labor of love be rewarded in Heaven above."

From the foregoing it will be reasonable to conclude that up to December 1853, there was an organized Baptist Church in Crockett, and that it did not employ a pastor, although the old Baptist Church building must have been erected about that time. So far as information can be obtained, the original church building was erected about 1850, or soon thereafter, and the organization was first known as "Mount Zion Baptist Church." We obtained this information from the record of a deed from A. T. Monroe to J. L. Lipscmb, James T. Heflin and E. Currie, as trustees of Mount Zion Baptist Church, dated April 18, 1866,

CROCKETT CHURCHES

and recorded in Book S, Page 66 of the Deed Records of Houston County. The witnesses to this deed were: W. A. Stewart, a distinguished lawyer of that day, and W. H. Cundiff, an extensive land speculator. Whether a deed was executed to the property prior to that date is not known, but the building had been in existence at least ten or fifteen years before that time. The consideration expressed in the deed was $150.00 and the lot conveyed is the one on which Miss Lena Woodson's home now stands. This property was later sold by the trustees of the Baptist Church to Dr. J. J. Woodson and the church building remodeled into a dwelling house. The name of the church was later changed to the Crockett Baptist Church.

THE GREAT DIVISION

The following report was sent to the Baptist Herald:

"Dear Brother Link:

"We, the committee appointed by the Baptist Church at Crockett to communicate to you the action which resulted in a consolidation of the two organizations, heretofore existing in this place, beg leave to say that while Bro. D. W. Steele was officiating as pastor of the Missionary Baptist Church of Christ at Crockett, Bro. J. G. Thomas was called to the charge of the Mount Zion Church. Both lamenting the unfortunate differences among the brethren, Bro. Thomas being guided by the Spirit of God was able to digest a plan by which all could come together and submitting it to Bros. Elders J. P. Pritchard and D. W. Steele, they cordially and fully cooperated with him in the glorious work. The three agreed upon the following plan, to-wit:

"1ST. That both the existing church organizations be merged into one.

"2ND. That all members humble themselves before God, and heartily confessing their sins, their failures in duty, their zeal and devotion to the cause of their blessed master, at the same time imploring him to be merciful unto them and bestow upon them his forgiveness and blessings.

"3RD. That they all acknowledge to the Church such errors and wrongs as they may have committed during the long continuance of the deplorable differences, in the spirit of meekness and Love, and that all such acknowledgments be received in the same spirit, full and free forgiveness being extended to each other.

"4TH. That the present names of both churches be dropped and a new one be selected and adopted and that all the records of both churches be turned over to the clerk of the consolidated church, and be thereafter her property.

"5TH. That all members pledge themselves to each other to be faithful and vigilant in the discharge of every church duty, and in the maintenance and enforcement of strict and wholesome discipline in accordance with the teachings of the Eighteenth chapter of Matthew.

"6TH. That all promise to discontinue both public and private card playing, the excessive use of ardent spirits, attendance of dancing parties, circuses, etc. and avoiding as far as possible all appearance of evil.

   J. G. Thomas
   J. P. Pritchard
   D. W. Steele."

"The pastors of the two organizations having called together their churches on Sabbath, April 9, 1871, Bro. D. W. Steele preached a very appropriate sermon for the occasion, and the church being filled to overflowing, and all seeming to take a deep interest, both Saint and Sinners. After the sermon Bro. Thomas presented the recommendations as above set forth which were unanimously adoptd by both organizations, Bro. D. W. Steele then preached a church covenant, prepared by himself and Bro. Thomas which was unanimously adopted, and the church was to be known as the Baptist Church of Crockett. A clerk was then unanimously elected. Bro. Currie then presented a resolution that the Church retain the ministerial services of both the former pastors, to-wit: Bros. D. W. Steele and J. G. Thomas, for the remainder of the year, leaving it with them to appropriate their labors, for the benefit of the church, which resolution was unanimously adopted. Bro. Thomas then proposed to the Brethren and Sisters to meet at the altar and bury all past differences there, extending to each other the right hand of Christian fellowship and love. Then followed such a scene as was never before witnessd in this part of God's moral vineyard. The grayhaired brethren who had been estranged for long years wept tears of joy, for God was pouring out his spirit upon them, not only God's people, but the wayward sinners of that large congregation, were made to weep at the manifestation of his love and mercy. Thanks be to His holy name, our church is at peace and grant, O Lord, to continue their loving kindness.

"The congregation was then dismissed, but assembled in the evening around the sacramental board to commemorate the wonderful love of Christ in shedding his blood to atone for our sins. The church was waited upon by Deacons Jas. Cason and Jas. T. Heflin, Bros. Steele and Thomas officiating, after which they sang a hymn, and again extended to each other the right hand of fellowship, then went out. This was truly a most solemn and interesting occasion and we feel that we are under renewed obligation for the manifestation of God's loving kindness unto us. Although our estrangement has been of years' standing, God has been able to overcome hardness of heart with mercy and love. We beg that you will say to your many readers that the Baptists of Crockett are now a united people, determined with the help of Almighty God to do better in the cause of their blessed Master."

"Yours in bonds of Christian Love,

J. F. Arledge
E. Currie,
Committee."

The foregoing article published in The Baptist Standard, contains such a complete report of the proceedings relating to the reconciliation of the two Baptist Churches that it is not necessary to give further explanation.

Following the reconciliation a protracted revival meeting was held, the preaching being by Elder Thomas H. Pritchard, of Raleigh, N. C., a son of Rev. Joseph P. Pritchard, assisted by Elders J. G. Thomas and D. W. Steele. As a result the record shows that on May 5, 1871, Helena Lacy, Hattie Arledge, Andrew Shivers, Mary Atkinson, Lou Long, Rosa Dalton, F. H. Wagner, Jr., Herbert Wagner, J. M. Odell, Mr. E. Currie, Addie Dailey and M. A. Lacy were received into the church, the ordinance of baptism administered by Elder Thomas H. Pritchard. The Revival continued and on May 14, 1871, R. J. Blair, Thos. Matlock, Mary Dalton, Edward Currie, G. W. Leaverton and J. R. G. Heflin were received into membership and baptized by Elder J. G. Thomas.

On May 21, 1871, G. W. Leaverton, John Erwin, Ellen Simpson, W. B. Otts, Jennie Collins, Lutitia E. Heflin and John Lee were received and baptized by Elder Thos. H. Pritchard. J. J.

Woodson was received by letter. At the evening service the Lord's Supper was celebrated—Elders Thos. H. Pritchard and S. G. Wall and Deacons J. L. Lipscomb and E. R. Helms, officiating.

On May 22, 1871, the folowing resolution was passed:

"We, the members composing the Baptist Church of Crockett, feeling the necessity of a more commodious and comfortable house of worship than the one we now have, RESOLVED, that we use our best efforts to procure the means and to erect a house of worship in which convenience, comfort and elegance will be so blended as to be an honor to the advancement of our Master's cause on earth." And J. F. Arledge, John McConnell and R. J. Blair were appointed to solicit funds, to which were added later James C. Wootters, John H. Burnett, B. W. Neal and J. T. Heflin, and the committee was authorized to purchase a lot and sell the old church property.

On August 6, 1871, a committee was appointed "to have such repairs made as will effectually prevent the nuisance we are now subject to from the cattle and hogs getting into the church lot."

On the First Lord's Day in October 1871, it was decided to connect the church with the Texas Baptist Association.

At this meeting resolutions were passed on the death of James Cason, a deacon in the church and E. R. Helms.

On November 28, 1871, Elder J. R. Jones of Tennessee preached.

First Lord's Day in December, 1871, Elders J. G. Thomas and J. P. Pritchard were elected pastors; Elder Thomas to preach on 1st and 3rd Sabbath and Elder Pritchard on the 4th and 5th Sabbath.

On the third Lord's Day in December 1872, it was agreed at a conference of the church to dispense with the services of a pastor, on account of the embarrassed condition of the church finances, and that the efforts of the church be centered on the erection of a house of worship, which was already under construction.

On the second Lord's Day in March, 1873, a resolution was passed to engage the services of Elder W. D. Beverly at a salary of $600.00 for half his time which offer was accepted by Elder Beverly on the Fourth Lord's Day in January, 1874, and at that time Elder Beverly, Mrs. R. A. Beverly, Ella J. Beverly, Ida A. Beverly, Lula Beverly and Willie S. Beverly were received into the church.

On the Fourth Lord's Day in May 1874, a sermon was preached by the celebrated Dr. R. C. Burleson, who was the same minister who had received Gen. Sam Houston into the church and baptized him. Reliable information has come to

CROCKETT CHURCHES

the author from Mr. John E. Monk that at the time of his baptism, General Houston saw a snake near by and made a characteristic remark about it.

There seems to be no record of the names of the pastors of this church from its organization in 1846 to about 1870. It is probable that it was served by a number of ministers during that period, but no minutes of the proceedings now exist and no person now living can be found to supply this information. It is fortunate that the records furnish authentic information of the names and terms of service from 1871 to date, as follows:

1871—J. G. Thomas and D. W. Steele, co-pastors.
1872—J. G. Thomas and J. P. Pritchard, co-pastors.
1873—J. P. Pritchard
1874-1877—W. D. Beverly
1878—W. W. Kone
1878—W. A. Whipple
1878-1884—A. J. Hill
1884-1886—W. D. Beverly
1888-1890—J. B. Armstrong
1891-1896—W. M. Gaddy
1896-1900—R. E. Morris
1900 —N. B. Graves
1901-1902—W. H. Sowell
1903-1904—J. A. Howard
1905-1906—O. C. Payne
1906—W. S. Roney
1907—H. W. Harris
1909-1912—L. T. Grumbles
1912—E. M. Francis
1914-1917—M. L. Sheppard
1918-1921—L. L. Sams
1921 to date—A. S. Lee

It is a matter of note that during the past 70 years, from 1871 to 1941, the present pastor had nineteen predecessors. So far he has served a period of twenty years constituting more than one-fourth of the seventy years. This speaks well both for the ability and popularity of Brother Lee. During his pastorate the church has probably doubled its membership and has progressed in many ways in the religious work in which it is engaged. His long pastorate will remind us of the pastorate of Rev. S. F. Tenney who was pastor of the Presbyterian Church for fifty-four years.

During these seventy years this church has had three church buildings. The first building was a wooden structure in which the members worshipped from the time that it was built in 1850 until about 1874, when a more pretentious building was erected on the site of the present church building. When the congregation had outgrown this building the present splendid brick church was built, about the year 1911, and the annex was built some time later. The present building will compare favorably with that of any other church in our community and, perhaps, with any other church in any city in Texas, with no greater population.

* * * * * *

HISTORY OF THE FIRST PRESBYTERIAN CHURCH OF CROCKETT, ALSO KNOWN AS THE TENNEY MEMORIAL CHURCH

Rev. Samuel Fisher Tenney, D. D., who was pastor of this church for more than fifty-four years, during his life time prepared a history of the church which is so complete and satisfactory that I have adopted it as a history of the church and which is as follows:

"History of the First Presbyterian Church, Crockett, Texas."

"At an early day there was in Crockett a Cumberland Presbyterian Church, with a brick building as a House of worship. The said building was located near the present residence of Mr. James E. Downes, or nearly in front of the Lipscomb residence. Tradition says that the said brick Church became unsafe and was abandoned. The Cumberland Organization seems not to have grown much and was abandoned at an early date. A record in the old Sessional Record Book of the Cumberland Church (as seen by this writer, the said book being in the possession of Mr. Daniel Murchison, who lived near Crockett), indicated that some of the members of the Cumberland Church were Presbyterians, and that when an opportunity was afforded to organize a Presbyterian Church these members were granted letters of dismission from the Cumberland Church, to enter the new Presbyterian Church at Crockett. The said record also shows that these letters were granted in May, 1854.

"The First Presbyterian Church was organized by Rev. W. C. Dunlap, D. D. who for a time not only preached, but also taught school in Crockett. Tradition says that Dr. Dunlap for a time lived in a house that then stood on our present Church lot. Dr. Dunlap passed through much affliction during his stay in Crockett, losing his wife by death.

"Mrs. Dunlap was before her marriage a Miss Gregg. Her remains lie in our town cemetery. Some of our old citizens remember that Dr. Dunlap for a time preached in the Baptist house of worship, a building which is yet standing, as the residence of

CROCKETT CHURCHES

Mr. G. W. Woodson on the opposite side of the street from our Church lot. Dr. Dunlap in a letter received by this writer in 1878, says that he organized the Church in 1854 or 1855, but he was persuaded that it was in 1854. Mr. A. C. King, one of the first ruling elders, in a letter written to the writer in 1878, states that he thinks the Church was organized in 1856 or 1857. But 1854 is according to Dr. Dunlap's recollection, and this agrees with the record of the Cumberland Presbyterian Church.

"This church was first organized as a New School Presbyterian Church, but in 1864 the New School and the Old School Presbyterian Church in the South, were united, and afterwards the Crockett Church was known only as a Presbyterian Church, or sometimes, popularly called Old School Presbyterian to distinguish it from the Cumberland Presbyterians.

The first records of the Church were probably burned in one of the destructive fires in the early history of the town. So we do not know certainly as to all the names of the first members of the Church. Mr. A. C. King and Col. W. A. Stewart were the first ruling elders. Mr. King remembers the following as the first members:

"A. C. King and wife, and two daughters; W. A. Stewart and wife; G. M. Hunter and wife; and John McGill and wife; ten persons in all. This so far as we know constituted the membership of the first organization. But it is probable that Mr. A. W. Bledsoe and his wife were either members in the first organization or were received into membership shortly afterwards. Mr. Bledsoe was a ruling elder in the Church at an early date. Not having any records we do not know as to what members were afterwards added to the Church in its early history. Mr. A. C. King states that Dr. Dunlap continued to supply the Church about two years. He was afterwards in charge of the Presbyterian Church at Marshall, Texas, and of a Presbyterian Church in New Orleans, and for many years was pastor to Shreveport, Louisiana, where he died. Mr. A. C. King also stated that Dr. S. A. King supplied the Crockett Church about two or three years, but he probably was mistaken as to the length of time, as Dr. King probably preached in Crockett a longer period than two or three years. It was during the ministry of Dr. King that the first house of worship of this Church was built, located near the present residence of Mr. A. W. McConnell. This house was a neat and substaintial structure.

"Mr. A. C. King stated that the first house of worship cost about sixteen hundred dollars, and that a large part of the money was raised by Dr. S. A. King when he attended the General Assembly and visited some of the Northern Cities, and also by help from the General Assembly's Church Erection Fund. It seems however that a debt was left on the Church, and it was about to be sold for this debt, but in 1870, was saved by the liberality of a few members and friends. This first house of worship was used for a time during the Civil War as barracks for Confederate Soldiers, and was considerably abused. The old house, however, still exists and stands on one of our hills as one of the Mary Allen Seminary buildings, and is still used in the service of Christ's Kingdom.

"After Dr. S. A. King removed to another field of labor the Church was left without any regular preacher for many months. In 1870, Rev. A. P. Silliman preached on fifth Sabbaths at Crockett (living at Rusk). During that year he was assisted in a protracted meeting by Rev. Hillery Mosely (then living at Cotton Gin, near Mexia). The result of that meeting was a glorious revival, leaving the Church with forty-five members, besides there were additions to the Methodist and Baptist Churches. Rev. A. P. Silliman and Rev. H. Mosely have long since gone to their reward.

"When the present pastor took charge of the Church in January 1871, there were forty-five members on the Church roll. Only two of these now remain as members: Mrs. Mary Douglas and Mrs. Hattie Collins, though about ten or twelve of these are still living. During the thirty-three years there have been added to this Church 397 members, more than half of them by profession. Sixteen other Presbyterian Churches have been organized in this County, mainly through the instrumentality of the Crockett First Presbyterian Church. Two of these Churches have been dissolved, but fifteen Presbyterian Churches yet remain in the County.

Our present house of worship was build in 1886. Of all those who constituted the Church when it was first organized so far as is known none are living except Mrs. King, wife of Rev. S. A. King, D. D.

"Three of its former members are now ministers of the Gospel, and many of its former members are now useful members in other churches in many places.

"Through the instrumentality of this Church the Mary Allen Seminary was established at this place, an Institution for the Christian education of colored girls, under the care of the Northern Presbyterian Church. There is also a Presbyterian Chuch in connection with the same institution. Several other Presbyterian Churches for colored people have been organized

CROCKETT CHURCHES

through the efforts proceeding from the instrumentality of the First Presbyterian Church.

"Rev. S. A. King, D. D. who ministered to this Church in its early history, and lived in Crockett, was then just beginning the work of the ministry. After serving the Church at Milford for several years, and the First Presbyterian Church at Waco for forty years, he is now Professor of Theology in the Austin Theological Seminary at Austin, Texas. (From sketch written and read at Centennial of Crockett Church, May 22, 1904, by S. F. Tenney).

"The foregoing sketch brings the history of this Church down to May 22nd, 1904. Dr. Samuel Fisher Tenney continued his fruitful ministry as pastor of this church until old age and infirmity induced him to be released from active duty, and he tendered his resignation as pastor of the church in the early part of the year 1925, after a continuous pastorate of 54 years. The pastoral relation was then dissolved by Presbytery, but Dr. Tenney continued to preach as long as his health would permit. In 1926, Rev. J. L. Spears accepted a call from this church and served as pastor acceptably for ten years, when he accepted a call from the First Presbyterian Church in Marlin, where he still holds the pastorate.

"In 1936 this church called its present pastor, Rev. R. Gage Lloyd, who has carried on a faithful and successful ministry up to this time and is still very dear to his flock.

"In this brief history, it is impossible to give the full story of the long and faithful pastorate of Dr. Tenney. In recognition of his eminent services, the name of the church was changed to 'Tenney Memorial Church' and so it will continue for all future time."

THE CHRISTIAN CHURCH

Prior to 1899 or 1900, there was no organized Christian Church in Crockett. About that time a small band of members of this denomination were accustomed to meet first in the Opera House and later in the District Court room in the courthouse and hold religious services, which were conducted by Rev. Virgil Graves. During the year 1901 Rev. Harry H. Hamilton, of Lovelady, began to visit this little flock and soon gathered quite a number of followers into a congregation that undertook the erection of a church building. Too much credit cannot be given Mr. and Mrs. W. V. Berry for their share in infusing new life into the church at this time. It is hardly an over statement to say that had it not been for the efficient efforts of Mr. Berry, at that time, it is probable that the present attractive church building would never have been erected. The following ministers have served this church since the erection of the church building:

Rev. J. A. Arnold, Rev. B. F. Trimble, Rev. Edmund S. Allhands, Rev. W. B. Parks, Rev. I. N. Jett, Rev. Albert T. Pitts, Rev. W. H. Marler, Rev. John A. Stephens, Rev. J W. Walton and the present pastor, Rev Marion Browning.

Among the members of this church who have had a large share in its organization and success are the following:

Mr. and Mrs. W. V. Berry, Mr. and Mrs. J. W. Brightman, Mr. and Mrs. S. E. Jensen, Mr. and Mrs. Major Sharp, Mr. John R. Sheridan, Mrs. M. J. Kelley, Mrs. E. Currie, Judge Porter Newman, Mr. and Mrs. Cal Beeson, Dr. M. A. Thomas, Mr. C. D. Towery, Mr. W. H. Long and many others who have been faithful and loyal members.

THE CONCORD PRESBYTERIAN CHURCH

The following history of the Concord Presbyterian Church was prepared by Dr. Sam M. Tenney, Curator of the Historical Foundation at Montreat, N. C.

About the first of the year 1875, S. M. Thompson, a ruling Elder of the Crockett Presbyterian Church removed with his family (six of whom were members of the above named church) to what is now known as the neighborhood of Concord Church, Houston County, Texas. At his request his pastor, Rev. S. F. Tenney, preached occasionally at his house, and afterwards monthly. Preaching was thus kept up about two years, and during which time a protracted meeting was held, lasting a few days, in which much interest was manifested, but resulted in no additions to the Presbyterian Church. Rev. J. D. Porter assisted in the meeting. About the first of the year, 1877, a Church building was erected and occupied for preaching early in Spring. Being furnished afterwards, it was dedicated on the first Sabbath of November, 1877, Rev. H. B. Boude preaching the sermon.

Soon after this house was occupied, a Sabbath School was commenced, of which S. M. Thompson was chosen Superin-

CROCKETT CHURCHES

tendent. This school "having obtained help of God" continued to the time of this writing, and is intimately connected with the history of the organization which is hereby recorded.

At this Church, a protracted meeting was held in the summer of 1877, in which Rev. Robt. Bell assisted and also Rev. D. P. Cullen, of the M. Episcopal Church South. This meeting resulted in two additions to the Presbyterian Church: Mr. John M. Simms and Mrs. Dolly Tunstall, the latter 83 years old, and the former a young man.

At the fall meeting of the Presbytery of Eastern Texas, 1878, Rev. S. F. Tenney and Elder S. M. Thompson obtained permission to organize a Church in this neighborhood, should the way be clear.

On Sabbath, November 10th, 1878, Rev. S. F. Tenney, commenced a protracted meeting, and was afterwards assisted by Rev. J. D. Porter and Rev. W. M. McElwee. God poured out His Spirit, Souls were converted. On Sabbath the 17th of November, the Lord's Supper was administered, four adults were baptized on profession of faith, and at the close of the afternoon service, a Presbyterian Church was organized, with seventeen members, the members answering affirmatively by rising, the following questions: "Do you, in reliance on God for strength, solemnly promise and covenant that you will walk together as an organized Church, on the principles of the faith and order of the Presbyterian Church, and that you will study the purity and harmony of the whole body?"

The presiding minister then said "I now pronounce and declare that you are constituted a church, according to the work of God and the faith and order of the Presbyterian Church in the United States. In the name of the Father and of the Son and of The Holy Ghost, Amen."

The following persons were included in the above organization:—

1. S. M. Thompson
2. Mrs. C. R. Thompson
3. Miss Sally M. Thompson
4. Miss Dolly V. Thompson
5. Miss Emma T. Thompson
6. Thomas W. Thompson
7. Mrs. Dolly Tunstall
8. Mr. N. O. Thompson
9. Mrs. E. A. Thompson
10. Miss L. C. Thompson
11. Edward L. Thompson
12. John M. Simms
13. Jefferson Simms
14. Miss Allie Simms
15. Miss Augusta Daniel
16. Miss Eugene Hale
17. Mrs. Angeline Craddock

HISTORY OF HOUSTON COUNTY

LOVELADY BAPTIST CHURCH

By Mrs. Ella Mainer Young

Shortly after 1870, the date not definite, a few earnest citizens of the little hamlet of Lovelady, realizing the urgent necessity of spiritual guidance and training of the young, as well as the adult of the community, came together for the purpose of organizing a Sunday School.

Since there were no church houses to serve the various denominations represented in the town, this earnest group, led by T. N. Mainer, of Baptist faith, and Mrs. Belle Barbee, of Methodist faith, met in the frame building then used for day school. Thus came into being the first religious organization of Lovelady, a union Sabbath School. Prominent among the names of teachers listed in an old class record book belonging to T. N. Mainer in 1876 were the following: Mrs. M. E. Cone, Mrs. Ida Adams, B. G. Freeman, Dr. H. L. Hogg, E. E. Larue.

Shortly after the organization of the Sunday School, those of Baptist belief, together with the Knights and Ladies of Honor, erected a two-story building on the site of the present church. In the upper story were held the meetings of the lodge, while the lower served for church auditorium and Sunday School room.

The early Lovelady church was served by pastors who lived in Crockett, dividing their time between the churches. Among these were such outstanding men as A. Armstrong and Bill Gaddy.

In 1909, during the pastorate of T. N. Mainer, a brick building was erected, and this since has housed a membership composed largely of the descendants of the early pioneers, who laid the foundation of a church that has sent forth from its protecting fold men and women embued with a fervid zeal for righteous service to humanity whether ministering in the high realms of the highest offices of our state or its halls of learning. Among these were Miss Myrtle Mainer, the wife of Hon. Pat M. Neff, former Governor, and now president of Baylor University, and Miss Mildred Collins, wife of Homer P. Rainey, President of the University of Texas.

BIOGRAPHIES

CAPTAIN ISAAC ADAIR

Captain Isaac Adair was born in 1823 and married Augusta Louise Smith, daughter of Captain John T. Smith about 1852. He died at Santa Fe, New Mexico while serving as Captain of a Company in the Confederate Army, on April 7th, 1862, at 4 P. M.

He held several important offices in Houston County during his life including the office of District Clerk for a short time.

A muster roll of his Company appears elsewhere in this history. He was survived by his widow, who later married James M. Porter. He was survived by two children, John Adair, who married Miss Alice Walsh, and Emma Adair, who married Alfred Brown.

All of these are now dead.

Altogether, he was a good citizen, a brave soldier and died a patriot in the service of his country.

COL. EARLE ADAMS

Col. Adams was born in Edgefield District, South Carolina, on September 7, 1847, being the son of a Baptist minister, Rev. Thomas Adams, and with his parents went to Louisiana in 1853. He enlisted as a volunteer in the Confederate army at the age of 14 years and served four years under General Nathan B. Forest, the great cavalry leader, surrendering in Alabama at the close of the war. Col. Adams laid the foundation of a classical education in a select school maintained by the patronage of Louisiana planters at Clinton, of which a Dr. Dembinski, a Pole and graduate of the German University of Heidelberg, was the head. His advanced education academic and professional, was secured at Centenary College, then located at Jackson, Louisiana from which he obtained his Master's degree and at 20 years of age he married Miss Emma Miller, a daughter of a Lutheran minister, a Rev. J. J. Miller, and a niece of Rev. J. C. Miller, president of Centenary College. He was admitted to the bar in

1869 and practiced law for five years in Louisiana, coming to Crockett on January 14, 1875, where he has since made his home. For two years, 1878-80, he served as county attorney of Houston County, and for six years as district attorney of the third judicial district. He then retired from active politics and engaged in the private practice of his profession, and at his death was recognized throughout the length and breath of Texas as one of the foremost lawyers, one almost without a peer in criminal practice. At the time of his death he was president of the Houston County Bar Association. Col. Adams united with the Baptist Church in early life, and in his more mature years was a very active member of that denomination.

Col. Adams was survived by his wife, who has since died; two daughters, Mrs. Emma Castleberg and Mrs. Denny Arledge and one son, Earle Adams, who has since died. His oldest son, Hon. Joe Adams, who was his law partner, preceded him in death. He is buried in Glenwood Cemetery, Crockett, Texas.

THE ALDRICH FAMILY

BIOGRAPHY OF THE AUTHOR

Armistead Albert Aldrich, the author of this history, was born in Crockett, Texas, on the tenth day of April, 1858, the son of Oliver Cromwell Aldrich and Eliza Jane (Masters) Aldrich, being the same day on which his father was first elected County Clerk of Houston County. The house in which he was born then occupied the site of the present Tenney Memorial Presbyterian Church. His first school was taught by Miss Margaret Hall, later Mrs. John S. Shivers, where he learned his alphabet. Later his teacher was Mrs. Jane Blair, the wife of Colonel John Blair, a veteran of the Mexican War. His next teacher was Mrs. Lucy Collins, who was his teacher in 1870.

In 1871, he was a student under Major John Spence, one of the noblest men who ever taught school. One year, 1874, he studied with George P. Miller. After that from 1875 to 1877, he was a student under Hon. W. B. Page, one of the ablest instructors who ever followed the profession of teaching. He finished his high school work under Mr. Page, and at his suggestion in 1877, attended the University of Virginia during the session of 1877-1878. He then began the study of law, in the well known offices of Nunn & Williams, and was admitted to the bar in 1883. His political life began as alderman of the City of Crockett, in

BIOGRAPHIES

1890, and he is now the only surviving member of that city council. In 1892, he was elected County Judge of Houston County and held the office for two successive terms. In 1900, he was elected as Representative to the 27th Legislature and served one term only, not offering for a second term. He attended many State Democratic Conventions and was chosen Presidential Elector in 1936, and attended the second inauguration of President Franklin D. Roosevelt.

He is a member and elder of the Tenney Memorial Presbyterian Church, a life member of the Knights of Pythias, an honorary member of the board of directors of the Crockett Chamber of Commerce, a charter member of Crockett Lions Club, and was for nearly thirty years a member of the board of trustees of Austin College, who conferred on him the honorary degree of LL. D on May 31st 1937.

ALBERT AUGUSTUS ALDRICH

The second son of Collin Aldrich, Sr. was born on Mustang Prairie about 1837 and spent his boyhood there, with but few school advantages. In 1860 he boarded with Tom Vaughan at Old Randolph and went to school to Judge S. M. Thompson. On July 4th he became a member of Currie's Company of Volunteers and marched away with that company on that day and reached Virginia in time to become a member of Company I of Hoods Brigade. He served for four full years in the Confederate army, and participated in the battles of Fredericksburg, and other hard fought battles including the battle of Gettysburg, where he was wounded and made a splendid record as a brave and fearless soldier. After the end of the war he returned to Crockett and engaged in the mercantile business for many years. About 1879 he married Miss Josephine Coleman, the daughter of Uncle Dan Coleman, soon afterwards they removed to Athens where his wife and their only child, a son named John died. He then returned to Crockett and for several years lived in the home of his brother Collin Aldrich, Jr. His last years were spent in the home of the A. A. Aldrich, where he died on March 18, 1917, at the age of eighty years. He is buried in the Old Crockett Cemetery by the side of his mother.

COLLIN ALDRICH

Collin Aldrich was born in Menden, Massachusetts, on Sunday May 2nd, 1801, the son of George Aldrich, a soldier of the

HISTORY OF HOUSTON COUNTY

War for Independence of the United States. He came to Texas in 1829 where his first son, Oliver Cromwell Aldrich, was born on January 5th, 1830 in what is now Red River County, near Clarksville. He removed to a place, then in Nacogdoches District, and now known as Houston County, where he located on the league of land, known as the Collin Aldrich League, and near the spot where his grave is situated. He was a volunteer in the army for Texas Independence, and Albert Sidney Johnston, Secretary of War in the days of the Republic, certified that "he fought bravely at the Battle of San Jacinto." His name appears on the San Jacinto Monument.

He had an active part in the creation and organization of Houston County on June 12th, 1837, and was elected the first Chief Justice of the County in September, 1837, which office he held until 1840. He married Mrs. Elizabeth Crownover, whose maiden name was Elizabeth Lawrence. He died in June 1842. He was survived by his widow who died in 1875, and the following children: Oliver Cromwell Aldrich, Albert Augustus Aldrich, Collin Aldrich and Ann Aldrich.

COLLIN ALDRICH, JR.

Collin Aldrich, Jr. was the third son of Collin and Elizabeth Aldrich, was born on Mustang Prairie, Houston County, 1840. He received his education in the country schools of Houston County and had scarcely reached his majority when he was mustered into the Confederate army on July 4th, 1860, at Old Randolph in Houston County, and marched off on that day as a member of Currie's Company and became a member of Hood's Brigade. He remained in the army until the end of the war and in 1865 returned to Crockett. In 1866, he married Bettie Kyle, a daughter of Matthew G. Kyle, of Augusta, and began business as a merchant at Augusta, with his father-in-law, under the name of Kyle & Aldrich. During his residence at Augusta his wife, Bettie, died leaving an only child, a son who was named Wace, a peculiar name, composed of the initials of his friends, who served as waiters at his wedding, Billy Wingfield, Gus Aldrich, John Collins and Dan Egbert. After the death of his first wife he married her sister, Julia Kyle, who survived him and they were the parents of three children, George, who died without having married, Jesse Kyle Aldrich, who married Ruby Godsey and Charm, who is the wife of B. L. Satterwhite, a prominent business man of Crockett.

BIOGRAPHIES

OLIVER CROMWELL ALDRICH

Was born on the 5th day of January 1830, in the Mexican State of Coahuila and Texas, on Red River, near where the City of Clarksville now stands, the son of Collin Aldrich, and Elizabeth Aldrich. In that early day he had scant opportunity for an education, and attended country schools for a few months, but was self educated and by his own efforts acquired a fairly good education and became what could be called a well informed man. When a young man he clerked and kept books for A. T. Monroe, a leading merchant of Crockett, and in that way became an efficient business man. In 1855 he was chosen County Treasurer of Houston County and served in that capacity for only a short time. On the 5th day of January 1857, he married Miss Eliza Jane Masters, daughter of Henry Masters, in the old Double Log house, where Henry Masters lived, on Masters Hill, about three miles east of the courthouse in Crockett, now known as Campbell's Hill. On the 10th day of April 1858, he was elected County Clerk of Houston County for the first time and held the office until 1868, when he was removed by the Reconstruction Administration. In 1873, when the Democrats regained control of affairs in Texas, he was elected District and County Clerk, the offices having been combined and held that office until the offices were separated under the constitution of 1876, when he was elected County Clerk and held that office until 1886. He was for many years a member of Lothrop Masonic Lodge and also a member of Palestine Commandery of Royal Arch Masons. His wife preceded him in death in 1874, and he died on September 1889, at the age of fifty nine years, and is buried in the Old Crockett Cemetery. He left surviving him the following children: Armistead Albert Aldrich, Mary Aldrich, later the wife of A. P. Moore, of Tyler, Collin Isaac Aldrich, Rush Oliver Aldrich, Elizabeth Aldrich, who married C. M. Newton, and Robert Lee Aldrich.

JACOB ALLBRIGHT

This pioneer was here before Houston County was erected or organized. In fact he was one of the organizers and was elected the first County Clerk of the county in September 1837 and held the office for more than one term. He later filled the offices of Notary Public and tax assessor and collector. His father, John Allbright, was also a pioneer and brought a large family with him to Texas in the early thirties. His father met a tragic death,

HISTORY OF HOUSTON COUNTY

soon after his arrival in Texas, at the hands of the Indians. Jacob Allbright was one of ten children of John Allbright, Sr. His brothers were:—Edward Allbright, William Allbright, Solomon Allbright and John Allbright, Jr. His sisters were: Sarah Strand, Margaret Ware, Mary Long, Nancy Long and Catherine Kirchoffer.

Jacob Allbright settled on a bluff on the East bank of the Trinity River and established a town there known as Alabama. This town became the business center of a thriving population and a commercial business. He established and conducted a ferry and did a warehouse and commercial business there. Trinity College was located there and he was one of the trustees, composed of the most notable pioneers of that day. The history of Trinity College is given elsewhere in this history. Jacob Allbright lived and died at Alabama and his grave is in sight of his old home.

MURDOCK McINTOSH BAKER

Murdock McIntosh Baker was born April 1st, 1838 in McNairy County, Tennessee near the town of Purdy. His parents were Archibald Baker and Mary Murchison Baker who had emigrated to Tennessee from Moore County, North Carolina. His father died when he was eight years old, leaving him the mainstay of the family consisting of his mother, his sister and himself. In 1852 when he was fourteen years old, the family came to Texas, overland from their home to Memphis, down the Mississippi by boat to a point below Natchez, thence overland to Crockett bringing their livestock, wagons and household goods with them and settled on a small farm three miles northwest from Crockett near Cook's mountain. Three years later he bought a farm 3½ miles north from Crockett on the Grapeland road where he made his home the rest of his life. He joined the 13th Texas cavalry soon after the beginning of the War Between the States, furnishing his own horse and saddle, and trained with the regiment for a few months on Mustang Prairie before leaving for the front. Soon afterward the cavalry regiment against the North regarding the War but he never forgot he being assigned to Capt. John Smith's company in Col. John H. Burnett's regiment, Walker's brigade.

At the close of the war he came home and again engaged in farming. In the later years of his life he felt little if any resentment against the North regarding the war but he never forgot or forgave the carpet baggers and their acts in the reconstruction period following the War.

BIOGRAPHIES

He joined the Cumberland Presbyterian Church in his early boyhood and was a consistent member as long as he lived and often walked from his home to Crockett to attend Sunday school and church services in the little brick church located where Miss Amelia Collins' home now stands. He married Miss Mittie Royall, of Athens, Texas, Feb. 8th, 1868 to which union seven children were born. He built and operated for many years a cotton gin and grist mill on his farm and it was always his practice to never charge a widow for ginning her cotton or grinding her corn. He served Houston County as County Treasurer for six or seven terms during the 1880s and 1890s. His wife died Oct. 26th, 1882 and in Sept. 1885 he married Mrs. Minnie Harris Murchison to which union two children were born. He died Feb. 6th, 1906 survived by the widow and nine children, as follows:

The first born, Dick Baker, who married a daughter of Judge, E. Winfree, and is now dead; Arch Baker, the President of the First National Bank of Crockett, is still living in Crockett; John F. Baker, who married Blanche, a daughter of Hon. F. H. Bayne, and is now dead; Tucker Baker, who married Miss Hattie Crook, and is still living; Rev. Henry Baker, a distinguished minister of the Presbyterian Church, is now dead; Lucy May, who married George H. Denny, a prominent citizen of Crockett, is still living in Crockett; Mittie, who married Rev. O. C. Payne and is now dead; Alwilda, who married Carter Anderson and is still living and Harry Baker, who still survives. Altogether they were a distinguished family.

DOCTOR JAMES G. BARBEE

Mrs. Fannie Mae Barbee Hughes of Wharton, a granddaughter of Dr. Barbee, gave the author the following family history:

"Dr. J. G. Barbee, came to Shelby County when quite a young man, practiced medicine there during the feud of moderators and regulations. In 1851, they were living in Crockett. My father, J. G. Barbee, Jr. was born there that year. The Barbee's were French Huguenots, and came to the United States from France, seeking life and liberty from religious oppression. Chappel Hill University, Chappel Hill, N. C. was largely promoted by our great, great grandfather, Christopher Barbee. He gave the first 241 acres. East and West Halls, the first buildings, were erected on this acreage and stand today in a fairly good state of preservation. Christopher Barbee's old law office building is standing nearby the campus, as is the old homestead, a gift from the Barbee family to the university.

"In Memorial Hall, the large center tablet was erected to the memory of Christopher Barbee. The Barbee history included in the history of Chappel Hill University, was written by the father of Dr. Battle, at one time president of the University of Texas. I visited the University of Chappel Hill last summer and felt quite humble, but had a thrill I shall never forget.

"My father, J. G. Barbee, met my mother at the home of her aunt, the wife of Col. M. C. Gallaway. Col. Gallaway served on Forrest's staff during the Civil War.

"The first Ku Klux uniforms were made and worn in Memphis. My mother's aunt, Fannie Gallaway, and other Memphis ladies made them. Being unable to finish them in time for the parade, my mother, Fannie Barker Fifer, and other Memphis girls, were sworn in, to sew on the buttons.

"Colonel Gallaway was the owner and editor of the Commercial Appeal and advocated the choice of Col. N. B. Burrow for the presidency of the Confederacy. Colonel Burrow was an uncle of Mrs. Miranda Burrow Barbee, wife of Dr. J. G. Barbee, and mother of my father, J. G. Barbee, Jr. Miranda Burrow was thrice married. At the age of 15 she married Dr. Barbee in Tennessee. They came by horseback to Texas. After Dr. Barbee's death, near Caldwell, she married a Mr. Keene, and after his death a Davidson.

"Mrs. Virginia Wall-Frymier was a sister of my father, Col. N. B. Barbee was his oldest brother. Another sister, Mary, married Tom Gay, a son of Tom Gay of Texas' heroic pioneers, at San Felipe, and Old Washington. Ab Keene, a half-brother, was nephew of George Keene of Jefferson, one of the Mier prisoners. He and a brother drew white beans in the lottery for life. I think you are undoubtedly acquainted with the many valorous deeds of George Lawson Keene in the World War, and know the story of how those medals, that were stolen from him, were replaced by the United States.

FIELDING HARVEY BAYNE

Fielding Harvey Bayne was born in San Augustine County, December 5th, 1846. His parents were Grafton H. Bayne and Harriet Kinley Bayne. They came to Houston County in 1854 and bought and settled on a farm on White Rock Creek, when Harvey was only eight years of age. Here he was raised from his early boyhood until he was sixteen when he volunteered in the Confederate Army and served in Company H, Fifth Texas Bri-

Cynthia Ann Parker
and
child

Hon.
Isaac Parker

UPPER LEFT: Cyrus H. Randolph. UPPER RIGHT: Gen. John F. Beavers. LOWER LEFT: H. F. Craddock. LOWER RIGHT: Mrs. Nancy Jane (Burton) Hail.

UPPER LEFT: Capt. A. D. Elam and Mrs. A. D. Elam. UPPER RIGHT: Andrew Edwards Gossett. LOWER LEFT: Mrs. Nannie Hansen Stuart. LOWER RIGHT: Edward Augustus Gause.

UPPER LEFT: Judge L. W. Cooper. UPPER RIGHT: Mrs. Dolly T. Worthington. LOWER LEFT: William B. Worthington. LOWER RIGHT: Judge Samuel Morris Thompson.

UPPER LEFT: Gen. Thomas P. Collins. UPPER RIGHT: James P. Collins. LOWER LEFT: Mrs. Emma Collins. LOWER RIGHT: Mrs. Mary Collins Douglass.

UPPER LEFT: Major John Wortham. UPPER RIGHT: Steward Alexander Miller. LOWER LEFT: Mrs. Lucy Atkinson Collins. LOWER RIGHT: A. LeGory.

UPPER LEFT: Henry J. Arledge. UPPER RIGHT: Monroe Thomas. LOWER LEFT: Daniel McIntosh Murchison. LOWER RIGHT: Mrs. Maud Sims Pence.

ABOVE: George B. Lundy. LOWER LEFT: W. B. Page. LOWER RIGHT: William McLean.

UPPER LEFT: Major John Spence. UPPER RIGHT: Capt. John H. Wootters.
LOWER LEFT: J. G. Barbee. LOWER RIGHT: Col. George English.

UPPER LEFT: Joshua J. Hall. UPPER RIGHT: Mrs. Adelle Robbins Spence.
LOWER LEFT: John Collins, Jr., LOWER RIGHT: Mahala Roberts Hall.

UPPER LEFT: Mrs. Rebecca Miller. UPPER RIGHT: Jacob Allbright.
LOWER LEFT: Mrs. Kitty Burnett. LOWER RIGHT: Dr. Albert Woldert.

UPPER LEFT: Mrs. Amelia Vann Collins. UPPER RIGHT: Hon. J. W. Madden. LOWER LEFT: Joe Adams. LOWER RIGHT: John McConnell.

UPPER LEFT: J. M. Hall. UPPER RIGHT: A. H. Wootters. LOWER LEFT: William J. Foster. LOWER RIGHT: W. H. L. Burton.

Upper Left: Mrs. Willie Rice. Upper Right: Joseph Rice. Lower Left: Eliza Jane Aldrich. Lower Right: Oliver Cromwell Aldrich.

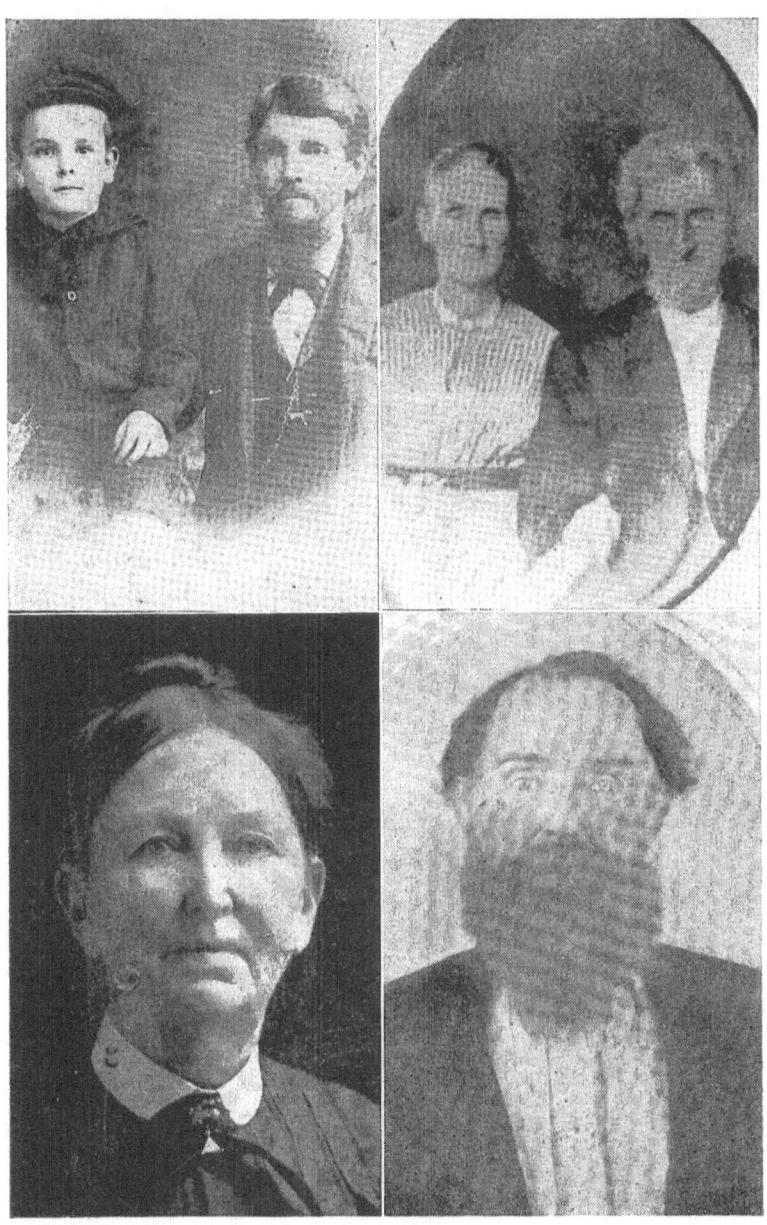

UPPER LEFT: Dr. Stephen T. Beasley & Son. UPPER RIGHT: George Washington Hallmark and wife. LOWER LEFT: Mrs. Virginia Barber Frymier. LOWER RIGHT: Daniel M. Coleman.

Upper Left: Mrs. Helen Williams Nunn. Upper Right: Col. David Alexander Nunn. Lower Left: Judge Frank A. Williams. Lower Right: Mrs. Corinne Nunn Corry.

BIOGRAPHIES

gade, Green's Cavalry. He fought in the battles of Baton Rouge, Monets Ferry, Mansfield and Pleasant Hill and participated in the Louisiana campaign.

In 1868, he worked on the farm of Wash and Porter Holley, near Pennington, and in 1869 and 1870, he attended Steel's Academy, at Pennington, taught and conducted by the celebrated teacher, Dr. Steele.

In January 1871, he came to Crockett and clerked for Major J. C. Wootters and resided there until his death on December 18th, 1937.

On January 5th, 1876 he married Miss Elizabeth Jones Long, a granddaughter of Col. John Long, a pioneer of Houston County.

He was elected Sheriff of Houston County in 1876 and served for fifteen years, during the greater part of the period his office included the duties of tax collector.

He was elected Representative to the Twenty-Third Legislature.

He is survived by his four children, Mrs. Narcie Crook, Mrs. Blanche Baker, Mrs. Josephine Barnes and his only son, Harvey Bayne.

In his earlier life he was a member of the Baptist Church, but later affiliated with the Presbyterian Church and was made an elder in the Tenney Memorial Church at Crockett, which office he held up to time of his death. His wife preceded him in death by several years.

DOCTOR STEPHEN THOMAS BEASLEY

Doctor Stephen Thomas Beasley was born at LaGrande, Georgia, March 11th 1840, the son of Dr. William Parks Beasley and Louisa Edwards Beasley. He was educated at the University of Georgia and graduated in 1858. He first studied law and taught school for a while. He then entered The Jefferson Medical School in Philadelphia in 1859, and was among the seceding students, caused by John Brown's raid at Harper's Ferry. He continued his medical education at Augusta, Georgia, then at Atlanta, Georgia, where he delivered the valedictory at his graduation. From there he went to New Orleans and became a private student of Doctors Schopin and Schupert, and was at the same time a student of the New Orleans School of Medicine, graduating in 1861. Immediately afterwards he entered the Confederate Army, as assistant surgeon of the Thirteenth Georgia Regiment, being a commissioned surgeon at 21 years of age. He was in a campaign in West Virginia with Generals, Floyd, Wise and Lee. On April 1st, 1862, he was wounded at White Marsh Island, near Savannah, Georgia. He afterwards joined his regiment and served until the end of the war.

Doctor Beasley came to Texas in 1865, and settled at Marshall for a year. From there he came to Porter Springs, in Houston County, where he carried on a successful practice. In 1885 the family moved to Crockett, where they resided until his death, December 3rd, 1916. He was married in 1862 to Miss Elizabeth Crook, who died in 1864. In 1867 he married Miss Grace Smith, of Porter Springs, a daughter of Captain John T. Smith. She died in 1872, leaving two children, Ada Louise, now Mrs. W. H. Denny, of Crockett, and Stephen T. Beasley, Jr., of Sealy, Texas. In 1874, he married Miss Kate Smith, of Huntsville, Texas. To this union there were born seven children, including the following: Mrs. John C. Millar, Mrs. G. Q. King, John Gordon Beasley, Sr. generally known as Jack, Miss Nell Beasley, of San Antonio. He was a member of the Methodist Church. He was Mayor of Crockett from 1887 to 1901, and his son Jack served for several terms later. He was County Health Officer for Houston County for several years.

H. W. BEESON

H. W. Beeson lived within three or four miles of Crockett for many years and a great many of his descendents are living in and around Crockett now. Although he had a large family of children, I believe that only three of these are now surviving. From these I have by diligent effort, obtained the information that follows:

He was born October 29, 1812, and died April 15, 1890. His full name was Horeston Wilson Beeson. He came to Texas from Alabama in 1847, and spent the remainder of his life at his farm home about three or four miles South of Crockett, a farm that was later owned and operated by his son-in-law, Bill Austin.

He was twice married and by his first wife, had the following children: Argayle Beeson, Billy Beeson, Walter Beeson, Jehu Beeson, Jennie Beeson, who married G. W. Woodson; Alvis Beeson and Cal Beeson. The last named died near Crockett only a short time ago.

His second wife was a daughter of Dr. W. A. Murchison, who once was a prominent citizen living northwest of Grapeland on Elkhart, near Dailey. His younger children were: Mrs. Willie

BIOGRAPHIES

Lovell, Mrs. Mack Hale, Mrs. A. M. Langston, Mrs. Anna Austin and Wilse Beeson.

One of his sons, Jehu Beeson, married a daughter of Judge R. N. Read, and lived on the old Read home place on Nevills Prairie, near what is now known as Prairie Point. The author is indebted to Dr. Sam P. Beeson of Weldon for much of this information. One of the remarkable facts in connection with his history is that both of his grandfathers, H. W. Beeson and Judge R. N. Read, were seventh sons. H. W. Beeson is a pioneer whose memory deserves to be perpetuated.

DR. JEHU ARMISTEAD BEESON

Dr. Jehu Armistead Beeson, pioneer doctor of Houston County, son of John and Priscilla Saunders Beeson of Guilford County, North Carolina, came to Texas about 1838 and settled near Crockett, Houston County, two miles north of Hurricane Bayou on the old Palestine, Texas, Road, about five or six miles from Crockett. He practiced medicine in what is now the Murchison Neighborhood and also practiced in the small town of Houston and in its Fort Houston, which was then in operation. He took out his headright grant in what is now Anderson County. He brought with him his mother, a widow, Priscilla Saunders Beeson, whose headright was in Rusk County, four miles north of the town of Henderson, and he also brought his niece Ann Eliza Lindsay, daughter of Jane Beeson, his sister. Ann Eliza married later Wm. Young Lacy of Cherokee County, son of Martin Lacy of Fort Lacy.

From all accounts his brother, Harston W. Beeson, had preceded him by several years, and had settled in Houston County about 1836, bringing with him his wife, Jane Shelley (of Mansfield, La.) and two children, Argyle and John, being one of the very early settlers of the district.

In 1844 Jehu Armistead Beeson went back to North Carolina, Guilford County and married Paulina Catherine Tatum. She was a niece of Richard G. Beeson's wife who lived near Greenboro and owned a tobacco plantation. She was reared by her aunt and uncle and educated at old Salem College, N. C.

Dr. Beeson did not live a year after he was married. He died from pneumonia, the effect of his swimming the Trinity River on a freezing night that froze his clothing. He left one child, Jane Armistead Beeson, who was born about two months after he died, which was on April 30th, 1845.

His widow, Mrs. Pauline Catherine Tatum Beeson, married

HISTORY OF HOUSTON COUNTY

Dr. W. G. W. Jowers (another pioneer doctor of Houston County) in Crockett, May 13th, 1846, and soon after they moved to Palestine in the newly created county of Anderson. She died on the 27th day of September, 1862 and is buried in Palestine. Her daughter, Jane Armistead Beeson, grew up in Palestine and married Nathaniel Wyche Hunter, a lawyer of Palestine and the son of a pioneer family, on September 6th, 1865.

WILLIAM V. BERRY

If a man's importance to his community is to be measured by his accomplishments, then W. V. Berry is to be rated as one of the outstanding citizens of Crockett and Houston County in his day. He was born in Louisiana on June 2nd, 1856, and came with his father, Dr. Henry Berry, to Houston County when only sixteen years of age. His father bought and settled on a farm near Dailey, and W. V. Berry worked there for a short time. Before he reached his majority, he was employed by Frank Edens, a merchant of Grapeland, at ten dollars per month and out of this meager salary, he saved enough money to send himself to Soule Commercial College at New Orleans, where he qualified himself for a business life, and returned to Grapeland and worked for B. F. Edens in an important capacity, until he went into business with Major Jas. F. Martin at Grapeland. This continued for a short time, after which he came to Crockett and bought out the Henry Grabenheimer stock of merchandise and went into the mercantile business, which he carried on for many years. On October 16th, 1888 he bought the Walter Coleman Farm about 4 miles southeast of Crockett and began farming operations on a large scale. This farm was later sold to some northern people and is now known as the Stockton Farm or Ranch.

Mr. Berry was instrumental in assembling a large body of land about five miles north of Crockett, at a place on the railroad, then known as Stark's Switch and which is now known as Latexo. He also purchased the old J. J. Woodson Place about three miles south of Crockett which later was known as the Clinton Farm.

In 1890 he purchased the hotel property previously known as the Collins & Douglas store and changed the name to the Pickwick Hotel, and operated the same for many years and as a hotel proprietor was known all over the State of Texas.

He had a unique and varied career. His mother was a devout Catholic and eloped from a convent to marry his father, who

BIOGRAPHIES

as a physician attended many a case of yellow fever. Mr. Berry as a boy served as altar boy to a Catholic priest in a famous church in New Orleans.

He died in Crockett on the 6th day of September, 1926, and is buried in Glenwood Cemetery. His widow, Mrs. Alice Lively Berry and his children still survive ,and his son, Mayes Berry is a prominent business man of Crockett.

JOHN ANDREW BOX

This pioneer is worthy of a place in this county's history, for he was a veteran of San Jacinto, and his name is inscribed in both bronze and marble, for it is listed with the other heroes, in the lofty San Jacinto Monument, and the Centennial Commission of Control has provided him a handsome marble marker at his grave.

He was born in Tennesse on July 2nd, 1803, and died at his home near Crockett on August 2, 1874. He is buried in the old Box-Beeson Cemetery about three miles south of Crockett. The author is proud of the fact that he assisted in locating his grave and in procuring the marker for it. He was a devout Methodist preacher and attended services in the Crockett Methodist Church. He was recognized also as a man of business ability, and when his friend, Col. William B. Stokes, died, he was made administrator of his estate as shown by the Probate Records of this county. He was a member of a large family of pioneers, his brothers being: Rev. Thomas G. Box, Stillwell Box and Nelson Box, all of whom were San Jacinto Veterans. The Box family was a distinguished family of Houston County pioneers.

C. W. BRACKEN

He was commonly known in his day as Charley Bracken. He and his family lived in Crockett for many years. His old home site is now owned by Thomas Self and is situated just east of the old W. B. Wall home. None of his family or descendants now live in Crockett. He belonged to one of the oldest and most prominent families in Houston County. His father was James R. Bracken, who lived and raised his family about 18 miles Northeast of Crockett, on the old San Antonio Road. Willie Holcomb now owns the old Bracken place, and lived there quite a while with his family. The old cedar trees that stood in the Bracken yard are still there. The creek just beyond this place is still known as Bracken Creek.

The history of the Bracken family would be a good subject for historical treatment by the students of Glover School, for the old home stood almost in sight of where that school is located. James R. Bracken was justice of the peace for the Augusta precinct in an early day. His oldest son, B. M. Bracken, commonly known as Ben Bracken, was a soldier in the war between Mexico and the United States and was a member of Captain John L. Hall's company. He married a daughter of G. W. Wilson, a pioneer, who lived and died on his headright league on which the town of Augusta is situated.

C. W. Bracken was born in Alabama, August 16, 1827, and came to Texas with his father in 1839, and served in both the Mexican War and the Confederate War. He was married to Betty Cummins on Valentine's day, February 14, 1858. They had several children; the oldest, Emma Bracken, born December 8, 1858; Dick Bracken, born October 21, 1866; Estelle Bracken, born August 15, 1871. All of the above were born in Crockett and the youngest, Bert Bracken, was born at Lampasas, August 10, 1879. In 1865 C. W. Bracken was deputy tax collector of Houston County under H. G. McDaniel. In 1875 he was deputy sheriff under J. L. Sheridan. This is just another case of a pioneer family whose history should be perpetuated.

MENDEL BROMBERG

One of the enterprising citizens of Crockett, who deserves to be remembered is Mendel Bromberg, who was born in Meretz, Russia, September 16th, 1844. He spent his boyhood in the City of Bromberg, Poland, (now annexed to Germany). He arrived in the United States in (1860, and lived first in Syracuse, New York. He married January 5th, 1868, and he and his family moved to Crockett in 1873, where he lived until his death on January 12th 1919. During his residence in Crockett, covering a period of 46 years, he was engaged in business and took an active part in the civic affairs of the City and County.

In 1890, when the City of Crockett was re-organized, he was chosen one of the alderman and served faithfully in the establishment of an improved public school system, and was a member of the city council, which also served as trustees of the public schools, and under its direction a splendid new school building was erected, which stands today as the Grammar School building.

BIOGRAPHIES

He accumulated a large estate and at his death owned many farms besides some very valuable city property.

He was survived at his death by his wife and the following children: Solomon Bromberg, (generally known as Sol) who is still living in Galveston; Mose Bromberg, who has ever been a forward looking citizen of Crockett, and had much to do with its advancement. His real interest in this city may best be illustrated by the fact, that when he was offered the position of manager of the Crockett Chamber of Commerce, at a handsome salary, he declined all compensation and actually served for a considerable period without compensation. Another son of M. Bromberg, was Doctor Perry Bromberg, who attained a very high rank in his profession and died in 1939, while at the height of his brilliant career. His three dauhgters are Mrs. Lena Klein, long an able teacher in our public schools, Sarah, who is now the wife of Hyman Harrison, of Los Angeles, California, well known business man of Crockett, before his removal to California. Pauline, the wife of Harry Weiss, who still makes her home in Crockett. Altogether Mr. Bromberg was one of the most enterprising citizens that Crockett ever had.

JUDGE JAMES RUSSELL BURNETT

James Russell Burnett was born in Summerville, Georgia, on June 20th, 1843, son of Silas E. and Malinda Howell Burnett. J. R. Burnett arrived at Crockett, Texas in April 1860 (An elder brother, Col. J. H. Burnett, had moved to Houston County, Texas, in 1854). He was at Rondo, Lafayette, County, Arkansas (where an elder brother, E. P. Burnett resided), a short time before the Civil War began. He volunteered as a private in the first company that was organized in Lafayette County, known as the "La-Fayette Guards" and commanded by Capt. Sam H. Dill who had served in Jefferson Davis' regiment in the Mexican War. He was elected second-lieutenant of his company. The venerable and gallant Capt. Dill was killed in the Battle of Shiloh and J. R. Burnett was unanimously elected captain to succeed him.

In August 1862 Capt. Burnett was compelled, on account of disability contracted in the service, to resign. Recovering, he again entered the service as adjutant of the 13th Texas Cavalry, organized by his brother, Col. J. H. Burnett and which had been made an infantry regiment. In the latter part of 1863 he was again compelled by disability to resign.

He returned to Lafayette County, Arkansas, where in 1864 he was married to Miss Mollie McCollum, daughter of Hon.

A. M. McCollum. Her brothers were confederate comrades of his. They moved to Crockett, Texas, where, in 1864, he established the Crockett Quid Nunc and published it until after the close of the war. In the meantime he read law in the office of Judge Wm. M. Taylor. At the first term of the district court held at Crockett after the War, September, 1865, he was admitted to the bar and was associated in the practice with Judge Taylor.

In 1868 he was elected a delegate with Gen. A. T. Monroe, to the Constitutional Convention held at Washington, D. C. and was a member of the judiciary committee. He moved to Huntsville, Walker County in 1870. In August, 1870 he became judge of the 30th district embracing Walker, Grimes, Madison and San Jacinto counties, and served six years. He was elected state senator in 1878 from these counties and among other bills that he introduced was the one establishing the Sam Houston Normal Institute at Huntsville, Texas. This was the first normal college in the State. Judge Burnett returned to Crockett in 1880 where Mrs. Burnett died on September 4th, 1881, leaving four daughters and one son.

The family moved to Galveston in 1883. In 1888 Judge Burnett was appointed attorney for the I & G N Railway Company at Palestine and held this position until receivers were appointed for the company. He was elected district judge of Anderson, Houston and Henderson counties in 1894 to fill the unexpired term of Judge W. Q. Reeves, deceased. After the expiration of the term, December 1896, he removed to Galveston. In July 1889 when the bankruptcy law went into effect, he was appointed referee in bankruptcy for the Houston and Galveston Division. He held this position until 1904. Early in 1900 he moved to Houston, Texas. In 1907 he was appointed Special Master in Chancery for the Kirby Lumber Company which was in the hands of receivers until 1909.

In June 1903 Judge Burnett and family moved to Kerrville, Texas, a change to a higher climate being necessary on account of ill health in the family, but he retained his office in Houston until the close of the receivership of the Kirby Lumber Company.

He organized the First State Bank at Kerrville in 1905 with which he was actively connected, most of the time being its president.

Judge Burnett died at Kerrville on April 30th, 1907. Two of his daughters had died previously at Kerrville. The two younger daughters still reside there. The son, Judge McCollum Burnett, resides in San Antonio where he has been County Judge of Court-at-Law No. 1, Bexar County, for twenty years.

BIOGRAPHIES

DANIEL M. COLEMAN

The subject of this sketch was born in Perry County, Alabama, on the 23rd day of August, 1818 and came to Texas with his mother, Nancy Dean Coleman in 1851, and settled on a plantation, about 4 miles southeast of Crockett on the Crockett and Sumpter (now Pennington) Road, which became known as the Coleman Plantation, and now known as the Stockton Farm or Ranch. His brothers, Frank and Lawrence, with their mother, settled in Anderson County and his brother, Nat Coleman, settled on a plantation in Henderson County, near Athens.

About 1858 or 1859 Mr. Coleman, then and ever after, known as "Uncle Dan" bought the house of A. T. Monroe in Crockett and lived there until 1880, when he sold the same to Oliver C. Aldrich, and moved to Henderson County and lived with the family of his brother, Nat Coleman, until his death on February 6th, 1895.

Before and during the Civil War, he was a planter on a large scale, and before his slaves were freed, he was very prosperous, and was surrounded by every luxury. Before coming to Texas, he married Louisa Matlock, and they had a large family of children, several of whom died while they lived in the country, and only three of them lived in the Crockett home. The oldest of these was Cornelia, who married Captain Albert Alford, who first moved to Galveston, and moved from there to Rice, Texas, and later to Wills Point, Texas. The second daughter, Josephine, married Gus Aldrich, and she died at the home of her uncle, Nat Coleman, near Athens. The third child, Walter Coleman, sold the Coleman plantation to W. V. Berry and moved to Houston, where he enlisted as a soldier in the Spanish American War, in 1898. Later he lost his health and entered the Veterans' Hospital in Kansas, where he died about ten years ago.

Many of the older people of Crockett will remember "Uncle Dan," when he lived in his old home in Crockett, and grew flowers, because he loved them, and spent his time in friendly greetings to his neighbors and friends, and delighted in making others happy. He was truly an apostle of sunshine.

JAMES COLLINS

James Collins was born in Ireland May 29th 1834, being the oldest of a large family of children. He came to the United States when only 12 years of age and lived in Philadelphia for seven years. He came to Crockett about the year 1854 and was associated with his relatives Thomas P. Collins and James P. Collins in business for many years. He was manager of the large business of Collins & Douglas for many years and as long as said business lasted. On February 14th, 1860 he married Miss Hattie Bond Stokes, a daughter of the pioneer lawyer, William B. Stokes, the ceremony having been performed by the distinguished Presbyterian Preacher, Dr. Samuel A. King. He was a member of the Presbyterian Church at Crockett almost from its beginning and was Superintendent of the Sunday School from January 1871, when Rev. S. F. Tenney came as pastor of that church, until his death November 14th, 1887. His two daughters, Rydie and Carrie preceded him in death. He was survived by his wife and his four sons, Robert Lee Collins, James Stuart Collins, Douglas Stokes Collins and Thomas Bell Collins. Only the last two still survive and both reside in Dallas. He was Quartermaster in the Southern Army during the Civil War.

JAMES P. COLLINS

James P. Collins was one of three brothers who were born in Cookstown, Tyrone County, Ireland, and all came to Texas in an early day, associated with Moses Warden, under the firm name of Collins & Warden. He was born on August 12, 1809, and died on Monday, May 9, 1881. His oldest child was John Collins, born July 17, 1838, and who married Lucy Atkinson, who taught school in Crockett for many years and was generally known as Mrs. Lucy Collins up to the time of her death. His oldest daughter was Eliza Collins, who married William McLean, and was the mother of the late Dan McLean, Judge Will McLean, Jim McLean, Mrs. Mary Davis, wife of W. A. Davis; Mrs. Daisy McConnell, who was the wife of W. V. McConnell, and Jennie McLean, who married W. V. McConnell, and Eula McLean, who married Rev. Riall.

James P. Collins, was also the father of Janie Collins, who married F. G. Edmiston, and was the mother of Charlie and F. G. Edmiston. He also had a son by the name of William Peacock Collins, who married Virginia Smith, whom we now know as Mrs. Virginia Collins. His second son was named Samuel B. Collins, who was born in August, 1844, and who served in the Civil War. His second oldest daughter was Susan B. Collins, born in 1846, and who married John W. Prewit. Many of our people today will remember James V. Collins, who married Miss Fanny Denny, and who was the father of Alfred Collins, Denny Collins, Brownie Collins and Mattie Col-

BIOGRAPHIES

lins, who married Will Ike Kennedy. These was not all of his children, but will give the reader some idea of the large family he raised in Crockett, and how many of them are still with us.

DOCTOR JOHN COLLINS

Among the three brothers who emigrated from Cookstown, Tyrone County, Ireland, about 1839, was Dr. John Collins, who was born August 24, 1811. He came to Crockett about 1839 and at once took high rank among the pioneers of the county. In 1840, he was serving as Chief Justice of the county, and from that time until he decided to move to Athens, in Henderson County, about ten years later, he was an influential citizen. His first wife was a daughter of Ed Wingate, one of the soldiers of the Texas Revolution, who fell with Fannin at Goliad.

The records show that on February 9, 1841, he was serving as deputy Clerk of the County Court of Houston County, under Jacob Allbright, the first County Clerk of Houston County.

While in Houston County, before moving to Athens, he engaged in the mercantile business and later practiced medicine. After moving to Athens he continued to practice his profession of medicine and also engaged in many business enterprises. In fact he became one of the leading citizens of Athens and Henderson County.

His first wife having died he married again and raised a large family of children in Athens. One of his daughters married Judge Gooch, who held the office of District Judge for the Third Judicial District for many years. One of his sons, W. E. Collins, now lives in Dallas, and is the manager of the large business of Padgitt Brothers Company. One of his sons was named Jim Tom, evidently for his two brothers, James P. Collins and Thomas P. Collins. A large picture of Dr. John Collins now hangs in the courthouse in Crockett, to preserve his memory as a former Chief Justice of the County.

He died on January 3rd 1890, in Athens and is buried in the cemetery there. He was highly educated and a lover of poetry, which he could quote by the page.

JOHN COLLINS, JR.

John Collins, Jr. was the son of James P. Collins and Amelia Vann Collins and was born July 17th, 1838. He received his education in Tennessee and later attended Baylor University at

Independence, Texas, where he met and later married Miss Lucy Atkinson on November 29th, 1866. He and his bride came to Crockett soon after his marriage and made that his home until his death. He was admitted to the Bar July 21, 1866, showing great promise of being a successful practitioner, when he died in the prime of life, August 16th, 1869.

There was a meeting of the Crockett Bar to take proper notice of his death, which was attended by all the members of the Bar, which included at that time Col. Steward A. Miller, Col. W. A. Stewart, Col. D. A. Nunn, Edward Currie and Judge William M. Taylor, and suitable resolutions were passed extolling his fine and amiable character. These resolutions were prepared by Col. D. A. Nunn, his law partner, and the original copy is still in existence. Later on October 11th, 1869, resolutions were passed by Lothrop Lodge, of which he was a member, the resolutions having been presented by a committee, of which Col. S. A. Miller was Chairman, and Richard Douglass, secretary.

He left surviving him his wife, Mrs. Lucy A. Collins, one daughter, Amelia, his father and mother and a number of brothers and sisters.

GENERAL THOMAS P. COLLINS

The subject of this biography was the oldest of the three brothers, who about 1839, left their native Ireland, and sailed for America, choosing Crockett, as his destination. He was probably the first merchant to begin business in Crockett; and built a large log store house, on the northeast corner of the public square, where the Crockett Hotel now stands. He was born in Cookstown, Tyrone County, Ireland, on January 12, 1800. He first married Miss Adaline Bishop, who was born July 3rd, 1809 and died July 24, 1861. He afterwards married Emma, sister of his first wife, who survived him. By his first wife he had one daughter, Mary, who first married Billy Moore, and after his death, she married Zacheus Wilson. Later she married Charles Douglas, who was killed in March 1883, accidentally. Mrs. Douglas was associated with her stepmother, in carrying on the business of her father, Thomas P. Collins, first under the firm name of Collins and Wilson and later under the name of Collins & Douglas.

Thomas P. Collins died July 6th, 1869. He first established his home in Crockett, where Mrs. Maud McConnell now resides, where his daughter, Mary, was born, on November 7th,

BIOGRAPHIES

1842. He later built one of the notable residences of Crockett, about one mile west of the town, which was ever after one of the show places of the town, known as "Park Hill," and is now owned by Col. Fain.

Gen. Collins was a man of high ideals. Mrs. Douglas, his daughter, was fond of repeating a statement made by her father, on many occasions, "Truth is such a beautiful thing."

He had a fine sense of humor and employed this in his business advertising. He was partial to the "Crockett Argus" and the following is a specimen of the humor that he mingled with his advertising in that paper:

"Nole Me (or My Property) Tangere, I implore you!

"The State of Texas, Houston County:—Be it known to all men (and the petticoats, also) by these presents that, whereas, certain persons, at the instigation of—I will not name the old rascal—and not having the fear of anything good before their eyes, have, in place of saying their prayers like good boys, concocted and put in circulation reports to this effect, viz: That I have been selling, alienating, enfeoffing and otherwise conveying my lands and hereditaments, and my colored bipeds, vulgarly yclep'd "niggers." Now, although I am a shade over twenty-one years of age; think I have a pretty good modicum of hard horse sense; consider myself strictly compos mentis, as there has not been a writ of "delunatico inquirendo" instituted in the premises, yet I will acknowledge their authority and plead guilty. "I have done the deed," but will promise not to do so pro tempore forturo, unless it suits me! Lest there should be misconceptions, anxieties, tribulations, or other bad feelings, impressed on the minds of my good friends and self-constituted guardians, on my behalf, I conceive it my duty to apprize them that I have had in my noodle, for some time past, some crude notions of peringrinations by "flood and field," and it is highly probable that I shall carry some of them into execution.

"Imprimis: I think of taking my daughter to Live Oak Seminary, in Washington County—a first-rate school—and the principal is a genuine Presbyterian. But hush! Not a word about the pig, for some of my Hard Shell or Methodist friends may be taxing me with sectarianism! Again: In my cogitations and ratiocinations, I have concluded it to be my duty to accompany my wife on a visit to her mother (very old and infirm) in Tuscombia, North Alabama, in November proximo, but fully calculate on achieving the trip within twenty-five days, as business matters will imperiously demand my presence at home, for I am importing a bully stock of goods—you'd better believe it—

and, as for prices, I will astonish the 'natives.' As I have made a clean breast of it, I beg you will not, during my absence, be harpies snort usis, fiery faces, or coram boguses issued against me—nor yet be taking out letters of administration on my estate, as had been done in our vicinity; for, if my health and life be spared, I will come back to you like a bad six-pence! As one of my neighbors is reported to have said, "I will stay with you until a certain hot place (which shall be nameless) will freeze over four feet thick!"

MRS. LUCY ATKINSON COLLINS

For much of this biography the author is indebted to an obituary, by Hon. J. W. Madden, published in the Crockett Courier in July 1925. The subject of this sketch was born in Middleburg, Tennessee, February 11th 1841, and died at Crockett, Texas, on July 18th 1925. When she was only a few years of age the family moved to the old town of Independence, Texas. There she received her finishing education, graduating from Baylor University in 1859, at the age of 18 years, and in which institution she taught during the Civil War. In 1866, she married Lieutenant John Collins, of Crockett, Texas, who later became a member of the Crockett Bar. Coming to Crockett as a bride she continued to reside here the remainder of her life. After two and one half years of happy married life her gifted and promising husband died. Thereafter she devoted her life to the honorable and useful profession of teaching, until the infirmities of old age compelled her to give it up. She taught school for about forty years. When she was a school girl she united with the Episcopal Church. In 1887, she united with the Crockett Methodist Episcopal Church South and continued a faithful member until her death. She left surviving her only child, Miss Amelia Collins, who still resides in Crockett; one sister, Mrs. Annie Peyton, of Trinity, who has since died. She has a nephew still living, Richard Atkinson, the son of her brother R. M. Atkinson, who was for many years a prominent business man of Crockett. Many members of her husband's family still live in Crockett.

JUDGE LEROY W. COOPER

Leroy W. Cooper was born of humble parents in Gwinnett County, Georgia, October 16, 1822, and died at his home at

BIOGRAPHIES

Crockett, Texas, October 25th, 1900, being at the time of his death 78 years and 10 days old.

His parents being very poor, his educational advantages were exceedingly limited, laboring on the farm and in the shop in the day, and studying at night by the light of a pineknot. In March, 1845, he received license to practice law, and arose to prominence and success in his profession.

In March, 1846, he was married to Miss R. A. Brazier, who survived him. In 1856 he moved from Griffin, Georgia to Texas, and located at Crockett, Houston County, reaching here on November 18, where he continuously resided and where by a life filled with energy and industry he accumulated considerable property.

On his arrival at Crockett he at once took high rank in his profession, and as a criminal lawyer he had few, if any, superiors in the state, being regarded as an able advocate. The emancipation of the slaves, of which he owned a considerable number, instead of depressing him only served to stimulate his energies to the struggles of a business life.

He left surviving him, his widow and the following children: Mrs. Nettie Wall, wife of W. B. Wall; Mrs. Georgia Moore, wife of H. W. Moore; Judge Louis N. Cooper, generally known as Nat Cooper; and Dr. J. L. Cooper of Fort Worth. All of these have since died, but a number of grandchildren still survive.

Judge Cooper was an admirer of Henry Clay, whom he had often heard speak and in whose policy of government he believed. Being a Whig, at the organization of the Republican Party, he drifted into it, and was a life long believer in the policy and principles of that party. In 1866 he was chosen a state senator, and in 1870 he was elected to the lower house of the legislature. During the administrations of Governors Hamilton and Davis, he was judge of the district court of this district, and dispatched the business of his office with rapidity and efficiency.

He was the nominee of his party for congress and for associate justice of the supreme court, and in 1876 was a Blaine elector. In the Seventies the governor offered him the position of associate justice of the supreme court, but the same was declined; the district judgeship which he was occupying at the time, being preferred.

He was a delegate to the national convention of 1876, which nominated Mr. Hays for the presidency and differed from the Texas delegation as to a suitable candidate, casting the only

HISTORY OF HOUSTON COUNTY

vote in his delegation for Roscoe Conklin of New York.

It is said of him that he never drank a drop of intoxicants, as a beverage in his life.

Among his descendants who are with us today, are: Mr. William C. Wall, Mrs. Ruby Decuir, wife of A. M. Decuir, and Judge Leroy Moore, present County attorney, and former County Judge.

Although he died forty-two years ago, many of our older citizens remember him.

DOCTOR W. F. CORLEY

Dr. W. F. Corley, was a practicing physician in and near Crockett during the years 1851 and 1852, and probably earlier than that time, and we know that he lived here much later than 1852. At one time he lived at the place four miles east of Crockett on the Kennard Road, at one time known as the John H. Burnett place and later known as the Sam Platt place. Later he moved into Crockett and lived in a brick residence where Mr. and Mrs. A. M. Decuir now live, generally known as the H. W. Moore place. This was the only brick residence in Crockett at that time. Before moving to Crockett and during the early days of the Civil War, W. F. Corley not only practiced medicine, but was a farmer and the owner of a number of slaves. One of his slaves was accused of entering the home of a white family here in Crockett and endeavoring to choke the wife of the owner, which resulted in a mob taking him and hanging him to the limb of a tree on the courthouse square. As Dr. Corley resented this action of the people, it is probable that this incident had something to do with his moving away from Crockett. At various times he was the owner of many tracts of land in the county and seemed to have been a first-class business man, as well as farmer and physician. While living at the Burnett or Platt place his children, Josie and Kit, attended school a short distance away at a school house in the Monk and Douglass neighborhood, probably known as the Monk School House at that time.

It seems appropriate at this time to take up and discuss the family of Dr. W. F. Corley, because his oldest daughter is still living in Kosse, Texas, and has recently celebrated her 87th birthday. This celebration was mentioned in a number of Texas papers. I think the following report of the celebration of her 87th birthday will be of sufficient interest to the people of Crockett to have a place in this history. It is as follows:

BIOGRAPHIES

"Kosse Pioneer Believed Oldest Baylor Graduate."

"Mrs. Josephine Ann Burleson, 87, has diploma dated 1870 and signed by school officials.

"Kosse, September 7 (spl.) —Mrs. Josephine Ann Corley Burleson, 87, long-time resident here, is believed to be the oldest living graduate of Baylor University, having a diploma dated June 23, 1870, for the degree of "Maid of Honor," signed by Dr. Rufus C. Burleson, President of Baylor, with the entire members of the faculty, indicating the degrees they held and the subjects taught in the school."

JAMES M. DANIEL

We do not have information showing when or where this pioneer was born, but we do know that he was a real pioneer, for the record shows that he was a member of Captain John L. Hall's Company in the Mexican War and that he enlisted as a private on June 19th, 1846. The next record that we have is where his name appears on Thomas P. Collins' day book on October 2nd, 1851. It is known that he married Sallie Platt, a sister of James Platt and Mrs. Adeline Hill. He was a member of Captain Isaac Adair's Company in the Confederate Army and was killed at the Battle of Mansfield, Louisiana, in the latter part of 1864. He left surviving him, his wife, and the following children: David Ratcliff Daniel, commonly known as "Dick" Daniel, who married Miss Sallie Thompson, the daughter of Judge Samuel M. Thompson. He was survived by no children. The next child was Jennie Daniel, who married Ike Smith and whose children are living in and near Crockett. The next child was A. F. Daniel, generally known as Frank Daniel. The next child was Albert Daniel, who never married and died a few years ago at Crockett. He was a large planter on a river farm. The next child was Mary Daniel, who married Bob Hardin and was the mother of Mrs. Sally Arledge, Mrs. Augusta Knox, Mrs. Effie Baker, Mrs. Clara Smith and Mrs. Buenna Foster. The next child was Isaac Adair Daniel, who was generally known as Ike Daniel and who was a prominent citizen of Crockett and Houston County and held both the offices of sheriff and representative of the Texas Legislature. His widow, Mrs. Ruth Daniel, still lives in Crockett, and a son, Hon. Albert K. Daniel has followed in his father's footsteps and recently served as representative in the Texas Legislature. Other sons are: Ike Daniel and Morris Daniel. There were two daughters:

Miss Nell Daniel, who married Max Hardy and Miss Carol Faye Daniel, who married Harvey Doran Oatman.

Another daughter of James M. Daniel was Augusta Daniel, who married H. F. Craddock. She is now dead and left the following children: Frank Craddock, Dan P. Craddock, Ike Craddock. The above sketch of James M. Daniel, a pioneer, shows how closely the past history of Crockett is connected with the present.

BRADFORD DAVIS

A pioneer, who met a tragic death, at the hands of Indians, came to Texas in 1839 from Jefferson County, Mississippi and settled upon a tract of land near what is now known as Ash, in Houston County. He owned two farms in Mississippi and about one hundred negro slaves, but brought only 22 with him to Texas. The story of his death is briefly this: He and his friend, Joel F. Leathers, were not only farmers, but bee hunters. They had baited the bees with some honey placed on a pole. Early one morning as they visited the bait, Leathers discovered that the Indians had been there and told Davis to run for his life. Leathers mounted his horse and made his escape. Davis not acting so rapidly was too slow and the Indians killed him. He sleeps in an unknown grave on Mustang Prairie. He left three children: John A. Davis, Bradford Davis, Jr. and James Franklin Davis. The oldest son, John A. Davis attended school in Crockett, and after the death of his father, Judge A. E .Gossett became his guardian and he lived in his home for a time. John A. Davis, son of Braford Davis, at his death left six children, one being John A. Davis, Jr., who was Justice of the Peace at Grapeland for many years, but is now dead. A son, Ed W. Davis, still lives in Grapeland and is a patriarch himself, with children and grandchildren gathering at his home frequently. The Davis Family had an important part in the development of Houston County.

COLONEL W. W. DAVIS

Colonel W. W. Davis was a native son of Houston County, born of pioneer parents, his father, Wm. P. Davis, coming from Mississippi to Texas in 1828, and his mother, Elizabeth Davis, was a native of Tenenssee. Colonel Davis was born in Houston County near the present town of Weches, on what was known

BIOGRAPHIES

as the old Davis place, on March 15, 1831. He was an only son and the youngest of four children. His parents died when he was quite young and his three sisters were reared by their maternal grandmother. It is a part of the family history that his oldest sister was to have been married to the famous Jim Bowie, but she died before the marriage was consummated.

Colonel Davis was married to Lucy Margaret Penick on August 25, 1850, when he was only 19 years of age. The Penick family were also Houston County pioneers and came to Houston County from Missouri. He spent his entire life in Houston County, where he was born.

He was a capable business man and when a young man he was a partner with William McLean in a mercantile business at Augusta, which continued for many years. After coming from Augusta to Crockett he also engaged in the mercantile business for many years.

He was a man of unusual intelligence and ability and represented Houston County in the Legislature. He died on June 22, 1910, and left surviving him a son, John Davis, a daughter, Miss Betty Davis, still living in Crockett, and Mrs. Alice Long, who resides in Tennessee, being the wife of a prominent business man, and statesman, who represented his district in the Tennessee Legislature. His son, Wm. A. Davis, who preceded him in death, was one of the outstanding lawyers of the Crockett bar, and held the offices of County Attorney and County Judge before his death. Colonel Davis was noted for his amiable qualities. His memory will be revered in Houston County for generations to come.

MISS ADINA De ZAVALA

Miss Adina De Zavala, research historian, was born at De Zavala's Point, Harris County, Texas. She was the daughter of Augustine and Julia (Tyrell) De Zavala and granddaughter of Lorenzo De Zavala, vice-president of the Republic of Texas.

She attended Ursuline Academy at Galveston, Texas; Sam Houston State Teachers College; and studied music in Chillicothe, Mo. She was the founder and president of the Daughters and Sons of the Heroes of the Republic of Texas; member of the Descendants of Signers of the Texas Declaration of Independence; Scientific Society, San Antonio; Texas State Historical Association (fellow and councillor) United Daughters of the

Confederacy; Witte Museum Art League.

She is the author of History and Legends of the Alamo and other Missions of San Antonio, as well as of various historical and biographical sketches, and edited collation of Kingsborough's Antiquities of Mexico. Her hobbies are perpetuation of Texas liberty, writing, travel. She is a member of Catholic Church and lives at 141 Taylor Street, San Antonio, Texas.

While she never resided in Houston County, she is entitled to a place in this history on account of her interest and activities in connection with the location of the site of Missions San Francisco and Santissimo Nombre de Maria, and of having obtained through the Historical and Landsmarks Association the imposing markers that mark the sites of these missions.

WILLIAM DICKERSON

This pioneer was born in 1796 and came to Houston County some time prior to January 11th 1841, for on that date he purchased the place on which he established his home and on which he lived until his death on October 7th, 1861. He owned a number of slaves and opened and cultivated a large plantation about two miles northeast of Crockett on the old Crockett and Rusk road. That place has gone by the name of the Old Dickerson Place ever since, and has been one of the landmarks of the County.

He brought some of his children with him when he came to Houston County, for his oldest daughter, Mary Jane, married John McConnell as early as 1851, for during that year the old day book of Thomas P. Collins shows that items were purchased by the wife of John McConnell.

When he died he left surviving him his widow, Jane, who lived only one week longer and died on October 14th, 1861. He also left surviving him six children, Mary Jane McConnell, wife of John McConnell; Elizabeth, who first married Burton Clark, and after his death she married W. E. Mayes; Susan, who married Salathiel Robert; his sons were John H. Dickerson, Van G. Dickerson and Charles Martin Dickerson, all of whom are now dead.

He still has many descendents living in Crockett and Mineral Wells, including the children of William V. McConnell, who are conducting the McConnell Dry Goods Company, and the children of John McConnell, for many years, a leading merchant of Crockett, and the children of Elizabeth Rice, who married Joe Rice.

BIOGRAPHIES

Mrs. Jennie Sample, a granddaughter of William Dickerson, and a daughter of John H. Dickerson, still resides in Crockett.

COLONEL GEORGE ENGLISH

Col. George English was born in Tennessee in 1808 and came to Texas in 1830 and settled in what is now Shelby County. On November 29, 1835, he was appointed First Lieutenant of Infantry of the general council of the provisional government of Texas. He commanded a company at the storming and capture of Bexar, on December 5 to 10, 1835, and for his service, he, on January 27, 1840, was issued Donation Certificate No. 1006 for 640 acres of land. At the same time he received Bounty Certificate No. 730 for 320 acres of land for having served in the army for a period of three months. On May 31, 1837, President Houston appointed him captain of a company of mounted gunmen for duty in Shelby County. He commanded a company of volunteers in 1839, and was at the same time president of the Board of Land Commissioners of Shelby County.

Captain English was lieutenant in Captain A. M. Truitt's Company in the Monterrey campaign in the Mexican War."

The name of Col. George English was already been recorded in history. In the history written by Dr. George L. Crockett, called Two Centuries in East Texas, the name and achievements of this hero are mentioned on several occasions. On page 84 of said history, the following statement is made:

"Neighbors of Jonas Harrison were the English brothers, one of whom, George English, was the first sheriff of the district in 1827, and was also first sheriff of San Augustine County under the Republic of Texas."

After having acquitted himself so bravely during the War of Texas Independence in 1836, and the Mexican War of 1846, this patriotic pioneer was ready for the third war and enlisted in the Confederate service and fought in the Civil War of 1861 to 1865. At that time he had long been a citizen of Houston County, having removed to Houston County from San Augustine County at an early day and spent his later years in this county. After the death of his uncle, Arch H. English, he took care of his children and widow, the children being Miranda English, who later married E. E. Barlow and died in Houston County only a short time ago. Another daughter of Arch English was Miss Lizzie English, who also died in Crockett not many years ago. A third child of Arch English is Elisha English, who recently died near Trinity, and was present at the family reunion held on September 1st, 1940. Colonel George English was a second father to these nieces and nephews, and Elisha spoke in the most loving terms of his noble qualities and goodness to his kindred.

He died in Houston County and was buried in the old English cemetery, about 11 miles East of Crockett, located on the old James English homestead tract of land, and the author was instrumental in securing a monument for his grave and in locating the same where a splendid marker now stands, showing the last resting place of this patriotic Texan. It is a shrine worthy of a pilgrimage by the present generation, who delight to honor the noble and the good.

CAPTAIN JOHN ENGLISH

The following sketch of Captain John English was furnished the author by Mrs. John E. Wright of San Antonio, who is a granddaughter of Captain John English.

"English, John—Born in Virginia, July 5, 1793, and came to Texas about 1825. In 1833 he was a delegate to the second convention of Texas, held in San Felipe. The following account of Captain English's life was written at his death by W. P. Sansom and published in a newspaper. It was pasted in a scrapbook by his daughter, Mrs. S. P. Tucker:

"Died at his residence in Houston County on Wednesday evening, December 30, 1868, at 4 o'clock P. M., Captain John English.' For several years Captain English has been laboring under a chronic disease by which he was greatly reduced. On Saturday night previous to his death he was attacked with acute pneumonia, which terminated fatally, after severe suffering, on Wednesday following. The subject of his life notice was one of the oldest living Texans. He was born at English's Ferry on New River, Virginia, on the 5th of July, 1793, his parents emigrating to North Carolina, thence to Tennessee, where he was married to Miss Elizabeth Choate in 1824, and immediately moved to Texas. In 1815 Captain English was a soldier under General Jackson and was captured by the enemy a few days before the memorable 8th day of January and was detained a prisoner for several weeks. In Texas he was a participant in all her early troubles. He was a member of congress of the Republic and always took deep interest in everything that concerned Texas or her welfare. No man excelled him in patriotism, in kindly feel-

BIOGRAPHIES

ing for his fellow men and in genuine social hospitality. His good qualities always shown out, his gentleness of heart, his disposition to hide or extenuate the faults of others. His accurate knowledge of the early history of Texas made his company very entertaining in the last years of his life, when the present was all forgetfulness, the past ever present in his mind. He bore a painful sickness without complaint and died at the advanced age of 75 years, 5 months and 25 days, surrounded by children, grandchildren and friends at peace with all men."

The following clipping from "The Sentinel" published Tuesday, January 5, 1868, in Crockett, was also found in Mrs. Tucker's scrap book:

"An Old Texan Gone, Last Wednesday Captain John English, an old Texan, valuable citizen, a good man and a survivor of the Texas revolution, departed this life at his residence 12 miles east of Crockett. Captain English was an old man and had for the past year been in feeble health. His last illness which culminated in his death, only lasted a few days. The announcement of his death carries sorrow to man."

Mrs. English was born in Tennessee, January 5, 1807, and died July 30, 1857. She was buried in what is now known as the Hicks cemetery, ten miles east of Crockett, Houston County. At his death, Captain English's remains were placed beside those of his wife. The State of Texas erected a joint monument at their graves in 1937.

Children of Captain and Mrs. English were Captain John C. English of the Confederate Army, who first married Jane Stuart of Crockett and after her death, Emma Day of Austin; Elvira Jane, who married Thornton Hollis; Eliza, who first married Dr. Dozier, and after his death, Baylor Owens; Irene, who married Thomas Hicks; Evlyne, who married Dr. Edward Curie; Willie, who maried Robert Beavers; Elizabeth, who married Seth P. Tucker; Rufus English, who married Maggie Calhoun, and James Denton English, who married Ella Beavers.

Emma English, a daughter of James English, married Barker Tunstall, but is dead and is survived by her husband, Barker Tunstall, and the following children: Erin Carnes, Vicory Durst; Beth LaBat; Elvira Bennett; Dolly Porter; Rebecca Orchard; Eugenia Francis; Barker Tunstall, Jr.; Thomas James Tunstall and Bobby Ray Tunstall.

There are other descendents of Captain John English living in other parts of Texas.

HISTORY OF HOUSTON COUNTY

THE GOSSETT FAMILY

The only surviving child of Andrew Edwards Gossett, Mrs. Josie Gossett Newton, of Galveston, has furnished such a complete history of the lives and families of her grandfather, Elijah Gossett and her father, Andrew Edwards Gossett, and their families that I have adopted the same for this history, as follows:

"My paternal grandfather, Elijah Gossett, was born on Rutherford Creek, Tenn. (I do not know County) Feb. 1st, 1788. He was married to Elisabeth Stone Edwards, who was born in Tenn. Sept. 1st, 1789. (Her mother was a Miss Lackridge). They reared a family of ten children, moved from Tenn. (date unknown) to Ill. where they lived for a short time (The city of Cairo, Ill. was later located upon his farm, so I have been told). They returned to Tenn. and in 1833, accompanied by his entire family, moved to Texas.

"They traveled with a large party, as was necessary in those days because of danger from marauding Indians, wild beasts, etc. They were more than 2 months en route, were camped on 'Grand Prairie' Ark. when the 'Stars' fell. I do not know what became of others of the party, but 'The Gossetts' settled in what was later to become Houston County, but was then a part of Nacogdoches County (and of course, all belonging to Mexico). Elijah selected a site for his home, on the Hurricane Bayou five miles Northwest of present town of Crockett, and lived there until 1837. He and his three oldest sons, namely, James Lackridge, Andrew Edwards (my father) and John Van Dyke, served in the 'Texas Revolution' for its entire duration as Volunteers under Capt. William Spurlock, Brigadier General Thomas J. Rusk, commanding. After Texas became a Republic they all four joined Capt. Elisha Clapps Company of 'Texas Rangers,' and served on the frontier. (These facts were furnished me by Miss Harriet Smither, Archivist of the Texas Library in the Capitol Bldg. Austin.) She also gave me copies of their Discharge Papers.) All rec'd Bounty Warrants for 320 acres of land for their military service. (Some of this information was copied from Comptrollers Military Service Records, Numbers 4909 and 4911. Some from Pension Papers, Archives.) They also rec'd Land Grants from the Mexican Government as Settlers.

"My grandfather, Elijah Gossett was elected Chief Justice (County Judge) in 1841 and he was one of the eleven trustees appointed for Trinity College, which was first established at Alabama in Houston County by the Senate and House of Rep-

BIOGRAPHIES

resentatives of the Republic of Texas in Congress assembled Jan. 30th, 1841. The act was signed by David S. Kaufman, Speaker of the House of Representatives, Anson Jones, President Pro Tem of the Senate, approved Jan. 30th, 1841, signed David G. Burnet. (Volume 2, Page 146, *Gammel's Laws of Texas.*)

"Elijah Gossett made a business trip to Van Zandt Co. where he owned land in Nov. 1848, became ill and died there Nov. 24th, 1848. His body was conveyed to Crockett in an ox wagon and he was buried in the first old cemetery there, as was his wife who died the following year, July 6th, 1849. In 1937 the Centennial Commission placed a beautiful marker at their graves.

"My father, A. E. Gossett, built his first little log cabin home at top of the hill North of the present Town of Crockett, where the Mary Allen Seminary, Negro college is now located; he chose that site because of the convenient spring at foot of the hill. (The Barbee pond). His nearest white neighbor was his father, five miles away; when he needed a pound of coffee or other supplies, he rode his Indian pony 63 miles over a rough dim trail to Nacogdoches, the nearest trading post. It was a hard day's journey, and necessitated his absence from home one night each time he made the trip. His wife and little children were thus left alone but friendly Indian squaws would go to her home and sit with her for company, though they were unable to converse, as neither could speak the other's language.

"My father built the house now standing 1¾ miles East of Crockett and still referred to as 'The old Gossett Place' in the spring of 1837. It is said to be the first weather-boarded house built in the Republic of Texas. The house is still in a good state of preservation and is occupied as a home. (The present owner has repaired and painted it). My father, however, didn't occupy his new home until 1848, because his parents were victims of malaria whilst living on the Bayou. He moved them to his new home where they remained until their deaths in 1848 and 1849.'

"Houston County was created from a part of Nacogdoches County on June 8th, 1837 and organized the same year. Crockett was incorporated Dec. 29th, 1837. My father, A. E. Gossett, donated the site for the town and because of this gift, he and his father were given the privilege of naming both county and town. In as much as both had served under General Sam Houston, hero of San Jacinto, they decided upon the name of Houston for the county, and, as David Crockett, Elijah's boyhood friend and neighbor in Tennessee saw and recognized Elijah as he passed through the village on his ill-fated journey to San Antonio where he met a tragic death but a few weeks later, Elijah suggested that the town be named 'Crockett,' which was done. (David Crockett spent the night with his old friend en route to San Antonio, but I do not know the date.)

"Andrew Edwards Gossett was born July 19th, 1812, in Maury County, Tennessee; married Rhoda E. Mulder, daughter of Koder and Rhoda Mulder, who was born in Halifax, N. C. Jan. 14th, 1812, and died at her home in Crockett, April 14th, 1853. They were married Dec. 27th, 1831 in Tennessee and were the parents of nine children.

"A. E. Gossett and Mary Margaret Murchison were married Jan. 22nd, 1857. She was the daughter of Simon Murchison, and Elisabeth Daily Ross, and was born in McNary County. Tennessee. Feb. 17th, 1832 and died Dec. 20th, 1904, age 72 years. Their children were: Andrew Edwards Simon (Tony) born Aug. 4th, 1858, died April 28th, 1928, age 69 years, 8 months, 24 days; and Margaret Josephine, born Dec. 22nd, 1862."

EDWARD ALEXANDER GAUSE

Edward Alexander Gause, was born August 8th, 1819 in Mobile, Alabama, of Welch and Scotch-Irish parentage. He graduated from a college in Ohio, where he had as his friend, the distinguished James A. Garfield, who later became President of the United States. It was through the influence of this eminent statesman that Mr. Gause was appointed Postmaster at Crockett on October 16th, 1879. He was married to Miss Catherine Neal Hall, a granddaughetr of Huguenot refugees. Mrs. Gause was born in Wilmington, North Carolina, and died in Crockett on October 16th, 1883, being the 23rd anniversary of her marriage.

Mr. and Mrs. Gause came to Crockett soon after the Civil War and he and his sister, Mrs. McCall, engaged in teaching school. At that time Crockett was noted for the unruly character of some of its older students, and they had hitherto fought and intimidated the teachers. In Mr. Gause they met their match. He was fearless and resolved not to be overrun by any of his students, however large physically. When it became necessary to punish one of these bullies, he brought his revolver to school and laid it on his desk. While his sister held the gun he thrashed

BIOGRAPHIES

the disobedient student and thereafter had no trouble in school.

He established a newspaper at Crockett, THE CROCKETT PATRON, and conducted it for several years. While thus engaged, he was associated for a time with R. M. Johnson, who moved to Houston and became prominent in newspaper work.

He was a devout Christian, an enterprising citizen, and a kind and devoted husband and father.

He was survived by three daughters: Mrs. Anna Gause Phillips, Mrs. Johnnie Dawes, and Mrs. Flora Gause Murchison.

JAMES H. GILLESPIE

Just when or where this pioneer was born the author has no information, but he was living in Crockett as early as 1841, as shown by records. They show that at that time he was serving as deputy County Clerk of Houston County, under C. H. Nelson, the second County Clerk of the county. In 1846 he succeeded C. H. Nelson as County Clerk and continued to hold that office until 1858, when he was succeeded by Oliver C. Aldrich.

He died in Houston County and William Wortham was appointed Temporary Administrator of his estate on January 29th, 1861.

He was a close friend of the family of Daniel Murchison and frequently paid his attentions to his daughter, Angeline, who later married H. F. Craddock.

An interesting bit of history connected with him is the fact that he followed the gold rush to California in an early day, and brought back with him a gold nugget, from which a ring was made that is now owned by Miss Minnie Craddock.

The deed Records of Houston County attest the fact, that during his more than ten years of tenure of the office of County Clerk, he wrote a good hand, took numberless acknowledgements to deeds and other instruments and recorded them in long hand. He seems to have died a bachelor as no relative is mentioned in the administration proceedings of his estate.

JAMES MADISON HALL

This pioneer was the son of Joshua J. Hall and was born February 22nd, 1819, probably in Maryland. He came with his father to Houston County as early as July 1st, 1839, for at that time he made out a deed to a large tract of land in Houston

County, which shows that he was living in the County then.

He married Cornelia A. Bracken, a daughter of James R. Bracken, as early as 1851, for during that year Ben M. Bracken, a brother of Cornelia, conveyed to her certain slaves as shown by a bill of sale still in existence.

He was elected District Clerk of Houston County in 1847 and held the office until 1857, when he was succeeded by Isaac Adair. He was the second District Clerk of the County, his predecessors having been L. E. Downes.

About 1858 he and his first wife were divorced and he later married his stepsister, a daughter of his Stepmother, Mahala Hall, with whom he lived until his death November 12th, 1866.

The most unfortunate experience in his whole career was when, in a fit of anger, he killed his friend, Isaac Peacock, who had assisted John McLemore in eloping with his daughter, Margaret. He was acquitted of the charge of murder for this killing.

He deserves to be remembered for having kept one of the most complete diaries that the author has ever seen. It covers the entire period of the Civil War, from 1861 to 1866. In this he has preserved some valuable history of that trying period.

CAPTAIN JOHN L. HALL

Captain John L. Hall was born on October 25th, 1809, and came to Texas in the days of the Republic. He was here as early as July 1st, 1839 and probably earlier. On that date he conveyed, as agent of his kinsman, Joshua J. Hall, 23, 654 acres of the Roman de la Garza Grant to James Madison Hall, a son of Joshua J. Hall. On February 28th, 1844, he purchased from Jesse Walling, a San Jacinto veteran, 76 acres of the A. E. Gossett Headright Survey and probably made his first home in Crockett there. Soon afterwards he raised a company of volunteers for service in the Mexican War, and the muster roll of this company shows that it was a part of the Second Regiment, Texas Brigade of Texas Mounted Volunteers Riflemen Militia, commanded by Col. George T. Woods, and ordered into service of the United States by the Governor of Texas from June 9th, 1846 to December 19th, 1846.

The names of the subordinate officers in Captain Hall's company were: George English, first lieutenant; Wilbur B. Young, second lieutenant; Selden L. B. Jasper, first sergeant; Samuel A. Burton, second sergeant; John A. Moncrief, third sergeant; John P. Saunders, fourth sergeant; Robert C. Dickson, first corporal; Thomas Hays, second corporal; Joseph Burnam, third corporal and George B. Lacy, fourth corporal.

On April 15th, 1849, he purchased from John I. Burton Lot No. 80 in Crockett on which his Hotel was afterwards located. This lot is now owned by Davy Crockett Chapter, Knights of Pythias and on which their castle hall is situated. This hotel, known far and wide as Hall's Hotel, was destroyed by fire in 1871.

John L. Hall was a prominent Mason and was buried with Masonic honors at his death on August 25th, 1857. He was survived by his widow, Mrs. L. L. Hall, a daughter of John I. Burton, and his two daughters, Mrs. Nancy Wortham and Mrs. Margaret Barbee, and two sons, Dr. John L. Hall and W. A. Hall. All are now dead, but his grandson, Bunk Barbee, is still living, and his great-grandson, Jack Barbee and great-granddaughter, Mrs. Charlie Neel, are still living in Crockett.

JOSHUA J. HALL AND MAHALA L. HALL

Just when Joshua J. Hall, left his Maryland home for Texas, is not known, but as early as July first, 1839 the records show that he was the owner of more than twenty-three thousand acres of land, on which he located his home and on which he lived up to the time of his death. The author has no information as to who was his first wife and the mother of his oldest son, James Madison Hall. It is known that he later married the widow, Mahala L. Sharp, the daughter of Elisha Roberts, a pioneer citizen of San Augustine County. Soon after reaching Houston County, he established a warehouse and business at a point on the bank of Trinity River, near his home, which has ever since been known as Hall's Bluff. Before the advent of the railroad to Crockett, Hall's Bluff was quite a business place where cotton was shipped to market on steamboats that plied the river to and from Galveston. The business of hauling cotton to that point, and goods from that point, to Crockett merchants, was a regular trade before the coming of the railroad.

He was the owner of several slaves and improved a large plantation on his large tract of land. He was fond of amusement and made frequent trips to Crockett to attend balls and other festivities. He was fond of the dance. All of this appears from his diary, which he kept from 1848 to 1854. He may have kept diaries covering other periods, but this is the only one that has come to the attention of the author. Besides his son, James Madison, by his first marriage, he had a daughter, Roberta, and a son, Horace, by his second marriage. This diary is worth far more than its weight in gold. The author is indebted to his grandson, Jim Hall, of Groveton, for a copy of this wonderful diary.

THE HALLMARK FAMILY

The progenitor of the Hallmark family in Houston County was George Hallmark, who lived on Mustang Prairie, and for whom a small creek is named. He was a prominent man in his day and accumulated a large estate during his lifetime. He made his will on August 16, 1848, which was probated in the County Court on October 25, 1852, and same was recorded in Book "I," of the deed records of Houston County, Texas. His estate was appraised at $17,000. In this will he bequeathed to his three youngest children, Richard M. Hallmark, Ephriam L. B. Hallmark and Alexander C. Hallmark, three negroes, named Solomon, Charity and Little Tom, stating that Little Tom was the youngest negro that he owned, and provided in said will that said negroes should work for the use, benefit and support of said three children until they shall be of age, or the youngest one marries, at which time they shall be equally divided among them. Just how this could be accomplished, the will does not undertake to provide. The rest of his estate is bequeathed to his children, Polly Box, William C. Hallmark, George W. Hallmark, Lee Anna Rosser, John B. Hallmark, James M. Hallmark, Alfred Hallmark, Aveline Hallmark, Stidham, Matthew D. T. Hallmark, together with Stillwell Box's six children, who, out of their part, shall put in $640, which, if they do, shall be entitled to an equal share of the property, together with seven negroes, Peggy, Big Tom, Harriett, Charles, Simion, Elizabeth and July. This same George Hallmark, in 1843, was postmaster at Mustang Prairie.

The William C. Hallmark, mentioned in said will, was a San Jacinto veteran and the Centennial Commission erected a marker at his grave, in the old Bynum graveyard near Shiloh. He also left a will, one item of which read as follows:

"I give and bequeath to Shiloh church, three acres of land, including the house of worship."

Some of these sons of George Hallmark deserve separate mention.

In addition to the above mentioned William C. Hallmark, his brother, Alfred Hallmark was also a veteran of San Jacinto, and his name appears in the report of the Centennial Commis-

BIOGRAPHIES

sion of Control and both names are engraved on the tablet of the San Jacinto Monument. Alfred and William C. Hallmark are simply listed among the veterans of San Jacinto. The inscription on the marker at the grave of William C. Hallmark reads as follows:—

"WILLIAM CALVERT HALLMARK

A veteran of San Jacinto. Born

in Tennessee, May 20, 1804.

Died January 26, 1880."

(Cemetery, 10 miles S. W. Crockett)

JUDGE JAMES T. HEFLIN

The following autobiography of Judge Heflin was written by himself:

"I, J. T. Heflin, was born August 19, 1816, in Smith County, middle Tennessee. My family moved to North Alabama, Lawrence County in 1821, and settled one and one half miles from Moultain, the county seat. My father died soon after settling here.

"I moved to Texas in the fall of 1846 and settled in Crockett, Houston County and with four others and my wife, organized the present Baptist Church.

"I was elected justice of the peace in 1848 and in 1850 was elected sheriff of the county. I refused to serve a second term as sheriff. I then was elected justice of the peace a second time by salutation of the precinct and in 1860 I was elected county judge. In 1861 I joined the confederate service and was elected captain of Company "E" of Gould's Battalion and at Camp McCollough was taken sick and had to resign.

"After I was able to attend to business I was appointed confederate assessor of Houston County and served as such to the close of the war. In 1867 I was again elected sheriff of Houston County. In May 1886, I moved from Houston County to Travis County."

In later life Judge Heflin moved from Crockett to Austin, where his sons, Frank and James lived, and resided there until death at the age of 84 years, six months and five days.

His oldest son, Frank, had moved to Austin, where he married and lived until his death. His younger son, James R. G. Heflin, also moved to Austin and lived there until his death. His oldest daughter, Emma, married a man by the name of Heath and moved away from Crockett and died elsewhere. Another daughter, Letitia, was adopted into the family of Dr. J. J. Woodson and lived many years in Crockett. Another daughter, Della, married Charles Ellis and is still living in Crockett. Another daughter, Mrs. T. J. Gossett, lives in Topeka, Kansas. A son, Mordeau, is still living at Panhandle, Texas.

In 1846, Judge Heflin organized the Baptist Church in Crockett, with six members, consisting of himself, his wife and four others, whose names are not known. He has a granddaughter, Mrs. Alta Heflin Wilder, still living in Austin and has a position in the Registrar's office of the University of Texas. Judge Heflin left his impress on Houston County.

DR. JAMES HUNTER

Dr. James Hunter, a pioneer doctor of Houston County, was born in the State of Georgia on April 23rd, 1812, and came to Texas with the retinue of General Nathaniel Smith in the winter of 1839. Dr. Hunter belonged to the Virginia (Fredericksburg) Family of Hunter, coming from William Hunter of Duns, Scotland, who married Martha Taliaferro in Spotsylvania County in 1744 by his son James (R. M. T.) Hunter of Virginia of Confederate fame, came from the other son, William Hunter.

He brought with him, his wife, Mary, daughter of General Smith, and two sons, Malcolm Kenmore Hunter and Nathaniel Wyche Hunter, the latter being only six weeks old when they started to Texas. They arrived at Fort Houston, then Houston County.

Dr. Hunter was the son of Archibald Russell Spence Hunter, and Elizabeth Wyche Lucas Hunter of Georgia. He was sent to school to study medicine at the University of Pennsylvania and his brother Nathaniel Wyche, went to West Point Military Academy the same year, 1831.

He was married to Mary M. Smith, daughter of General Nathaniel Smith of Athens, Tennessee on May 31st, 1836 in Athens.

In February 1837 he was appointed physician to the Cherokee Indians of East Tennessee. When they arrived in Fort Houston there were a number of families living in and around the Fort. The times were so troublous that sentinels were stationed to guard the Fort and women stood at the guns while the men

UPPER LEFT: Hon. Charles Collins Stokes. UPPER RIGHT: Mrs. Lucy Hancock Stokes. LOWER LEFT: Charles Stokes. LOWER RIGHT: Dr. Edgar B. Stokes.

UPPER LEFT: Lodowick E. Downes. UPPER RIGHT: Major James C. Wootters. LOWER LEFT: Judge James Taylor Heflin. LOWER RIGHT: Dr. S. J. Collins.

UPPER LEFT: William Johnson. UPPER RIGHT: Col. Armistead Thompson Monroe. LOWER LEFT: J. R. B. Barbee. LOWER RIGHT: Wilson Edwin Hail.

ABOVE: Mrs. Emma Adams and Col. Earle Adams. LOWER LEFT: Rev. J. L. Spears. LOWER RIGHT: Dr. John Collins.

UPPER LEFT: Mendel Bromberg. UPPER RIGHT: M. M. Baker. LOWER LEFT: Judge George F. Moore. LOWER RIGHT: Daniel Murchison.

UPPER LEFT: Dr. William H. Denny. UPPER RIGHT: Dr. James L. Lipscomb. LOWER LEFT: James R. Burnett. LOWER RIGHT: Captain John T. Smith.

UPPER LEFT: John W. Arledge. UPPER RIGHT: Judge William B. Wall.
LOWER LEFT: F. H. Bayne. LOWER RIGHT: Miss Adina De Zavala.

UPPER LEFT: Mrs. Isabelle Taylor. UPPER RIGHT: Rev. R. Gage Lloyd.
LOWER LEFT: W. M. Taylor. LOWER RIGHT: Hon. Nat Patton.

BIOGRAPHIES

were away, his wife Mary, being one of them, and only nineteen years of age.

In a letter to his father in North Carolina, soon after they arrived, Dr. Hunter states that he and one other man furnished the meat for the inmates of the Fort by hunting, while other men were ploughing the fields.

He practiced medicine in and around the Fort and gave succor to the sick and wounded—the depredations of the Indians were at their height at this time. He died September 26th, 1840, less than a year after his arrival, of what they called "the fever." His father-in-law, General Smith, and his wife, both died the year following, 1841. They are all buried in Fort Houston Cemetery. While in Texas such a short time, Dr. James Hunter left his impress on Texas by a number of grandchildren and great-grandchildren who are loyal Texans.

His wife, Mrs. Mary M. Hunter, after his death, married Col. James Carr, a pioneer lawyer of Crockett, Texas. She lived to a good old age, rearing the two sons of James Hunter, both of whom served in the Confederate Army. Mary M. Carr was co-founder (with Col. J. J. Word) of the Episcopal Church in Palestine, and there is a tablet in the church to the memory of her and Col. Word. She was a woman of rare strength of character and accomplishments.

Miss Mary Kate Hunter, of Palestine, a lineal descendant of Dr. James Hunter, furnished the author with the above biography, for which he acknowledges his indebtedness.

TILMAN INGRAM

Probably few now living in Houston County ever heard of this pioneer, yet he lived here in 1862, and probably much earlier. The record shows that on Februaury 22, 1862, he was enrolled at Crockett, Texas, as a private in Captain George English's Company, Burnett's Regiment Confederate States Army. At that time he was 35 years of age. He has a grandson, J. C. Ingram, now living at Groveton, Texas.

WILLIAM JOHNSON

This pioneer of Houston County, who was a cousin of President Andrew Johnson, came to this county in 1853, with his wife and one child, Florence Josephine, who was only 2 months old at the time. This family came from Greenville, Tennessee, the home town of Andrew Johnson, in company with his brother-in-law, Alfred Bitner, and Susan Bitner, the sister of William Johnson.

For a short time both families settled and lived near old Shiloh where Bitner and his family lived, and where Bitner died after raising a large family, who still live in the same neighborhood. Mr. Johnson came to Crockett some time about 1855 and boarded with A. T. Monroe, in the house where George W. Crook now resides, and where his son, Samuel Hays Johnson was born on December 26th, 1856.

Mr. Johnson moved to a two-story house where B. F. Chamberlain now lives, and made that his home until he erected a new ten-room dwelling house just across the street where the Henry Arledge home now stands. He engaged in the mercantile business in Crockett for many years and also operated a gin and grist mill on his home place, about where the home of Dr. J. S. Wootters now stands. During the Civil War he held the office of County Treasurer.

He was born on May 25th, 1825 and was married to Mary Isabella Dunwoody on June 3rd, 1850 in Tennessee. Their first child, Florence Josephine (later Mrs. Florence J. Arledge) was born on November 6th, 1852. They had eight children, only two of whom are now living: Miss May Johnson and Walter Everett Johnson, both of whom now reside in Marlin. William Johnson and wife both died in Crockett and are buried in Glenwood Cemetery.

DOCTOR WILLIAM GEORGE WASHINGTON JOWERS

Dr. W. G. W. Jowers, prominent citizen of East Texas during the days of the Republic, and after, was born in Wadesborough, North Carolina. In 1835 he was graduated from Transylvania Medical College, Lexington, Kentucky. In 1839 he came to Texas and stopped at Nacogdoches, enlisting in the Texas Militia for six months. During this same year he accompanied Martin Lacy, of Fort Lacy, Cherokee County, Indian Agent, and John H. Reagan, as bearers of the letter to Chief Bowles, of the Cherokee Indians, from President Lamar, saying that the Cherokee Indians must go. He was married to Ann Lacy, daughter of Martin Lacy, May 20th 1840, and soon thereafter moved to Crockett, where he practiced the profession of medicine. Ann Lacy died and he married Pauline Catherine Tatum

BIOGRAPHIES

Beeson, widow of Dr. Jehu Armistead Beeson, May 13th 1846.

When Anderson County was cut off from Houston County in 1846, and Palestine made its county seat, he removed thereto, with his family, which consisted of his wife, Pauline, her daughter, Jane Armistead Beeson, one year old, and Annie Jowers, daughter by his first wife, Ann Lacy, near the same age. Here he practiced his profession, but just before the Civil War went into the merchandizing business. When the Civil War broke out he raised and was Captain of a company from Anderson County. His wife, Pauline, died during the Civil War, in 1862. Before this, in 1848, he was elected Representative of Anderson County and served in that capacity and later in the State Senate for sixteen years.

In 1863, he married Mrs. E. W. Gardner, widow of Judge Gardner. By this union there were no children.

In 1865, he was commissioned Adjutant General by President Houston. In 1869, he married Mrs. Bettie A. Lamon Hill and from this union there were five daughters, all real Daughters of the Republic of Texas and all now living: Mrs. Frank T. Rennie, Mrs. Sam S. Smith, Mrs. W. B. Flanagan, Mrs. R. E. Doyle, Mrs. Waites Bowdon.

Dr. Jowers probably held public office as long and as continuously as any man in Texas. After his service for sixteen years in the Legislature of Texas, he was elected County Judge, which office he held until he died. From 1868 to 1892, he was County Judge of Anderson County. Daughters of his son, Richard Beeson Jowers, are living: Mrs. George D. Hunter of San Antonio; Mrs. D. B. McKenna, and Mrs. J. P. Burkhead, of Palestine, and Mrs. Ed Burkhead, of Houston, and a great number of great grandchildren are citizens of Texas. Doctor Jowers, or Judge Jowers, as he was called, later in his life, was a prominent Mason. Being a member of the first lodge organized in Palestine.

He is buried in the old (pioneer) Cemetery of Palestine. He died after his long and useful life, on July 30th, 1892.

The author is indebted to Miss Mary Kate Hunter, of Palestine, for the above biography of Dr. Jowers, and is glad to have this opportunity of helping to preserve the memory of a worthy pioneer of Houston County.

The location of Dr. Jowers home, while he lived in Crockett, is not definitely known, but there is a strong probability that he lived where the Schmidt House now stands, as the author has in his possession an original unrecorded deed, from Dr. Jowers to J. H. Gillespie, dated July 2, 1852, conveying lots 138 and 140 in Crockett. J. H. Gillespie in turn conveyed the same to John

HISTORY OF HOUSTON COUNTY

E. Helms the same year, and that is where John E. Helms lived and where his widow lived many years later.

ADAM COLUMBUS KING

Was the son of Adam King and Fanny Glass King, and was born in Virginia May 3, 1813 and married Jane Catherine Bone, in Rutherford County, Tennessee, August 15, 1837. Their children were: Athelia Ann, who married Dr. Samuel Alexander King; Harriet Rebecca, who married W. M. King, Jr.; James Cadwallader Jones King, who became a prominent physician in Waco, Texas, John Bone King, who enlisted on February 22, 1862, at Crockett, Texas, in Company B, 13th Texas Cavalry, of the Confederate Army. About June 1, 1862, he was transferred to Captain McLean's Company C, Gould's Battalion, Randall's Brigade, Walker's Division, Texas Volunteers. James Cadwallader Jones King, enlisted at Crockett, April 15, 1861, Co. A, 2nd Texas Cavalry, Hood's brigade and served until the end of the war. Christina Jerusha married William Coleman. Other children were David Williamson, Catherine Maclin, who married C. T. Hogan, Andrew Columbus and Mary Jane.

Adam C. King moved to Crockett about 1849 or 1850, and soon became identified with the business, social and religious life of the town and county. In 1852 he purchased a large and valuable tract of land, on the western edge of the town, and there built a substantial home, and reared his family. In 1853 he was serving as county coroner, an important officer in that day. He was an elder in the Presbyterian Church. Before his death he moved to Waco, Texas, and died there October 26, 1893. Two of his daughters, Mrs. S. A. Burney and Mrs. H. A. Wilson, now reside at College Station, Texas. A granddaughter holds an important position in A. and M. College.

REV. SAMUEL ALEXANDER KING

The subject of this biography, although a citizen of Houston County and Crockett for only a few years, deserves a place among the pioneers of the County. He was born in Woodford County, Kentucky, October 11th, 1834, the son of Rev. William M. King, a Presbyterian minister, and Lucy Woodson King, a relative of Thomas Jefferson. He received his education through

BIOGRAPHIES

academic and seminary courses conducted by his father, who was a teacher and preacher in Illinois, before coming to Texas in 1851. He was licensed to preach and ordained by Presbytery at San Marcos, Texas, on April 5th, 1856. He became stated supply for the new school Presbyterian Church in Crockett and the Old School Presbyterian Church in Centerville, and served both churches from 1857 to 1861, living at Crockett and preaching twice a month in each church.

It was during this ministry that he married Athelia Ann King, daughter of Adam C. King, an elder in the Crockett Church, and Jane Bone King. Athelia Ann King was born in Williamson County, Tennessee on September 9th, 1838, and died in Wisconsin on September 12th, 1913, and was buried in Waco, Texas. During the years 1861 to 1863, Dr. King engaged in evangelistic work, going out from Garden Valley, Smith County.

In 1863 he lived in Milford, Texas and was stated supply for the church there and also for the Waco Church. In 1864, he became a Mason while at Milford, and took the Royal Arch degrees. In 1867 he moved to Robinson, supplying Robinson and Waco Churches.

In 1875 he moved to Waco and gave his full time as pastor of the First Presbyterian Church of Waco. In 1877 he was sent as a delegate from the General Assembly to the Pan-Presbyterian Council which met in Edinburgh, Scotland. He completed a pastorate of forty years with the Waco Church in February 1903.

In the fall of 1902 he moved to Austin to fill the chair of Systematic Theology in the Austin Presbyterian Theologican Seminary, occupying that chair until he reached the age of 80 years, when he asked to be released from active duty. He remained as Professor-Emeritus until a short time before his death which occurred on September 21st, 1918 at Austin. He was buried in Waco.

THE KYLE FAMILY

When a single family can claim four pioneers of Houston County, that family deserves a place in its history. This is the claim of the Kyle family for a place in the sun. Mrs. Mary Kyle Tucker of Elkhart has so ably told the history of her family that it is adopted for use in this history. She writes as follows:—

"About 1842 four brothers, J. H. B. Kyle who was our grandfather, John Kyle, W. R. W. Kyle, and Matthew G. Kyle, together with their mother and the families of the two older brothers left South Carolina to come to Texas. They came to Pickens County, Alabama where they settled temporarily. In 1844 W. R. W. Kyle married a Miss Kirkpatrick and came on to Texas with members of that family. He settled by homesteading, the homesite and farm where John Reagan now lives.

"My father was born in Pickens County, Alabama on October 5th, 1845. When he was four years old his father and uncle Matthew came on to Texas and settled out near Augusta. About 1856, our grandfather, J. H. B. and Uncle Bill, W. R. W. exchanged farms. Later, W. R. W. moved west of Elkhart and his two remaining sons live there.

"These two of his sons are S. B. Kyle, aged 87 and T. J. M. Kyle, who is quite a bit younger. They aren't sons of the former Miss Kirkpatrick however.

"My father was the next to the youngest of the seven sons of J. H. B. and Lou Spencer Kyle. They were: James, Joe, Henry Eli, George Spencer, John, William Polk and Matthew. With the exception of the last named, all reared families, though I believe Uncle Eli had no sons. There were also in this family five daughters who were: Margaret Jones, _____Driskill, Betty Hallmark, Vina Clinton-Smith, Lou Smith and Willie Tunstall.

"My father and his five older brothers were in the same company during the Civil War. Uncle Jim was killed at Blair's Landing, Tenn. in the fighting preliminary to the Battle of Shiloh."

Matthew G. Kyle, mentioned above as one of the four pioneers, lived for many years near Augusta, and was such a factor in the development of that community, that the following additional facts are recorded about him: He was the father of five daughters and two sons. His oldest daughter, Betty, married Coll Aldrich, son of Collin Aldrich, San Jacinto Veteran. After her death he married her sister, Julia. His next daughter, Martha, married Zack Douglas, and was the mother of two daughters and Joe. His third daughter, Fannie, married D. S. Williams, and is still living. His youngest daughter, married Jim McLean, and is still living in Crockett. His oldest son, Jessie, died many years ago unmarried. His youngest son, Sam, is still living.

A. LeGORY

A colorful career was that of A. LeGory, who was born at Vicksburg, Mississippi, October 10th, 1840. His parents were

BIOGRAPHIES

John B. and Margaret (Conley) LeGory. His father was a native of Genoa, Italy and his mother was a native of Ireland. As early as 1855, he came to Crockett with a man by the name of Daniels, and became a citizen of this place. Early in the days of the Civil War he enlisted, on February 1862, in the Lubbock Guards, a cavalry regiment which was later dismounted. As a member of Walker's Division he saw active service and was in the battles of Mansfield, Pleasant Hill, Carrion Crow, Lake Providence and Yellow Bayou. As a soldier he had never missed a day from the ranks of company.

After the war he returned to Houston County and lived with the family of Captain John T. Smith and while there traveled on steamboats plying their trade on the Trinity River. Among the boats on which he was engaged was Indian No. 2 and the Roofborn, besides he conducted business on a number of flatboats, plying their trade on the Trinity River. Later he operated a line of freight wagons between Crockett and Houston and betweent Crockett and Navasota.

He was a pioneer in the cultivation of the famous Stewart papershell pecans and also introduced a fine herd of Jersey cattle.

On January 7th, 1875, he married Miss Eliza Hortense Wortham, a daughter of Major John Wortham and his wife Cary Ann (Vaughan) Wortham.

A biography of Major Wortham will be found elsewhere in this history. To this union were born six children, John LeGory, a prominent citizen of Crockett, who has taken high rank in civic, fraternal, business and religious matters; A. LeGory, Jr., generally known as Gus; C. W. LeGory, generally known as Wortham; Lipscomb, who still lives in Crockett; Hortense, who is now Mrs. Hortense Sweet; and Cary Ann, who is the wife of our well known druggist, W. P. Bishop. These children and their families can well be proud of their noble father.

COLONEL JOHN LONG

In the old cemetery at Crockett there is a grave, marked with a large marble monument, covering the entire grave, which was once the most outstanding monument in the old cemetery. This monument has been broken and has lost much of its original attractiveness, but still attracts attention. On it is recorded the fact that Col. John Long was born May 7th, 1792 and that he died October 17th, 1859. The records show that on April 26th,

1850 he was Chief Justice of Houston County. In an early day he was the owner and proprietor of a hotel in Crockett, situated on the Southeast corner of the public square, which was known as the "Long Hotel," and which was destroyed by fire in the early sixties. He was associated with L. E. Downes in the mercantile business as early as 1851, on the lot now owned and occupied by Frank Chamberlain as a drug store.

He was married twice. Some of the children by his first marriage were S. J. W. Long, known as Sam Long; and W. E. Long, known as Bill Long. S. J. W. Long established his home on Hurricane Bayou, on the Hall's Bluff road, about seven miles west of Crockett, where he raised a large family of children, including Joseph Long and Charley Long, Jonie Long, who married F. H. Bayne, Mollie, who married A. A. DeBerry, Emma, who married John Taylor, Sallie, who married Tom Bayne.

W. E. Long, mentioned above, was the father of two daughters, Lou and Jennie. Lou, the elder of the two, married John M. Dunwoody and Jennie, first married Taylor J. Hail and after his death married his brother, Edley E. Hail.

Col. John Long was married a second time, his last wife, Miss Emily Cash, survived him, and later married Major James C. Wootters.

Col. Long, by his last marriage was the father of Miss Bettie Long, who married Dr. John B. Smith, and a son John Long who died without having married.

Hugh Long, a brother of Col. John Long, came with him to Texas, but settled in Harrison County. His descendents later came to Houston County and settled near Augusta, where some of them still reside.

GEORGE BRINSON LUNDY

This influential citizen of Houston County was born in Randolph County, Georgia, August 3rd, 1840, and after living a short time in the States of Florida and Mississippi, he moved with his father's family to Texas, in 1857 and settled near Moscow, in Polk County. On May 5th, 1862, he enlisted in the Confederate Army and became a member of Hood's famous brigade and served during the entire period of the war, except when being treated for a bad wound in the leg that came near proving fatal.

He was with General Lee at Appomatox and witnessed the surrender of his gallant leader. He had followed General Hood

BIOGRAPHIES

in many of the most celebrated battles of the war, including Chicuamauga, where he was wounded, he was a member of Company M (Captain Howard Ballinger), First Texas Infantry, having enlisted at Old Sumpter, in Trinity County, and the record shows that he was paroled at Appomattox on April 9th, 1865.

In 1867 he married Miss Mary Worthington, and to this union there were born three children, Ralph G. Lundy, Mrs. Ione Legory, and W. Q. Lundy, all of whom are still living.

After the death of his first wife he married Mrs. Sallie M. Daniel, a daughter of Judge Samuel M. Thompson, who survived him but has since died.

In 1872, he moved to Nevil's Prairie in Houston County where he met and married his last wife. He was a charter member of the Lovelady Masonic Lodge. After moving to Crockett in 1893 he affiliated with Lothrop Lodge.

He was an honored elder of the First Presbyterian Church of Crockett, (Also known as the Tenney Memorial Church), which he served until his death on December 27th, 1915. He is buried in Glenwood Cemetery in Crockett.

JAMES WILLIAM MADDEN

"Born in the Town of Augusta in Houston County, Texas, June 16, 1856; received his education in the common schools of his county, and at the Academy of Prof. Logan at Tyler, Texas, attending the latter Institution during the session of 1875-*; reared on the farm and followed farming until he was 26 years old; never attended a college or university; read law "at home" and without any instructor, except in the summer of 1877, when he taught school near Waco and read under Col. Tom Harrison while he was teaching; spent three years teaching through the summers and two years regularly; moved to Crockett, the county seat, in 1882; served three years as deputy Tax Collector under his father; was for six years deputy county and district clerk, serving in both capacities concurrently, keeping the minutes of all the courts in the county except the Justice Courts, and regarded this as his "law school," and was admitted to the Bar in April, 1891; edited the "Crockett Economist," a weekly newspaper, for three years after his admission to the Bar; practiced his profession until his appointment as Private Secretary to Governor Culberson in February, 1896, and promoted to the office of Secretary of State in December, 1896; served there until the close of the Culberson Administration in January, 1899, when he returned to his home in Crockett where he has been in the active practice of his profession ever since; served as Supervisor of the Census in his congressional district in 1910, under appointment of President Taft, and as a member of the Local Exemption Board during the War with Germany and Austria under appointment by President Wilson; and served in three cases as Special Associate Justice of the Supreme Court of Texas under appointment of Governor Neff."

Mr. Madden continued in the active practice of his profession, with his partner, Judge Sam A. Denny, until his health so completely failed that he was forced to spend the latter portion of his life in the retirement of his home. Until the last he manifested a deep interest in public affairs, and died on the first day of June, 1936, and will always be remembered as one of the most outstanding citizens of Houston County. His funeral was conducted in the First Methodist Church of which he had been a member and a steward for many years and rarely has so many lofty tributes been paid to any citizen of Houston County, as was paid to him on this occasion. He left surviving him: one son, Wilson Erls Madden, Lieutenant Commander in the Navy of the United States, and one daughter, Addie, who is the wife of Mr. S. M. Boone. A number of grandchildren survive him as well as numerous relatives.

N. J. MAINER

Some of the outstanding business men of Houston County conducted their business in Lovelady and exercised a wide influence in their communities as well as in the entire county. Prominent among them was N. J. Mainer, who was born in Polk County, Texas, on the 28th day of July, 1848. He received his early education in the common schools of Polk County. Later he had a year at Baylor University.

He clerked for Thos. H. Nelms, Sr. of Pennington from about 1870 to 1872. He married Ella Nelms, daughter of Thos. H. Nelms in 1872.

When the railroad came through Lovelady about 1873 he moved to Lovelady and with L. P. Nelms went into general merchandise business under the firm name of Nelms and Mainer. This business continued until L. P. Nelms' death, when the firm was dissolved and a new partnership formed with J. O. Monday, the firm named Mainer & Monday. This business

BIOGRAPHIES

continued until his death on May 31st, 1897 at Lovelady. The business was continued under the name of E. Mainer & Sons until Ella Mainer's death in 1912.

Besides the store, he accumulated a large estate in land and cattle. He was active in political life of this section, and in public affairs. He was a deacon of the Baptist Church and one of the pillars of the church as long as he lived.

Names of children: Myrtie Mainer Neff; Clyde Mainer (deceased) T. Nelms Mainer; J. R. Mainer; Hayne Mainer (deceased) Ella Mainer Young; Lucille Mainer McMurry; and Roy Mainer.

THE MASTERS FAMILY

The Patriarch of this family, Jacob Masters, Senior, and his wife, Elizabeth Shaw Masters, started on a trek from North Carolina, some time as early as 1828, with their two sons, Jacob, Jr. and Henry, and their daughters, Mary, who married Lemuel Rice, and who was known as "Polly"; Fannie, who married Solomon Allbright; Sallie, who married John D. V. Gossett; Eliza, who first married Alex Shaver, and after his death married_____ Cawthon; Elizabeth, who married Sanford Shaver; Willie, who married Joseph Rice.

Jacob Masters, Senior, located his league of land, on the King's Highway, known also as the Old San Antonio Road, about ten miles northeast of Crockett, and there established his home, which was a landmark for years thereafter, and where he entertained the traveling public. An old pecan tree, standing on the highway, more than a hundred years old, now marks the site of this pioneer home.

The exact date when Masters arrived in Houston County is not known, but that he was here as early as 1828, is borne out by an entry in the Diary of Adolphus Sterne, published in the *Southwestern Historical Quarterly*, which is as follows:

"Wednesday June 2nd (1841) fine weather-left Col. Bean's early in the morning traveled slow to Jacob Masters another old friend of 13 years standing, this day is the 13th anniversary of my marriage with my dear wife."

Previously Sterne had written in his Diary under date of Tuesday, April 23rd, 1839, as follows: "reached Masters at 7— —having some 42 miles this day. Masters is a timid old Dutchman, has built a Block House and makes all the members of the establishment sleep there at night."

HISTORY OF HOUSTON COUNTY

Jacob Masters, Senior was married to Elizabeth Shaw on February 28th, 1800. His sons Jacob and Henry evidently had families in Texas before the days of the Republic, for both received grants of leagues and labors of land from the Mexican Government as early as 1835.

JOHN McCONNELL

Old Ireland furnished Houston County some valuable citizens, who contributed largely to the development of the county, but none more outstanding than the subject of this sketch. John McConnell was born in Ireland on January 28th, 1818, the son of Patrick and Bridget McConnell. He landed in New York on January 1st, 1839 and went from there to New Orleans and, after a short time, he moved to a place near Nacogdoches. From there he came to Crockett on his way to Galveston, September 27th, 1847, but found the place so inviting that he decided to locate, and immediately opened a blacksmith shop, being a blacksmith by trade. Soon afterwards he married Mary Jane Dickerson, daughter of a pioneer, William Dickerson, who lived near Crockett. After her death, he married Martha Lovelady, the daughter of Cyrus Lovelady, also a pioneer of Houston County.

He was successful in his business career and having accumulated a competency in his blacksmith business, he opened a hardware store and built up a large and successful business in that line. Although not a politician, he held the office of County Treasurer of Houston County for twelve years and later the office of city alderman for four years.

He was a prominent and influential member of the Baptist Church and a suit that he brought against a Baptist minister for a debt resulted in a division of the church. He was also prominent in Masonic circles, both in his local lodge and in the Grand Lodge of Texas. He was a member of Palestine Commandery, Knights Templar. He died in Crockett.

He died September 7th, 1898 and so highly was he esteemed by the people of Crockett that a public meeting was held at the courthouse at which Col. W. W. Davis was chosen Chairman and Geo. W. Crook, Secretary, and J. E. Downes, W. D. Pritchard, A. LeGory and A. A. Aldrich a Committee on Resolutions. In these resolutions he was commended as "having exemplified in his life all the best qualities of a citizen, and was by his

BIOGRAPHIES

sterling worth and eminent usefulness, endeared himself to our people."

By his first marriage Mr. McConnell was the father of three children: Elizabeth, generally called Lizzie, who married Joe Rice, and whose children are with us today; second, William V., generally called Bill who built up a large mercantile business which continues as the McConnell Dry Goods Company, and third John A. McConnell, who was also a successful merchant and whose widow and children are well known citizens of Crockett, one being our sheriff. By his last marriage, Mr. McConnell was the father of four children: Henry Grady, Esther, who married Arch Burton, Robert Emmett, whose family still live in Crockett and Dan McConnell, whose widow and daughter also live in Crockett.

THE McLEAN FAMILY

A pioneer of pioneers was Daniel McLean, who was a native of North Carolina and first came to Texas as a member of the Magee Expedition in 1814, which was one of the most important of the early incursions of Americans in Texas. He was one of the ninety-three survivors of the famous battle of the Medina River. He escaped the Massacre and traveled to Natchitoches, Louisiana, going by night and stopping by day with friendly Indians, who at that time were almost the only people living between the San Antonio River and the Sabine. Not many years later he came into Texas again as a regular member of Austin's colony and finally located his home about twenty miles northeast of the present site of Crockett on the Old San Antonio Road. Here he settled in 1821 and was granted a league and labor of land on which his home was located, the old home site has ever since been in the McLean family. In 1837, some Indians stole his horses and he and his brother-in-law, John Sheridan, in company with others pursued them to a point near the present town of Elkhart where both McLean and Sheridan were killed by the Indians. The Centennial Commission of Control erected an imposing monument at the site of this massacre. His body was brought back to the old home and buried there and a suitable marker stands at his grave, erected by the family. He was survived by two sons, James McLean and William McLean and daughters.

His son, William McLean, became one of the leading citizens of Houston County. He inherited the old Daniel McLean homestead from his father and later moved his family to

Augusta and engaged in the mercantile business with Col. W. W. Davis, the firm being McLean & Davis, and was known far and wide, and continued for many years. He raised a large and influential family. His oldest daughter, Mary, married Judge W. A. Davis, for several terms, County Judge of Houston County. Jennie and Daisy married William V. Connell, a most singular coincidence is that Mary and Jennie died on the same day, February 3rd, 1888, and were buried the same day in the same cemetery. A funeral card issued by the family reads: "In loving Remembrance of Two Sisters, Jennie and Mary McLean, consorts of W. V. McConnell and W. A. Davis. Died in Crockett, Texas, Feb. 3rd, 1888, age drespectively 20 and 27 years." Another daughter of William McLean, Eulah, married Rev. Riall, and died recently at her home in Grapeland. She was the mother of our well known citizen, William Alfred Riall.

WILLIAM McLEAN

The name of this pioneer, native son of Houston County, has been mentioned in connection with the history of the McLean family, elsewhere in this history. His picture also appears in its proper place.

He was the youngest of the three children of Daniel and Hannah McLean. He was born on the Old Daniel McLean home place, on the Old San Antonio Road, about twenty-two miles northeast of Crockett, in 1829, and his father was killed by the Indians when he was only eight years old. His father and mother came from Moore County, North Carolina, before his birth.

After his father's tragic death, his Uncle Archibald McLean, came to Texas, thinking that the family would need his assistance, but his older brother, James McLean, who was then only sixteen years of age told him that he was man enough to take care of the family, and his uncle returned to his home in New Orleans, and the family knew nothing more of him.

The family continued to occupy the old home place, on his fathers headright league, and in the division of the estate the old house was awarded to him. After the death of William McLean, this place fell to his son, Jim McLean, whose family still own it.

After reaching manhood, William McLean moved to the town of Augusta and engaged in the mercantile business with Col. W. W. Davis, the firm known as McLean & Davis.

He died in November, 1904 and was survived by the following children: Dan McLean, Jim McLean and Will McLean, the

BIOGRAPHIES

present County Judge; Mary McLean, who married Judge W. A. Davis, Jennie and Daisy, who, in succession, married W. V. McConnell, and Eula, who married Rev. Riall. William McLean is buried in the Cemetery at Crockett.

DOCTOR FRANCIS LEWIS MERIWETHER

This distinguished pioneer and eminent physician was born in Abbeville District, South Carolina, July 29, 1804, and moved with his parents when quite young to Alabama, where he grew up and received his medical education. From there he moved to Harrison County, Texas, where some of his children were born. It is not known just when he came to Houston County, but it was some time prior to 1851, for his name appears on the old Thomas P. Collins day book on November 3, 1851, and he became a regular customer after that date. While living in Alabama he married Miss Ethelinda Dunlap, who was the mother of all his children. While living in Houston County he made his home on Elkhart Creek, about fifteen miles northwest of Crockett, where he did an extensive medical practice as long as he lived. His children were: a daughter, Huldah, who married Dr. Frank Rainey; another daughter, married Judge Anson Rainey; another daughter, Jessie, married Tom H. Dailey, and his youngest daughter, Willie, married Frank Edens. His oldest son was Dr. Lewis Meriwhether and his youngest son was Frank Meriwether. None of his children are now living. Dr. Meriwether died on February 9, 1881, and is buried in the old cemetery near Dailey, and his wife, Ethelinda, died on the 26 of December 1876, and they both sleep side by side in the same cemetery. A granddaughter, Mrs. Robert M. Hamby, now lives in Austin, and several other grandchildren live in and near Grapeland. The widow of Dr. Lewis Meriwether lives in Washington with her children.

COL. STEWARD ALEXANDER MILLER

The subject of this biography was a pioneer of Houston County, who had such a distinguished career, and left his impress on the life of his day, that he deserves to have his memory preserved for the benefit of posterity. He was born in Campbell County, Virginia, and was left an orphan at an early age. He learned the trade of a tanner and later taught school. He came to Texas in 1839 and settled in Crockett, where he resided, continuously, until his death on March 27th, 1893. He engaged in business in Crockett, and while pursuing his business, studied law under James Carr, who was probably the first lawyer to locate in Crockett. In 1843, he heard the call of his country, and enlisted in Col. Jacob Snively's Expedition. While on this expedition, through north and northwest Texas, and even farther, he kept a complete diary of the events that occurred, which is one of the most valuable diaries that the author has ever seen, and it is gratifying that the public will share the benefit of it, as his daughter ,Mrs. Amelia Comer, will soon have it published in *The Southwestern Historical Quarterly*.

It is a fact worthy of note, that Hon. Henderson Yoakum, drew on this diary for material in his well known *History of Texas*, and mentions the same in a note in his history. It was while on this expedition that Col. Miller gained the title of "Colonel."

He returned to his native Virginia in the fall of 1850, and on June 24th, 1851, was married to Miss Rebecca F. Whitten, of Bedford County (now Liberty County), Virginia. Ten children were born of this union, the only one surviving at this time is Mrs. Amelia Miller Comer (now Mrs. C. C. Comer) of Carthage, Texas, who is a worthy descendant of a noble father, and is a leading spirit in her community. Carthage can well be proud of its inheritance from Crockett.

Col. Miller had a distinguished career in both the fields of law and politics. He was one of the outstanding lawyers of his day and the author has heard it said that the eminent jurist, Judge Geo. F. Moore, in his early life, said that if he made as good a lawyer as Col. Miller, he would be satisfied.

Col. Miller was at one time associated with the eminent Judge Royall T .Wheeler, one of the distinguished Chief Justices of the Supreme Court of Texas, and Judge Wheeler in a document, still in existence pays him a high tribute as both lawyer and upright citizen. The earliest case found in the Texas Supreme Court Reports, in which the name of Col. Miller appears, is the case of Allbright vs. Aldrich, 2 Texas Reports, page 166, tried in the Supreme Court at the December Term, 1847. In this case the names of three of the most outstanding pioneers of Houston County appear; Jacob Allbright, first county clerk, Collin Aldrich, first chief justice, and Elisha Clapp, noted Indian fighter and hero of San Jacinto. All three had a prominent part in the organization of the county in 1837.

When Texas was admitted to the union Col. Miller was

BIOGRAPHIES

elected the first Representative from Houston County and served on the First and Second Legislatures in 1846 and 1847. Then he was a member of the State Senate in 1851, 1854 and 1861, when he had to make some of his trips on horseback. On one of these trips his wife started with him in a carriage but could not get across the Trinity and had to turn back leaving Col. Miller to finish the trip on horseback. He was a member of the Senate when Sam Houston refused to take the oath of office and was deposed as Governor. When the Constitution of 1876 was adopted he was elected County Judge of Houston County and held the office for two terms.

ARMISTEAD THOMPSON MONROE

The following sketch of Col. A. T. Monroe is furnished the author by his only living son, A. T. Monroe, Jr. of San Antonio.

A. T. Monroe was the son of Augustine Garnett Monroe, who was a nephew of President James Monroe.

"My father had three brothers, named, John and Joseph. James was a general in the northern army and his regiment guarded the capital at Washington during the Civil War. He died in harness and his remains lie in the National cemetery at Washington. A life-like painting of him is now hanging in the armory in New York City. John, his brother, was a trader and left his family well provided for in New York City. His brother, Joseph, was a priest in New York City. Mrs. Douglas Robinson of New York City, who was a grandchild of President James Monroe, was a first cousin of my father, and her son married a sister of President Theodore Roosevelt.

"My father left Virginia when he was 18 years old and went to New York City, and my recollection is that he came to Texas in 1842 or 1843, landing at the west end of Galveston Island, instead of the east end, which is now Galveston City. A short time after this he went by ship to Liberty and took a steamboat to Alabama Crossing, on Trinity River, in Houston County. There he remained and went into the mercantile business. He met my mother there, who was a daughter of Jacob Allbright, and was married in 1846. He was the oldest child in the family and was the only one who came south.

"My father had the first wood cook stove that was in Houston County, and had it put up at home, but the negro cook said she couldn't cook on that thing, and the only way he could get her to use it was to have the fireplace walled up.

After that she would sneak out to her cabin and cook things in the fireplace. It took our family a long time to get her to use the stove."

A. T. Monroe was one of the most enterprising men who ever lived in Crockett. Soon after moving to Crockett from Alabama Crossing he built a home on the main street of Crockett—the very house is still standing in good condition. It is now the home of Geo. W. Crook and was built in 1854. The large hewed oak sills in the house are as sound today as when the house was built. The outer walls were weather boarded with good, heart lumber, sawed by H. F. Craddock and dressed by hand. The ceiling was of the same character of lumber. The space between the walls was filled with brick and lathing placed on the inside for plastering, which was never completed. In 1880, a daughter of Uncle Dan Coleman sold the place to Oliver C. Aldrich, who lived there until his death in 1889. After that the author became the owner of the property and sold it to Geo. W. Crook and his wife in 1911 .The author has heard the old man Salathiel Robert, a brick mason, say that he built the chimneys to the house, and they are standing today in good condition.

JUDGE GEORGE F. MOORE

Houston County is justly proud of one of her most distinguished citizens, the eminent jurist, Judge George F. Moore, who came to Crockett as a young man and lived there for eight years.

He was born in Georgia on the 17th day of July, 1822, being the seventh son of his parents. Growing up in Alabama, he studied in the University of that state, and the University of Virginia, though he was a graduate of neither. At the age of eighteen he began the study of law, and received his license to practice from Judge Shortridge, then a circuit judge of Alabama. I am informed by Gov. Roberts who first knew him as a boy, that in his youth he was distinguished by a taciturn, retiring manner, and an application to study that marked him through after life.

Removing to Texas in 1846, he brought with him poverty, that priceless gift to the young, which made labor a necessity, and gave spurs to his desire for independence. He first settled in Crockett, and made that his home until 1854 when he removed to Austin, and afterwards to Nacogdoches where he resided until appointed a reporter of the decisions of the Supreme Court. After the breaking out of war between the states, he was

BIOGRAPHIES

elected Colonel of the 17th Texas cavalry, which position he resigned in 1862 on receiving news of his election as an Associate Justice of the Supreme Court. In 1866, when Texas was in the process of what was termed Reconstruction ,he was again elected to the supreme bench, and was by his Associate Justices made Chief Justice, from which position he was removed by military power, on the 10th day of September, 1867, in a period of profound peace, and under circumstances which redound to his credit.

On November 17th 1883, before the Supreme Court of Texas, Judge A. W. Terrell paid a wonderful tribute to Judge Moore, from which the following excerpts are taken:

"From 1867 to 1874 he practiced his profession in Austin, and when in 1874 the people for the first time in nine years after the war resumed peaceful control of the State, he was appointed again associate Justice of the Supreme Court. After the constitution of 1876 was adopted he was elected to the same position by the people. In 1878, on the resignation of Chief Justice Roberts, he was appointed to succeed him, and soon afterwards was elected Chief Justice by the people by over one hundred thousand majority."

Again he says: "An ardent love for this mighty State, that had honored and elevated him, was a part of his nature. Her soil, climate and expanding greatness, as an undivided empire from the mountains to the sea, I have often heard him refer to, with pride and exultation. But as a Supreme Judge of Texas, his most lasting reputation was achieved. We know not which most to admire in him, a rigid regard for established law, or the boldness with which he would attack its semblance, whether reposing in precedent or fortified with the names of great men. I am not alone in believing that he was the best chancery practitioner in Texas; and thus when justice required that what seemed the harshness of law should not prevail, his quick sense of right recognized the demand, while his knowledge of equity applied the remedy."

The following tribute was paid his memory by his long time friend, Col. A. T. Monroe, of Houston County, which was published in the Austin Statesman on September 5th 1883:

> "*I seek, however weak, with heart sincere,*
> *To twine one wreath to deck his honored brow,*
> *Whose memory bright, the country will revere,*
> *While love of worth controls mankind, as now,*
> *His name is written on her proudest page,*

HISTORY OF HOUSTON COUNTY

Indented there in characters of light—
A soldier true, a jurist, just and sage,
He leaves no blot to dim his record bright,
Beloved the most by all who knew him best,
The first sad tear he ever caused—or sigh,
Was when he laid him down in death to rest,
And she who loved him dearest, saw him die.

A. T. Monroe,

San Pedro, Houston County,

September 1, 1883."

DANIEL MURCHISON

Daniel Murchison was born on the 12th day of January, 1804 probably in the state of Tennessee, and died at his home about six miles north of Crockett on the Palestine road on the 5th day of June, 1882. He is buried in the old Crockett cemetery by the side of his wife, Lucindy Teague Murchison, who was born January 5, 1831, and died August 30, 1900. Before coming to Texas he removed from the state of Tennessee to Mississippi, and came to Texas in an early day.

He was chosen tax collector and assessor soon after coming to Houston County and the records show he collected taxes in 1851, in 1852, 1954 and 1855. At that time taxes were paid in specie, that is, either silver or gold, and there were no banks in which a collector could deposit his collections. Evidently there was not much robbery or burglary at that time and valuables were generally regarded as safe when kept in trunks or other places about the house. It is a tradition in the Murchison family that when Daniel Murchison had to transport his tax collections from Houston County to Austin, that he carried huge sums of money in his saddle bags and made the trip on horseback. The highjacker was unknown in that day and there was little danger of a traveler being molested by any highway robber. So far as we know the tax collections made by Daniel Murchison during the entire tenure of his office were transferred in a saddle bag and on horseback, and it is not known that any attempt was ever made to rob him.

His first home was near Cook's mountain, about three miles

BIOGRAPHIES

northwest of Crockett, and he later moved to the home where he died on the Palestine road.

He was an elder in the Cumberland Presbyterian Church and must have been a prime mover in organizing the Bethel Cumberland church on the Palestine road, about four miles north of Crockett. After Judge S. M. Thompson came to Houston County in 1855, he was also an elder in the Cumberland Presbyterian church and he and Daniel Murchison often met in the meeting of Presbytery, where each represented his respective church.

The oldest daughter of Daniel Murchison was Angeline, who married H. F. Craddock, and who was the mother of a large family of children. Her oldest child was Miss Alice Craddock. The next was H. F. Craddock, Jr. who is still living in Commerce, Texas. She had a son by the name of Ben, who died without ever having married; a son, Thomas D. Craddock, born in 1861, and who married Jennie Numsen, who still lives in our community. Other children of Mrs. Angeline Craddock were: Goodwill Craddock, Peacewill Craddock, Stonewall J. Craddock, Miss Minnie Craddock, Sue Craddock, who is the wife of Dr. J. S. Wootters, and Daniel Craddock, who now lives in Dallas. Another son of Daniel Murchison was Weldon J. Murchison, who conducted a mercantile business on Neville's Prairie, and gave his name to the town of Weldon. He died some years ago, leaving two daughters, Mary Belle Murchison and Ella Murchison both of whom removed from Houston County.

Another son of Daniel Murchison was Daniel M. Murchison, generally known as Mack Murchison, who conducted a large mercantile business in Crockett and who died many years ago, leaving as his descendants Mrs. Hallie Crook, wife of George W. Crook; Sydnor L. Murchison, a prominent merchant in Crockett today, and Mrs. Birdie O'Dell, wife of D. W. O'Dell, who spent most of her life in Cleburne and Fort Worth, and who now lives at Handley, Texas, near Fort Worth. Another son of Daniel Murchison, Thomas F. Murchison, lived and died in Athens, Texas.

DANIEL McINTOSH MURCHISON

Daniel McIntosh Murchison was the son of Daniel Murchison and Mary Killough Murchison, and was born near Holly Springs, Marshall County, Mississippi, October 16th, 1841 and died in Cleburne, Texas, in 1882, at the home of his sister, Mrs.

J. M. Odell. He came to Texas with his father and his family February 11th, 1848. He was a soldier in the Confederate army. He married Miss Sallie Arledge, by whom he had one child, a daughter, Hally, who married George W. Crook, and died recently in Crockett. He afterwards married Miss Gertrude Lipscomb, by whom he had three children, Birdie, who married Weldon Odell, Snydor, who is a prominent business man in Crockett, and Albert, who died young.

He was a member of Lothrop Lodge, Masonic Fraternity, and at his death resolutions were passed by the lodge and published in the Crockett Patron. These extol his virtues in the highest terms.

He was an influential and useful member of the Crockett Baptist Church and had much to do in the erection of a new church building.

Probably no merchant who ever lived in Crockett displayed greater business ability than he.

COL. D. A. NUNN

The following biography of Col. Nunn appeared in the National Cyclopedia of American Biography, and is so complete and so splendidly expressed that it is adopted for this history of his home county:

"David Alexander Nunn, lawyer, was born at Summerville, Noxubee County, Miss., October 1st, 1836, son of John and Jane (Tubb) Nunn. His father was a pioneer Mississippi planter, and served as a soldier under Andrew Jackson (q.v.) in the war with the Choctaw Indians.

"David A. Nunn received his education in the private college and at the University at Murfreesboro, Law School at Lebanon, Tenn. and later studied law at New Orleans; was admitted to the bar in 1857, and in that year began the practice of his profession in his native county. In his father's home he had known and admired such great Southerners as Jefferson Davis (q.v.) Albert G. Brown (q.v.), William Barksdale (q.v.) and others; from them he imbibed his old school conception of politics and civic and social relations. These ideals and ideas remained his characteristics throughout his political life.

"In 1858 he settled at Crockett, Texas .In this new community he soon acquired a place of distinction, and was voted into the office of Mayor (Crockett's first mayor) which carried no salary, and was then a post of onerous responsibility. The entire country about Crockett was infested by a dangerous and

BIOGRAPHIES

lawless element, and it required all the courage and firmness of his character to maintain peace and order in the community. Occasionaly, with the assistance of the town marshal, and with revolver or shotgun, he personally coped with lawlessness, and he soon became celebrated as a force for the preservation of peace and the regnancy of the law.

"With the beginning of the Civil War he raised a company and went to the front, continuing an actual soldier of the Confederacy until the end of the war. He was in the early campaigns of the Texas Troops in Arizona and New Mexico ,subsequently was transferred to Arkansas and Louisiana, and saw hardships and fighting in many of the campaigns of the Southwest. In the Confederate war records (series I, part II, vol XXXIX, p. 627) in the report of Gen. William Steel, who commanded in the Red River country, is the following:

" 'Captain Nunn, of Morgan's battalion, succeeded in getting a good position with his squadron and delivered an effective fire at close range.'

"In these records (series I, vol. IX, p. 515) Lt.-Col. William Scurry of the 4th Texas Cavalry mentions him with others as conducting the last brilliant successful charge 'which decided the fortunes of the day' in an engagement in New Mexico, near Fort Craig.

"After the war he resumed his law practice and soon rose to rank among the foremost lawyers of Texas. The firm strength and ability which he had displayed as a soldier he again exhibited during the dark days of reconstruction. He was sent as a delegate to the Convention of 1875 which drafted the new Constitution for the State after its re-admission to the Union, and in that Convention was an acknowledged leader.

"He included in his friendship nearly all the great men of Texas of his day. Col. Nunn was especially beloved by his old comrades in Co. I, 4th Texas Cavalry.

"He married at Macon, Miss., June 8th, 1858, Helen, daughter of Bryan T. Williams, a planter of Noxubee County, Miss:; she survived him, with two children: David A., a lawyer of Crockett, and Corinne, widow of R. E. Corry, and one grandchild, Robert R. Nunn, son of Robert W. Nunn. Mrs. Helen W. Nunn died at Crockett, Texas, Oct. 9, 1917.

"David Alexander Nunn died at Crockett, Texas, August 13, 1911."

MRS. HELEN WILLIAMS NUNN

The following is taken from memorial resolutions adopted by the D. A. Nunn Chapter of the Daughters of the Confederacy, on November 7th, 1917, the anniversary of the birth of Mrs. Helen Williams Nunn:

"We meet today with bowed heads and sorrow stricken hearts to speak of one most tenderly loved by each one present—Mrs. Nunn.

"Mrs. Nunn was born in Macon, Mississippi, in 1836. She is described as having been a most beautiful, joyous and happy girl, giving evidence in her youth of that wonderful ability that has in her mature years crowned her efforts with marked success.

"She married, early in life, the Hon. D. A. Nunn, for whom this chapter is named. They lived a life of unusual happiness for over fifty years. As a wife and mother she was most devoted, finding her greatest pleasure in the happiness and comfort of her loved ones. Her relation to her brother, sister and grandson, was ideal.

"In the work of the D. A. Nunn Chapter she was leader and guide, impressing the fact that this work was not carried on through any feeling of animosity toward the North, but rather, that this work might cause our Northern brethren to see and know the feeling and principle that inspired the South, and to create kindly feeling between the sections of the country. She lived to see this hope largely realized, and was most happy in feeling that we were at last a United Nation, and that this union was in a large measure due to the efforts of the Daughters of the Confederacy. She was largely instrumental in securing the Woman's Confederate Home in Austin, where many happy, contented women have found a refuge for their old age, and will cherish and revere her memory.

"She was ever the friend of the Confederate Veteran, sincere and true. Through her efforts most of Houston County's veterans have their 'Crosses of Honor,' and on the 3rd of June she was always untiring in her efforts to provide suitable entertainment for them.

"She worked long and faithfully to secure the law making Jefferson Davis' birthday a legal holiday in Texas, and her joy was unbounded when the law was finally passed. It has been well said of her: 'She was a great woman.'

"The Texas Division of the Daughters of the Confederacy, delighting to honor her, created for her the office of First and Only Past President of the Texas Division daughters of the Confederacy, and later when the convention met, soon after she had passed her 70th birthday, she was presented with a most beautiful loving cup, as a token of their appreciation of what she had accomplished for the cause so dear to her. She was indeed a noble woman, tender and true, a most faithful friend, thoughtful for all.

BIOGRAPHIES

"The graves in Glenwood cemetery bear silent witness to this fact, all cared for, and with but few exceptions, mainly through her untiring efforts. Many of these graves are the last resting places of those who long since gone, had almost passed from the remembrance of man. But she remembering, had them most tenderly cared for. Her last charity and love seemed to embrace the entire town. The citizens of Crockett were indeed 'her people,' and as such she loved and honored them.

She had passed over eighty years—a long life; a life full of sunshine as well as shade. A life in which smiles and tears were blended. A life devoted to duty, kindly acts and charitable deeds, striving ever for what was right, loving and beloved."

HON. WILLIAM B. PAGE

This distinguished citizen, of Houston County, was born in Virginia, where he received a thorough education in the best institutions of that renowned State, and came to Crockett, in 1873, well equipped to take charge of the Crockett Academy, as a successor to Major John Spence, who as Superintendent, had raised the institution to the highest rank among private schools. His educational qualifications would have well fitted him for a place in the best universities of the country. He left his impress on the youth of Crockett and Houston County, which has survived until this day. Many of our most successful men, in every walk of life, owe their success to the excellent instruction received from him.

After having taught for twelve years or more in this Academy, he entered politics and distinguished himself as a Statesman of high rank.

But his best work was done as journalist and proprietor and founder of the Crockett Courier. He established this well known paper in January 1890, and at once placed it in the forefront of weekly newspapers of Texas.

Late in life he married Miss Annie Saunders, who survived him, and whom he had known in his boyhood days. They are both buried in their beloved Virginia soil.

HON. NAT PATTON

It is a long stretch of years between the days of the Republic of Texas and the date of the Seventy-Fourth Congress of the United States of America, and yet that was the interval between the dates when Houston County had one of its citizens in Congress. Isaac Parker, the famous pioneer citizen of Houston County, represented his district in several sessions of the Congress of the Republic from 1837 to 1845, and the next time that Houston County had one of its citizens so honored was when Nat Patton was elected to the 74th Congress in 1934, succeeding Hon. Clay Stone Briggs.

According to his own statement, prepared for the Congressional Record, Nat Patton was born in a log cabin at Tadmor, in Houston County, on February 26th, 1884, the son of Frank M. Patton and Bessie Bland Patton. He received his early education in the common schools of Houston County and in 1901, the author of this history, while a member of the 27th Legislature of Texas, gave him an appointment to Sam Houston Normal, at Huntsville. Later he was a member of the Texas House of Representatives and attended the law school of the University of Texas. He was admitted to the Bar in 1918, and practiced law at the Crockett Bar. He served two terms as County Judge of Houston County, and was a member of the Texas State Senate during the Forty-first, Forty-second and Forty-third Legislatures. He was tendered the appointment as comptroller, but declined. He was elected to the Seventy-fourth Congress in 1934, and has been reelected to each succeeding Congress. He is known both nationally and internationally as "Cousin Nat." An incident in his career is quite characteristic. When the King and Queen of England made their historic visit to Washington, he met them at a reception and greeted them as "Cousin George" and "Cousin Elizabeth." He was married to Miss Mattie Taylor, his childhood sweetheart in 1907, and they have four children: Bessie Louise, the wife of Joe Gus LeGory; Weldon, who has just been admitted to the bar; Nat, Jr., a practicing lawyer of the Crockett Bar; and Bonnie, the baby of the family, who still lives with her doting father and mother.

MRS. MAUD SIMS PENCE

Among the educators of Crockett, one who deserves to take a high rank is Mrs. Maud Sims Pence. She was born in Mississippi on November 8th, 1874, and on the death of her father, came to Crockett about 1886 and lived with her Aunt and Uncle, Mr. and Mrs. W. A. R. French. In 1887, she returned to her mothers home in Illinois, and was married there. In 1902, she came to Crockett and soon thereafter was selected as a teacher in the Crockett City School. She was noted for her efficiency as a teacher and also for her scholarship and brilliant intellect. She

BIOGRAPHIES

later taught school in Boise, Idaho, and in Huntington, West Virginia, but later returned to Crockett and again taught for several years here. She was active in church and Sunday School work and after her death a church museum, which she was instrumental in establishing, was named the MAUD PENCE MEMORIAL, and a suitable bronze marker is placed in the room to her memory.

She was a niece of Rev. Samuel Fisher Tenney, who was pastor of the Presbyterian Church at Crockett for fifty-four years.

She was fatally injured by a motor car and died at Crockett, Texas on August 3rd, 1937, leaving surviving her an only son, Edward Pence, who now lives in Wheeling, West Virginia. She also has many other relatives in Crockett and elsewhere. She is buried in Glenwood Cemetery, Crockett, Texas.

CYRUS HALBERT RANDOLPH

C. H. Randolph was a son of Jesse Nathaniel Randolph of Rowan County, North Carolina, but was born at St. Claire, Ill. as the family was moving westward, on December 9th, 1817. C. H. Randolph lived in Missouri in 1820, later in Tennessee, and in 1828 moved to Alabama. He came to Houston County in 1838, the year following the county's organization. An attorney, but practicing very little, he was Chief Justice (County Judge) in 1844-45 and Sheriff in 1847-48. He served three terms in the Legislature and was State Treasurer from 1858-65. Later public service included recorder fo the Supeme Court and employment in the land office and the State Teasurer's office. Judge Randolph did not return to Houston County after going to Austin. He had married Susan Nowlin, daughter of Peyton Wade Nowlin of Hyde Park, Austin, about 1853, probably while in the Legislature.

Old Randolph, in Eastern Houston County, was once one of the most important towns of Houston County, rivaling Crockett, which had been made the county seat in 1837 when A. E. Gossett donated the land for the town and county seat. It is often heard that Randolph, which doubtless got its name from C. H. Randolph, tried to get the county seat in 1837, which probably is a confusion of county history. The information by the grandson is that Cyrus Randolph did not come to Houston County from Alabama until 1837. The town grew up and became Randolph after the county was organized, probably reaching its peak shortly before the Civil War, according to Judge Aldrich. Crockett and Randolph became natural rivals and the latter wanted the

HISTORY OF HOUSTON COUNTY

county seat, which Crockett had. Probably an election was held to move the county seat, but lacked the necessary two-thirds vote to move it. Crockett had the county seat and kept it. Randolph flourished a-while and began to dwindle. The winds now blow through the tall trees where once stood a flourishing town.

Having entered politics at the age of 23, papers found in Judge Randolph's box, certifying his election to various offices were signed by President David G. Burnet, President Sam Houston, Governor Albert C. Horton, Governor P. H. Bell, Governor T. Wood and Governor Richard Coke.

The oldest document found was dated February 13, 1841, which certified his appointment to an office to which he had been elected Dec. 21, 1840. Another document was signed by Anson Jones, then Secretary of State, which certified his election to the "office of Chief Justice, in and for the County of Houston, in said Republic," and the closing paragraph reads: "Given under my hand, at Washington, the Fourth day of December, A. D., 1843, and of the Independence of the Republic, the eighth."

Judge Randolph was granted a license to practice law by the District Court of Houston County, and the document was governor.
signed by "O. M. Roberts, District Judge," who later became governor.

JUDGE ROBERT N. READ

His full name was Robert Newton Read. He was one of seven sons. We do not have the date of his birth, but he came to Texas in 1843 and settled a few miles south of Crockett, on the Huntsville Road. He cleared and put into cultivation a large plantation, which, even today, is known as Read's Opening. His children were: Ben F. Read, who was associated with him in business and who moved with him to Mineola when he left Crockett. His daughter, Lizzie, married H. A. Long. A daughter, Julia, married Nelson Garner; a daughter, Emma, married Dr. Wortham. A daughter, Corinne, married P. F. Comba; a daughter, Louella, married R. N. Stafford, who served many years in the Texas senate; a daughter, Louise, married R. P. Jiles; his other sons were John Read, Bob Read and Sam Read. John Read was born October 16, 1844, and died August 2, 1899. Sam Read was born December 25, 1847 and died September 19, 1919.

In 1870, Judge Read purchased a stock of merchandise from

BIOGRAPHIES

John H. Burnett, which was situated in a store building then located where the Crockett State Bank now stands. Mr. T. W. Thompson was present when this deal was consummated in the back room of the store building, and said that it was the largest sum of gold and silver that he had ever seen. I think the consideration was $5000 cash.

A number of the descendents of Judge Read are still living in Houston County, among them Dr. Sam P. Beeson, of Weldon, who is a successful physician and farmer, and seems to have inherited some of the business ability of his grandfather. As stated in another article, his two grandfathers were Judge R. N. Read and H. W. Beeson, both of whom were seventh sons. I am told that the widow of Ben F. Read still lives in Mineola. Judge Read was one of the most prominent citizens who ever lived in Houston County and I take great pleasure in perpetuating his memory for the benefit of Houston County people who honor and esteem its history.

THE RICE FAMILY

Joseph Rice, Senior, was born May 24th, 1805. He married Willie Masters, a daughter of Jacob Masters, Senior. As a colonist he was entitled to a league and labor of land, under the Mexican colonization laws. He had a part of this located on the Old San Antonio Road, about five miles northeast of Crockett, and there made his home. He kept a Stagecoach Inn at his log house home and this site is now marked by a granite marker placed there by the Centennial Board of Control. Here he managed a large plantation which was worked by slave labor until the close of the Civil War. His wife was born August 17th, 1809. He died August 11th, 1866 and he and his wife are buried in the Old Rice Cemetery, on his home place.

He and his wife were noted for their hospitality.

He was survived by his wife and the following children: Joseph Jr. who established his home on the Old San Antonio Road, just beyond the home of his father and there raised a large family, many of whom are still living, one, John Rice occupying the old home of his grandfather, known as the Stagecoach Inn. Another known as Shink is living in the Concord neighborhood. A daughter, Willie, married Jim Saxon and resides outside the county; another daughter married Jim Brown and also resides out of the county.

Another son of Joseph Rice, Senior, George, established his home also on the Old San Antonio Road and raised an interesting family, one of his daughters, known as Banie, married Ike Lansford, and died several years ago; another daughter, Willie, married Dr. Ben Elliott and still resides in Crockett. Another daughter, Clara, married Chester Kennedy and they reside at Grapeland, Houston County.

Henry Rice, a son of Joseph Rice, Sr. established his home on the Rusk Road, about five miles northeast of Crockett and his son, Lonnie Rice, still lives near there. Jessie, a daughter of Henry Rice, married Judge John Spence, and still resides with her family in Crockett.

Elizabeth (Betty), a daughter of Joseph Rice, Sr., married Thomas J. Monk, and died many years ago, leaving several children, among them, John Monk, Jim Monk, Frank Monk, Dick Monk, Willie, a daughter, who married Jim Lacy, Beulah, who married Cal Beeson. All the children of Betty Monk are now dead.

Joseph and Willie Rice, Sr. had another daughter, Willie, who married Jeff Dawson, and her children are with us today, including Mrs. Nora Dean, wife of John L. Dean, and Lena, wife of Carlos Robbins, and mother of our County Clerk, J. Dawson Robbins.

Joseph and Willie Rice had a son, John, who died in the Civil War.

The Old Rice Cemetery, located just in front of the Old Stagecoach Inn, is still preserved and holds the dust of many members of the Rice family.

CAPTAIN JOHN T. SMITH

New York may justly be proud of her contribution to Houston County's honor roll of pioneers. On March 5th, 1815 Captain John T. Smith was born in the State of New York and later moved to Georgia, where he served in the Legislature of the State before coming to Texas in 1849 to begin a memorable career as a citizen of the Lone Star State. He served in the Texas Legislature during three sessions in 1866, 1873 and 1874. He died in Austin on February 16th, 1874, while serving in the Legislature and a delegation of Representatives escorted his remains to Crockett for burial. Dr. Frank Rainey, one of his best friends, also served with him in 1874, and at the memorial services held in the Legislative Hall, paid him a high and glowing tribute and accompanied his remains to Crockett. Among other things, Dr. Rainey said: "During the Civil War, he served

BIOGRAPHIES

in the Confederate Army, and his services proved him to be worthy. He was the head of a family who almost idolized him for his many virtues. One of Texas noblest sons had died. His character was irreproachable.

Captain Smith also served several terms as Chief Justice of Houston County. At one time he operated the steamboat "Ida Reese" on the Trinity River. His family was hardly less distinguished than himself. His oldest daughter, Augusta Louise, first married Isaac Adair, who died while serving in the Confederate Army. She later married J. M. Porter, one of the outstanding citizens of Houston County, who gave his name to the town of Porter Springs. His next oldest daughter, Georgiana, married Captain B. B. Arrington, and they have a number of descendants still living in Crockett. His third daughter, Elizabeth, married B. F. Chamberlain, the father of our fellow-townsman, B. F. Chamberlain. His fourth daughter, Grace, married Dr. S. T. Beasley, and was the mother of Mrs. W. H. Denny and Stephen T. Beasley. His fifth daughter, Mollie, married I. W. Murchison and she was the mother of Smith and Gaines Murchison. The one son of Captain Smith was Dr. John B. Smith, an eminent physician, who also served as Representative in the Texas Legislature.

ZACHARIAH STIDHAM

Zachariah Stidham was not only a farmer, but he was in the habit of hauling freight from Houston for Crockett Merchants. He was also a soldier in the Confederate Army. I have in my possession a letter from Mr. J. C. Ingram of Groveton, Texas, in which he stated: "I have my grandfather's furlough, issued to him in October, 1863, by Captain White, but signed by Z. Stidham, acting commander of the company at Tarkington Prairie. I find this same Zachariah Stidham serving as a private soldier in a Georgia Company in the Indian wars in 1836."

I also have in my possession a letter from Miss Harriet Smither, archivist in the State Library at Austin, as follows:

October 1, 1835.

"Z. Steadham, private, enlisted July 1861, in Captain J. R. Barbee's Reserve Company, Beat No. 11, Houston County, 11th Brigade, Texas Militia."

Then I find from old records in my possession that he married a daughter of George Hallmark, Adeline Hallmark, and she was named in the will of George Hallmark as Adeline Stedham.

The records show that on February 1, 1856, Zachariah Stidham received a patent from the State of Texas to 232¾ acres of land, situated about five or six miles southeast of Crockett, where he resided for many years thereafter.

In later life Mr. Stidham moved to West Texas and was visited there by Mr. George Taylor of Austonio. who remembers seeing him and his family after they had removed from Houston County. It is supposed that he died in West Texas.

THE STOKES FAMILY

So many members of this pioneer family have left their impress on the business, social and religious life of Houston County that the author has decided to give a history of the family, rather than single out some individual member for treatment.

The patriarch of the family was William Benson Stokes, who was born in Georgia on June 4th, 1804, and came at an early day to Texas and located in Crockett, where he practiced his profession as a member of the Crockett Bar and was recognized in his day as a leading lawyer. He was noted for his physical energy and when he had occasion to come to Crockett he cared nothing for a conveyance and made the journey on foot. At his death his estate was administered by his pioneer friend, John Box, and when his land was sold, it was purchased by his fellow lawyer, Col. S. A. Miller. He was survived by one son, Charles Stokes, and two daughters, Harriet (generally called Hattie) who married James Collins, and Mary, who married Joseph Atmar.

His son, Charles Stokes has a distinguished career of his own. He was born in Georgia on the 15th day of May, 1834, and came to Texas with his parents in his young manhood and engaged in both farming and the lumber business. At the beginning of the Civil War he enlisted as a Confederate soldier and served in both Texas and Arkansas. About 1880 he was elected tax assessor for Houston County, and held the office for eighteen years. About 186— he married Lucy Hancock, daughter of Major J. R. Hancock, an extensive planter and slave owner, and a more congenial couple would be hard to find. There were born to them eight children, five of whom lived to maturity and had families of their own. First, there was Dr. Edgar B. Stokes, who, after spending his early years on a farm, became one of the leading physicians of Houston County and East Texas. He

SAM HOUSTON
After whom Houston County was named.

DAVID CROCKETT
After whom Crockett (County seat Houston County), was named.

A GROUP PICTURE: Mrs. T. D. Craddock, Mrs. Dan McLean, Mrs. Lucy Collins, Mrs. W. A. R. French, Mrs. H. J. Castleberg, Mrs. S. F. Tenney, Mrs. Emma Adams Castleberg, Mrs. A. R. Spence. Mrs. Gussie Worthington Shivers, Mrs. Mabel Hail, Mrs. Denny Arledge, Mrs. Sue Wootters, Mrs. Hennie Millar, Mrs. Mary C. Douglas, Mrs. Virginia Frymier, Mrs. Angeline Craddock, Mrs. Bettie Chamberlain, Mrs. J. L. Lipscomb, Mrs. Nannie Morrison, Mrs. J. H. Wootters, Mrs. Geo. W. Crook (with back to camera), Mrs. Florence J. Arledge, Mrs. John R. Foster, Mrs. Margaret Grace, Mrs. Mary Wootters Morris, Miss Missouri Adcock, Mrs. Julia Barbee, T. D. Craddock, Alfred Lee Foster, Marian Foster, Mrs. Margaret Woodson.

BIOGRAPHIES

graduated from the University of Louisville in 1892 and practiced his profession for a while at Elkhart in Anderson County, where he met and married Miss Cora Davis, an accomplished and attractive lady, who still survives him. He died at Crockett, December, 1931, and besides his widow left a son, Dr. Paul B. Stokes, himself an eminent physician, who with his partner, Dr. John L. Dean, owns and operates a magnificent hospital in Crockett. A daughter of Dr. Edgar B. Stokes, Alta, is the wife of the genial proprietor of the Crockett Hotel, Raymond Cornelius. Another daughter, Mrs. Hattie Stokes Wootters is a teacher in The Crockett High School. Another daughter, "C. C." married E. A. Ellison. Robert C. Stokes, a son of Charles and Lucy Stokes is a prominent business man of Crockett, who has raised an interesting family, and has acquired large property interests in the city and county.

Mrs. Hattie (Stokes) Young, is a daughter of Charles and Lucy Stokes and has always been regarded as one of the most attractive ladies of our community.

Hon. Charles Collins Stokes, gifted as lawyer and statesman, died in the prime of a promising career, while serving his state as senator.

Lucy, another daughter of Charles and Lucy Stokes, married T. R. Deupree, and raised an interesting family.

Annie, a daughter of Charles and Lucy Stokes, married Rev. George W. Davis.

Charles Stokes died at Crockett on August 15th, 1916 and his wife, Lucy Hancock Stokes died January 22nd, 1927 and both are buried in Glenwood Cemetery.

JUDGE WILLIAM M. TAYLOR

He was born in Lancaster, Ohio, in 1817, and finished his education and was graduated from Miami University of Ohio. He came to Texas in 1844 and first located in Houston. Later he moved to Huntsville and in 1848 formed a law partnership with Col. Henderson Yoakum, author of the well-known *History of Texas*. This partnership continued until the death of Col. Yoakum, their professional card appearing in the Crockett Printer, the firm having offices in both Huntsville, where Col. Yoakum resided, and Judge Taylor residing at Crockett and carrying on the law business of the firm there, he having moved to Crockett in 1850. In 1854 he was elected to the state senate and served as senator for four years. He was a delegate to the

HISTORY OF HOUSTON COUNTY

Reconstruction Convention in Austin, which was under the supervision of Governor Jack Hamilton, the military governor.

During the Civil War he was appointed brigadier general and recruited a brigade for service, but on account of other duties did not enter the actual military service. In 1862 he was elected district judge and held that office until he was removed by the military government, which removed all civil officers.

In 1850 Judge Taylor married Miss Isabella A. Moore, daughter of S. M. Moore and Eliza Houston Moore, her mother being the youngest sister of General Sam Houston. She bore a strong resemblance to General Houston and was nicknamed "Little Sam."

Judge Taylor was one of the most outstanding Masons in the history of masonry and held high office in masonic circles and died while attending the general encampment of Knights Templar on September 23, 1871, at Baltimore. As a member of the Grand Lodge of Texas, he traveled over Texas as lecturer and inspector and compiled Taylor's Monitor, which is still recognized as authority among Masons everywhere. His wife survived him for many years and spent the latter part of her life in the home of James W. Hail, an old friend of the family. She died in Crockett at the advanced age of 92 and is buried in the old Cemetery in Crockett.

MONROE THOMAS

Many people of Crockett and Houston County will remember this venerable, kindly old gentleman, who died in the home of his son, Dr. M. A. Thomas, in Crockett, more than twenty years ago. He was born in North Carolina, January 5th, 1814, and moved from there to North Mississippi, when very young. He married Amelia Howell, in Mississippi, and came to Houston County in 1878. He first occupied a place on Nevils Prairie, belonging to Dr. S. J. Collins. He next moved to a place belonging to W. J. Murchison, also on Nevils Prairie.

Later he purchased his home on Nevils Prairie from Charles Little, where he lived until he came to Crockett, to live the balance of his life with his son.

He died at the home of his son, January 18th, 1918, at the advanced age of 89 years, full of honors and good deeds.

He and his wife are both buried in Antioch Cemetery about five or six miles west of Lovelady.

BIOGRAPHIES

He left surviving him three children, Fletcher Thomas, who still lives on Nevils Prairie; Dr. M. A. Thomas, a well known physician of Crockett and a daughter, Mrs. Sallie Magee.

THE THOMPSON FAMILY

In November, 1853, a covered wagon caravan set out from Lawrence County, Alabama for Texas, consisting of twenty-nine persons, old and young. Among the older members of this caravan were David Thompson and his family and William Vicory Tunstall and his family. Among the members of the Thompson family were Samuel Morris Thompson, and three of his children: William Porter Thompson, Thomas Wilson Thompson and Sallie Thompson, the first born October 11th, 1845, and the latter August 6th, 1852. Elsewhere in this history, the biographies of the Tunstall family appears.

Samuel Morris Thompson, son of David Thompson, was born in East Tennessee on July 13th, 1813, and died at Crockett, Texas, February 23rd, 1894. He married Caroline Tunstall, daughter of William Vicory Tunstall and Dollie Vaughan Tunstall, about 1845. He moved from Tennessee to North Alabama in 1820 and resided there until he came to Texas in 1853. On arriving in Texas he first stopped at Larissa in Cherokee County, and taught school there in 1854. During Christmas week, 1854, he moved to Houston County and settled in Old Randolph, about twelve miles east of Crockett. There he lived in a log house and taught school during the years 1855 and 1856. He later taught school at Cochino and other places in Houston County. In 1869 he was Chief Justice of Houston County and also served as Deputy District Clerk under R. J. Blair. He moved to Crockett in 1870 and first occupied the Dr. James A. Corley home, where the Ritz Theatre now stands and later moved to the McDaniel place in South Crockett, where he resided until he returned to his home in the country.

He was a member of the Cumberland Presbyterian Church and an elder in said church before coming to Texas. Later he joined the Crockett Presbyterian Church, when Rev. S. F. Tenney became pastor in 1871 and served as elder in that church until he moved back to his home in the country in 1875. He then became a member of the Concord Presbyterian Church and served as Superintendent of the Sunday School there and was the Bible teacher also.

He left surviving him the following children: Thomas W.

HISTORY OF HOUSTON COUNTY

Thompson, Mrs. Sallie M. Lundy, Mrs. Dollie V. Worthington, Mrs. Emma Freeman. Since his death Mrs. Sallie M. Lundy has died and the other three children are still living—Mrs. Freeman making her home in Denver, Colorado, and in Texas. Thomas W. Thompson and Mrs. Dollie V. Worthington are the two oldest members of the Tenney Memorial Presbyterian Church in Crockett.

WILLIAM VICORY TUNSTALL

William Vicory Tunsall was born in Pittsylvania County, Virginia, on December 19th, 1785. He was educated at Danville, Va., learned the printing business in the old State Gazette office at Nashville, Tenn. He was married at the age of 25 years in North Carolina to Miss Dolly Hall Vaughan. He edited and published the first newspaper in Halifax, N. C., called the "Informant," established in 1812. From North Carolina he went to Kentucky, and his uncle Buck Tunstall being Clerk of the Federal Court, he became his deputy. From Kentucky he went to Indiana and published a paper in Vincennes. From thence he again went to Kentucky. During his second residence there, he taught school in Frankfort. From Kentucky he went to Fayetteville, Tenn. where in 1823 he established, edited and published the "Post Boy." At the time of his death he was perhaps the oldest printer in the United States. From Tennessee he went to Alabama, where he resided 25 years, and then came to Texas in 1853. Here he spent his time in teaching, with his son-in-law, Judge S. M. Thompson.

He died at Crockett, Houston County, Texas, at the residence of his son-in-law, Judge Thompson (the house Dr. Corley lived in and where the present Ritz Theatre now stands) on December 14th, 1870 at the age of 85 years. He was the father of Thomas B. Tunstall and Caroline U. Tunstall, the wife of Judge Thompson, who was the mother of Thomas W. Thompson.

JUDGE WILLIAM BENJAMIN WALL

Judge William Benjamin Wall deserves to be remembered as a fearless, tireless, determined man, who had a will of his own and was uncompromising in support of his judgment. He was born in Amite County, Mississippi on August 3rd, 1837, the son of Rev. William B. and Sarah (Holden) Wall. The author of *Texas and Texans* pays this tribute to Judge Wall: "Reared under the sturdy and invigorating discipline of the old homestead plantation and in an environment of distinctive culture and refinement, Judge William B. Wall waxed strong in mental and physical powers, gained full appreciation of the precepts and example of his honored father and mother and found his ambition quickened by his purpose."

As soon as he reached his majority, in 1859, he left the old homestead and sought greener fields and enlarged opportunities in the comparatively new state of Texas. He landed in Houston County and for a year taught school, at the same time pursuing his study of law. Then came the call to arms, he entered the Confederate Army and became a member of the First Texas Infantry in General Wigfalls Battalion, which eventually became a part of General Hood's famous brigade. He was promoted to the rank of Captain after he had received a serious wound from a shot in the arm which necessitated the amputation of his thumb. After the close of the war he entered the mercantile business with Col. John H. Burnett and carried on this business for several years.

In 1878 he was elected County Judge of Houston County and held this office for eight years. During his incumbency of this office, the courthouse was destroyed by fire and he managed the erection of a new courthouse, which was completed in 1883.

In 1896 he was elected to the Texas Legislature and was instrumental in securing the submission of a constitutional amendment in favor of increased pensions for Confederate Veterans, and later in having a plank in the Democratic Platform in favor of a Home for Confederate soldiers and their widows.

He was a Mason and a member of Lothrop Lodge and of Trinity Chapter of Royal Arch Masons. He was a member of Crockett Camp of Confederate Veterans, and held the office of commander for several years.

On December 6th, 1866, he married Miss Nettie Cooper, the daughter of Judge Leroy W. Cooper, who was born in Monroe County, Georgia, March 30th, 1847. Of this marriage there were six children, the following five having lived to maturity: Miss Minnie Evelyn, a gifted musician who died without having married; William Cooper, who was a leading business man for many years, and still survives; Annie Pauline, who married Reeves Jordan, and is dead; Charles J. who is also dead and

Walton B. who is a banker in Stuttgart, Arkansas. Judge Wall died at Crockett and was buried in Glenwood Cemetery with Masonic honors.

JUDGE FRANK ALVAN WILLIAMS

Houston County, in its one hundred and five years of existence, has furnished Texas with two members of the Supreme Court, George F. Moore and Frank A. Williams. For that reason the County should be proud of these distinguished jurists.

Judge Williams was born October 6, 1851, at Macon, Mississippi, where he received his education before coming to Crockett in 1872. Here he studied law under his distinguished brother-in-law, Col. D. A. Nunn, and on being admitted to the Bar became his law partner. This able firm carried on a large practice until 1884, when Judge Williams was elected District Judge of the then newly created Third Judicial District. He held this office until 1892, when he was elected to the judgeship on the Court of Civil Appeals ,at Galveston. In this office he so distinguished himself, and showed such ability, that in 1899, he was elected Associate Justice of the Supreme Court.

In 1911, he voluntarily retired from this position to re-enter the law practice, associated with Judge N. A. Stedman under the form name of Williams & Stedman, at Austin, Texas. In 1913 he moved to Galveston to enter the newly created firm of Williams, Neethe & Williams, where he still resides.

On November 24th, 1880, he married Miss Laura Fisher, of Waverly and they are the parents of Bryan F. Williams, who is associated with his father in the law practice. Fred L. Williams, an able lawyer of Houston, Robert N. Williams, and two daughters, Rosamond and Helen.

Judge Williams takes rank among the ablest jurists of Texas.

DR. ALBERT WOLDERT

Albert Woldert, physician, was born at Tyler, May 9th, 1867 son of John George and Alma Edelina (Richter) Woldert. He is a graduate of New York College of Pharmacy, 1889 and received his M. D. degree from University of Pennsylvania in 1893. He married Elva Buford on May 6th, 1923.

He was a pharmacist for 4 years and has been in private practice of medicine at Tyler since 1893. He was formerly asso-

BIOGRAPHIES

ciated with patient departments of Howard Hospital; St. Josephs Hospital and Polyclinic, Philadelphia. He is a member of American Medical Association; is former councilor of Texas Medical Association and former president of Smith County Medical Association. He is also a member of Texas State Historical Society.

He has contributed to Gould and Pyles, Cyclopedia of Medicine and Surgery Journals, American Medical Association, Texas State Medical Association, Journal Medical Sciences, Investigation on Conveyance of Malaria by anopheles mosquito (Journal American Medical Association, 1901); believed to have been 2nd successful result in America. Was awarded 2nd prize by Texas Centennial Commission for oldest relic, "rabadoquines" (cannon, about 1690) found near location of Mission San Francisco de los Tejas; located sites of San Francisco, Santissimo Nobre de Maria missions, Houston County; also located several historic spots in Smith County where granite markers will be erected.

His recreations are: fishing and hunting. He is a Democrat, Episcopalian and his address is Gary Buildings, Tyler, Texas.

Dr. Woldert was never a resident of Houston County, but his contributions to its history entitle him to a place in any history of the county.

MAJOR JOHN WORTHAM

Among the pioneer citizens of Houston County, who contributed to its development, no one stands out more prominently than John Wortham. He was born on May 10, 1800 and came to Texas in the early thirties. His ability and fine character were recognized at once and he was appointed to responsible positions. There are so many historic documents that tell the story of his early life that the author will let these speak for themselves.

The oldest of these is a commission signed by Sam Houston as President of the Republic of Texas, dated December 18th, 1837, as follows:

"IN THE NAME AND BY THE AUTHORITY OF

THE REPUBLIC OF TEXAS

TO ALL TO WHOM THESE PRESENTS SHALL COME OR

MAY CONCERN—GREETING.

"Be it known, That I, SAM HOUSTON, President of said Republic of Texas, reposing special trust and full confidence in the honor, patriotism, fidelity, skill and capacity of J. Wortham, do by these presents, constitute and appoint him the said J. Wortham to the office of associate commissioner of the Board of Land Commissioners for the County of Houston to which he has been duly elected by the joint vote of both Houses. Giving and hereby granting to him, the said J. Wortham, full power and authority as such, to exercise and discharge all and singular, the duties, obligations, and trusts to his said office, in anywise appertaining, by the Constitution and Laws of this Republic.

TO HAVE AND TO HOLD the same and all and every the honors, fees, perquisities and dues thereunto belonging, for and during, and until the full end and term of his said appointment.

Given under my hand and the Seal of my office, at the City of Houston ,this 18th day of December, A. D. 1837, and of the Independence of said Republic the Second.

SAM HOUSTON

By the President,

R. A. Irion, Secretary of State."

* * * * * *

The folowing document dated June 15th, 1839 should be of general interest:

"Crockett, June 15th, 1839.

"We, the undersigned appraisers by authority of Major John Wortham to judge a lot of beeves, furnished by Collin Aldrich & Jacob Allbright, for the use of Gen. Burlisons Command, do hereby certify that we have this day judged the weights of 31 beeves on said contract and judge them to weigh 15,460 lbs. and that we judge them to be sound and wholesome beef.

"GIVEN under ourhands this date above written.

A. E. Gossett"

BIOGRAPHIES

On April 27th, 1839, he issued an appeal to the citizens of Houston County to enroll as members of a Battalion of Rangers which he signed: "John Wortham, Major, Houston County Rangers."

At the January Term 1846, Major Wortham was appointed road overseer by Order of the Commissioners Court as follows:

"REPUBLIC OF TEXAS   "Co. Com. Court.
HOUSTON COUNTY.   Jany. Term. 1844

"ORDERED BY THE COURT, That John Wortham be and he is hereby appointed of Precinct No. 1, Crockett & Ft. Houston Road from Crockett to Greenwood and the following hands are apportioned to work said road, to-wit: C. R. Pruit, A. E. Gossett; J. R. Brackin & son; John Wortham & hands; E. Cheatham; R. A. Walker; M. A. Walker; Mobley Roan; II. E. Roan; Widow Brents Hands; D. Doubt; E. T. Powell & hands; James Fortune; Alfred Range & S. Adams.

A True Copy.

C. H. Nelson, C. C. H. Co.
By H. Nelson, Depy."

* * * * * *

On July 1st, 1842, he was appointed Quartermaster of the 4th Regiment of the 3rd Brigade, Texas Militia by James Carr, Colonel Commanding said Regiment.

Correspondence shows that he was an intimate friend of Hon. Isaac Parker, Congressman from Houston County in the Congress of the Republic of Texas as early as 1839. He was one of the original trustees of Trinity College located at Alabama on Trinity River.

Later he married Miss Cary Ann Vaughan, and settled on a large plantation four miles northwest of Crockett, where he led the life of a country gentleman for many years and where he died November 10, 1867 and is buried. His grave is marked by a beautiful marker, erected by the Centennial Commission of Control. After his death his family moved to Crockett and acquired a good house, which was later known as the Brauner Place, now occupied by Smith Murchison. He and his wife raised a large family of children, the oldest being his son, William, known as "Billy" Wortham, who married Miss Nancy Hall, a daughter of Capt. John L. Hall; Jennie, who married John C. Lacy; "Bud," who met a tragic death in Crockett; Eliza, who married A. LeGory; and Lucina, who married Joe Long. Many descendents of this worthy pioneer are still living in Crockett.

WILLIAM BRANCH WORTHINGTON

The subject of this sketch was born on the 22nd day of February 1848, in Arkansas. His father moved, with his family in 1863, to a farm near Old Sumpter, then the county seat of Trinity County, his farm located on what was known as Piney Creek. At that time Mr. Worthington was a boy of about fifteen years of age. There he grew to manhood, had many experiences of frontier life while living there. Such animals as panthers and other kinds of "varmints" were then abroad in the land. He resided in Trinity County during the Civil War and during Reconstruction days and during that time was a member of the original KU KLUX KLAN, and assisted in preserving law and order in the county. During this period he held the office of tax collector of Trinity County and carried his money to the State Capital on horseback.

In the early seventies he moved with his brother Jim and his mother to Nevils Prairie in Houston County and engaged in farming and later operated a saw mill and grist mill with his partner Ben Speer.

On September 13th, 1879, he married Miss Dollie Thompson, a daughter of Judge S. M. Thompson and she survives him. To this union there were born four children, Augusta, now known as Mrs. Gussie Shivers, Eleanor, known as Ellie, who died many years ago, Morris, who still survives and is a prominent business man of New York City, and has traveled to South America in pursuit of his business, and Ruth, who is now Mrs. Ruth Harris.

He was prominent in Masonic circles, having been first a member of Lovelady lodge and later a member of Lothrop lodge at Crockett. He was a devout, conscientious and faithful member of the Church of Christ, and often preached to churches of that faith, and was regular in his attendance on the services of his church. Altogether he was a good man, a good citizen, a good father, husband and friend.

INDEX

INDEX

A

A. & M. College, 164
Acock, Nathaniel D., 19
Acree, Robert, 92
Adair, Billy, 66
Adair, Emma, 121
Adair, George, 66
Adair, Capt. Isaac, 31, 121, 145, 156
Adair, John, 121
Adair, Dr. W. W., 66
Adams, Earl Porter, 93, 97
Adams, Col. Earle, 87, 121-22; children of, 122
Adams, Mrs. Ida, 118
Adams, Joe, 87, 93
Adams, John, 8
Adams, S., 201
Adams, Rev. Thomas, 121
Aiken, W. W., 61, 93
Alabama School, The, 75
Alabama, Texas, 17, 63, 64, 75, 126, 134
Alabama University, 178
Alamo, The, 3
Aldrich, Ann, 124
Aldrich, Albert Augustus, 56, 65, 123
Aldrich, Armistead Albert, 5, 45, 93, 96, 97, 122-23, 172
Aldrich, Bettie (Kyle), 124
Aldrich, Collin, 5, 8, 16, 17, 56, 63, 64, 65, 123, 125, 176, 200
Aldrich, Collin, Jr., 123, 124; children of, 124
Aldrich, Elizabeth (Lawrence), 124, 125
Aldrich, Eliza Jane (Masters), 122, 125
Aldrich, George, 16, 17, 18, 19, 30, 123
Aldrich, Julia (Kyle), 124
Aldrich, Oliver Cromwell, 31, 48, 76, 122, 124, 125, 155, 178; children of, 125
Aldrich Post Office, 17
Alexander, G. G., 81
Alexander, Robert, 99
Alford, George G., 18, 19, 20, 23, 82, 83, 84, 85
Allbright, Albert, 8

Allbright vs. Aldrich, 176
Allbright, George, 8
Allbright, Jacob, 7, 16, 17, 19, 30, 63, 64, 125, 126, 139, 176, 177, 200; children of, 126
Allbright, John, 7, 8
Allbright, Solomon, 8, 31
Allen, Clinton, 31, 34
Allen, John, 35
Allen, Mrs. Robert, 94
Allen, R. D., 87
Allhands, Rev. Edmund S., 116
Alto, 42, 56
Alto Springs, 47
American Medical Association, The, 199
Amite County, Miss., 196
Anderson County, 11, 12, 21, 22, 23, 29, 47, 131, 163; boundaries of, 12; creation of, 12
Anderson Mail, The, 46
Andrews Bishop, 41, 102
Angeline County, 21, 22, 23
Anglin, Elish, 8
Anglin, William, 7
Antioch Cemetery, 195
Antrem Church, The, 46
Antrim School, The, 80, 81
Appomatox, 168, 169
Arcangel San Miguel River, The, 3, 4
Archer, B. T., 11
Archer, Dr. F. W., 70
Archer, Dr. P. W., 60
Arledge, E. C., 93, 96, 97
Arledge, Hattie, 109
Arledge, Henry, 162
Arledge, Florence (Johnson), 67
Arledge, John F., 35, 66, 109, 110
Arledge, Mrs. Johnson, 94
Arledge, S. C., 34
Arledge, Sam F., 95
Armistice, The, 46
Armstrong, A., 118
Armstrong, J. B., 111
Arnold, H., 9, 10
Arnold, Rev. J. A., 116
Arnold, L. H., 93, 97
Arrington, Bunnie, 72
Ash School, The, 79

Athens Mission, The, 102
Athens, Texas, 28, 29
Atkinson, Mary, 109
Atlanta, Ga., 129
Augusta, 6, 55, 74, 75, 77, 92, 124, 134 147, 166, 168, 169, 174
Augusta Ga., 129
Augusta, School, The, 74
Austin, 5, 25, 26, 27, 32, 34, 42, 46, 80, 99, 159, 165, 178, 179, 180
Austin College, 123
Austin Statesman, The, 179
Austin, The, 88
Austin Theological Seminary, The, 115, 165
Austonio, 79, 80, 192
Austonio School, The, 79, 80

B

Bailey, Joseph W., 26
Baker, Arch, 87
Baker, John F., 93
Baker, M. M., 61
Baker, Mittie (Royall), 127
Baker, Murdock McIntosh, 126-27; family of, 126-27
Ballinger, Capt. Howard, 169
Baptist Church, The, 49, 104-112, 114, 122, 129, 159, 160, 172, 182; school taught in, 68, in Grapeland, 78
Baptist Herald, The, 107
Baptist Standard, The, 109
Barbee, Belle, 118
Barbee, C. H., 76
Barbee Christopher, 127
Barbee, Fannie Barker (Fifer), 128
Barbee, Jack, 87
Barbee, Dr. James G., 127, 128; children of, 128
Barbee's Reserve Company, 191
Barbour, Reverand, 81
Barksdale, William, 182
Barnett, Albert G., 20
Barns, Jas., 8
Barrett, David, 19
Barrett, H., 8
Barrow, Allie, 69
Barrow, Prof. J. W., 68
Battle, Doctor, 128
Baylor University, 118, 139, 142, 170; oldest graduate of, 145
Bayne, Elizabeth Jones (Long), 129
Bayne, Fielding Harvey, 61, 128; children of, 128

Beagle, J. A., 100
Beasley, Elizabeth (Crook), 130
Beasley, Grace (Smith), 130
Beasley, J. G., 87, 93
Beasley, Louisa Edwards, 129
Beasley, Dr. tSephen Thomas, 129-130; children of, 130
Beasley, Dr. William Parks, 129
Beaty, W. A., 93
Beavers, Billy, 67
Beavers, Joseph, 34
Beavers, William B., 34
Bedi, 47
Beeson, Cal, 116
Beeson, Mrs. Cal, 116
Beeson, Horeston Wilson, 130-131, 189; children of, 130-131
Beeson, Dr. Jehu Armistead, 131-132; family of, 131, 163
Beeson, John, 131
Beeson, Pauline Catherine (Tatum), 131; also see P.C. Jowers
Beeson, Priscilla Saunders, 131
Belew, George H., 84, 85
Bell, James H., 53
Bell, Peter H., 27
Bell, Gov. P. H., 188
Bell, Rev. Robert, 117
Bennett, Miles, 8
Bennett, Stephen, 8
Bennetts, 46
Bennick, George E. W., 31
Berglund, John V., 101
Berry, Alice Lively, 115, 116, 133
Berry, H. T., 93, 94, 95
Berry, M. L., 95
Berry, Mayes, 133
Berry, W. H., 35
Berry, William V., 115, 116, 132-133, 137
Bethel Church, The, 70
Bethel Cumberland Church, The, 181
Bettict, Frances, 8
Bever, Jennie, 79
Beverly, Ella J., 110
Beverly, Ida A., 110
Beverly, Lula, 110
Beverly, Mrs. R. A., 110
Beverly, W. D., 110, 111
Beverly, Willie S., 110
Big Brothers, The, 95
Big Cieek, 79
Big Pine Creek, 10
Bidwell, Dr. A. W., 6

INDEX

Bishop, W. P., 87, 93, 94
Bishop, Judge W. R., 29
Bitner, Alfred, 162
Bitner Susan, 162
Blackstone, Prof. T. B., 78
Blair, Jane, 122
Blair, John, 20, 34, 36, 37, 44, 82, 85, 122
Blair, R. J., 109, 110, 195
Blakey, Joseph, 92
Bland, Prof. Earle, 71
Blandenship, Guy, 95
Bledsoe, A. W., 113
Blind Institute of Austin, The, 23
Board of Land Commissioners, 17, 200
Bodenhamer, F. D., 20, 31, 40
Bodenhamer, J. W., 31
Boise, Idaho, 187
Bolton, B. R., 100
Bonner, William N., 42
Boude, Rev. H. B., 116
Bowers, Col. Tom M., 61
Bowles, Chief, 162
Box, A. M., 100
Box-Beeson Cemetery, The, 133
Box, C., 100, 101
Box, John, 7, 17, 192
Box, John Andrew, 133
Box, Nelson, 7, 133
Box, R. W., 17
Box, S., and Brother, 50
Box, Samuel C., 13, 100, 101, 102
Box, Stephen, 8
Box, Stillwell, 8, 18, 31, 133
Box, Thomas G., 8, 133
Boyles, F. M., 101
Bracken, Ben M., 156
Bracken, Charley W., 31, 133-134; children of, 134
Bracken, James R., 19, 20, 86, 90, 133, 134, 156, 201.
Bradshaw, J. W., 92
Branch, Mr., 9
Braughton, Rev. D. W., 41
Brauner Place, The, 201
Brazier, Groves M., 23, 49
Brazoria, 14, 15, 99
Brazoria County, 15, 27
Breckenridge, Mr. 46
Briggs, Hon. Clay Stone, 28, 189
Brightman, J. W., 116
Brightman, Mrs. J. W., 116
Bromberg, M., Jr., 87
Bromberg, Mendel, 134-135; children of, 135
Bromberg, Mose, 93, 97
Bromberg, Poland, 134
Brooks, Prof. G. H., 80
Brown, A. B., 87
Brown, Albert G., 182
Brown, Alfred, 121
Brown, Claude, 97
Brown, D. M., 91
Brown, Jim, 87, 93
Brown, Mrs. M. J., 60
Brown, Robin, 7
Browning, G. W., 16, 18
Browning, Rev. Marion, 116
Broxson, Enoch, 61
Bryan, 60, 75
Bryan, Earl, 95
Bryan, Guy M., 27
Bryan, W. D., 59
Buge, Alfred, 8
Burch, James, 34
Burkes, Napolcon W., 103
Burks, N. T., 100
Burleson, Dr., R. C., 110
Burnet County, 13
Burnet, David G., 64, 153, 188
Burnett House, The, 60
Burnett, Judge James Russell, 23, 29, 60, 135-136
Burnett, John H., 21, 23, 33, 34, 36, 37, 91, 110, 135, 144, 189, 197
Burnett, Joseph P., 19, 20
Burnett, Malinda Howell, 135
Burnett, Judge McCollum, 136
Burnett, Mollie (McCollum), 135
Burnett, Oscar, 69
Burnett, Silas E., 135
Burnett, W. E., 34
Burton, D. L., 31
Burton, Prof. F. H., 77
Burton, Isaac W., 20
Burton, John I., 31, 35
Burton, Nathaniel W., 31
Burton, W. H. L., 31
Burns, Senator Gordon M., 5, 6
Butler, Dr. C. W., 79, 92
Butler's Hospital, 79
Butts, Andrew, 43
Butts, James F., 51, 92
Byrne, Bishop Christopher E., 5

C

Caddell, John W., 23
Cain, Prof. A. W., 78

HISTORY OF HOUSTON COUNTY

Cairo, Ill., 152
Caldwell, James M., 17
Caldwell, Robert W., 20
Calhoun, Thomas J., 34
Callahan, E. J., 96, 97
Callaway, C. H., 87, 93, 95
Camp McCollough, 159
Campbell County, Va., 175
Campbell, J. M., 87
Campeche, Mexico, 88
Canada, 1, 73
Caney Creek, 79
cannon barrel, Discovery of, 3, 199
Cannon, Mr., 77
Cantey, Sam B., 84
Carl, Daniel, 99
Carleton, J. S., 91
Carr, James, 63, 161, 176, 201
Carr, Mary M., 161; also see M. M. Hunter
Carthage, Texas, 176
Cartwright, J. S., 92
Cartwright, James, 90
Cartwright, W. G., 93, 95, 97
Cary, A. J., 79
Cason, James, 109, 110
Cason, Joseph, 8
Cass County, 48
Cassidy, Richard, 87, 93
Casteel, A. H., 92
Castañeda, Prof. Carlos F., 2
CCC Camp, 4
Centenary College, The, 121
Centennial Commission of Control, The, 133, 158, 173, 189, 199, 201
Center Hill Community, 73
Center Hill School, The, 73
Centerville, 47
Centerville Herald, The, 54
Centerville Mail, The, 47
Chamberlain, B. F., 93, 162
Chamberlain, Frank, 168
Champion, W. A., 61
Chappell Hill, N. Carolina, 127
Chappell Hill University, 127, 128
Cheairs, Elijah, 8
Cheairs, Frances, 8
Cheairs, John, 8
Cheairs, John F., 8
Cherokee, 101
Cherokee County, 2, 12, 21, 22, 23, 42, 44, 104, 162, 195
Chicamauga, Battle of, 169
Chillicothe, Mo., 147
Chilton, Horace, 26

Chisolm, E. P., 103
Christian Church, The, 115-116
Christian, Prof., 77
Church of Christ, The, 202
Church Directory, The, 1890), 61
Churches, see names of
City Hotel, The, 49
Clapp, Capt. Elisha, 7, 63, 64; Company of, 152, 176
Clapp, John E., 8
Clapp, Jowell, 8, 18
Clapps Creek, 47
Clark, Judge Amos, 28
Clark, Barton, 7, 18
Clark, John A., 31
Clark, William, 63
Clarksville, 12, 27, 124, 125
Clarksville Standard, The, 45, 52
Clay, Henry, 143
Cleburne, 181
Clerlosky, Samuel, 8
Clinton Farm, The, 132
Clinton, La., 121
Coahuila, 2, 125
Cochino Bayou, 55, 66
Cochino School, The, 66, 71, 195
Coke, Richard, 25, 26, 188
"Cold-Blooded Homicide," 57-59
Coleman, Daniel M., 123, 137, 178; children of, 137
Coleman, Josephine, 123
Coleman, Louisa (Matlock), 137
Coleman, Nancy Dean, 137
Collard, E., 31
Collard, James H., 100
Collard, James R., 86
Collins, A. C., 87
Collins, A. D., & Brother, 42, 43
Collins, Adaline (Bishop), 140
Collins, Amelia, 127, 140, 142
Collins, Amelia Vann, 139
Collins & Douglas, 138, 140
Collins, Emma (Bishop), 140
Collins, Hattie Bond (Stokes), 114, 138
Collins, James, 35, 137-138; children of, 138
Collins, James P., 54, 138; children of, 138
Collins, Jenny, 109
Collins, Dr. John, 43, 139; children of, 139
Collins, John, Jr., 18, 124, 139-140, 142
Collins, Lucy (Atkinson), 68, 122,

INDEX

140, 142; family of, 142
Collins, Mildred, 118
Collins, Dr. S. J., 194
Collins, Thomas P., 17, 20, 31, 43, 53, 65, 68, 80, 138, 140-142, 145, 148, 175; daughter of, 140-141
Collins, Rev. W. C., 48, 100
Collins, W. P., 61
Collins & Warden, 138
Collison, Samuel C., 8
Coltharps, 47
Columbus, Christopher, 2
Comer, Amelia, 176
Concord Church, The, 116
Concord Presbyterian Church, The, 116-117, 195
Cone, Mr. M. E., 118
Conklin, Roscoe, 144
Connally, Tom, 26
Conner, A. J., 92
Conner's Ferry, 50
Constitutional Convention, 136
Cook, G. L., 87
Cook, J. S., 93
Cook, John T., 59
Cook, Loch, 95, 97
Cook, T. J., 34
Cook, Mrs. T. S., 4
Cookstown, Ireland, 138, 139, 140
Cooper, Colonel, 49
Cooper, Judge Leroy W., 23, 36, 48, 76, 142-144; children of, 143, 144
Cooper, Mrs. R. A., 143
Cooper, Samuel B., 28
Cordova-Kickapoo Expedition, The, ix
Corley, Dr., James A., 47, 48, 195
Corley, Dr. W. F., 40, 47, 144-145; children of, 144-145
Coronado, 2, 5
Corsicana, 26
Cortes, 2
Cotton, Senator Clay, 6
Cotton Gin, Texas, 114
Court Directory, The, (1890), 61
Courthouse, Burning of, 33, 34, 35, 36, 37
Cox, R., 92
Craddock, Angeline, 117
Craddock, H. F., 50, 155, 178
Craddock, Minnie, 155
Craddock, T. D., 93
Craddock, T. W., 51, 59
Craddock's Wheelwright Shop, 51
Crawford, E. L., 100

Crawford, Jacob, 100
Crawford, Robert, 99
Creek Community, The, 79
Creek School, The, 79
Crist, Capt. John, 16
Crist, Reason, 7
Crist, Stephen, 7
Crockett: Incorporation of, 14, 68; selection as county seat, 14, 17
Crockett, Academy, The, 67, 68, 69, 185
Crockett Argus, The, 51-54, 74, 141
Crockett Baptist Church, The, 107, 108, 109, 110
Crockett Bar Association, 140, 142, 186, 192
Crockett Cemetery, The, 43, 123
Crockett Chamber of Commerce, 4, 5, 6, 80, 96-98, 123
Crockett City School, The, 186
Crockett Courier, The, 61, 68, 142, 185
Crockett, David, 153, 154
Crockett, Democrat, The, 62
Crockett Economist, The, 169
Crockett, Enterprise, The, 61
Crockett, Dr. George L., 149
Crockett High School, The, 68, 69; Auditorium of, 4
Crockett Hotel, The, 42, 95, 140
Crockett House, The, 49-50
Crockett Lions Club, The, 93-95
Crockett Methodist Church, The, 99-104, 133; Pastors of, 100-101
Crockett Methodist Episcopal Church, The, 99
Crockett Patron, The, 60, 155
Crockett Presbyterian Church, The, 117, 164, 194
Crockett Printer, The, 38-51, 52, 54, 74, 75, 89, 90, 91, 92, 104, 193
Crockett Rotary Club, The, 95
Crockett Sentinel, The, 55-60, 68, 70, 151
Crockett Shrine Club, The, 96, 97
Crockett State Bank, The, 43, 189
Crockett Weekly Courier, The, 61
Crook, George W., 87, 162, 172, 178
Crowson, Henry P., 8
Culberson, Chas. A., 26
Culberson, Governor, 169
Cullen, Rev. D. P., 100, 102, 117
Cumberland Presbyterian Church, The, 41, 112, 113, 127, 181, 195; Sessional Record Book of, 112

HISTORY OF HOUSTON COUNTY

Cundiff, W. H., 35, 107
Currie, Mrs. E., 116
Currie, Edward, 35, 49, 106, 108, 109, 140
Currie & Ford, 49
Currie's Company of Volunteers, 123
Cutler, T. N., 92

D

Dailey, Addie, 109
Dailey, Daniel, 31
Dailey, Sydney, 34
Dallas, 5, 46
Dallas County, 12
Dalton, Mary, 109
Dalton, Oscar, 38, 40, 48, 51, 76, 89, 92
Dalton, Rosa, 109
Daniel, Rep. Albert K., 5
Daniel, Augusta, 117
Daniel, Prof. J. Buford, 80, 81
Daniel, James M., 145-146; children of, 145
Daniel, Sallie (Platt), 145
Danville, Va., 196
Daughters of the Confederacy, The, 147, 183, 184
Daughters of the Republic of Texas, The, 163
Daughters and Sons of the Heroes of the Republic of Texas, The, 147
David Crockett Memorial Association, The, 97, 98
David, Jesse, 31
Davidson County, Tenn., 102
Davis, B. F., 51
Davis, Capt. B. W., 16
Davis, Bradford, 81, 146; children of, 146
Davis, C. H., 55, 65, 66, 67
Davis, Elizabeth, 146
Davis, George W., 101
Davis, Jefferson, 135, 182, 184
Davis, John A., 81
Davis, Lucy Margaret (Penick), 147
Davis, W. A., 61
Davis, Wm. P., 146
Davis, William W., 23, 90, 146-147, 172, 174; children of, 147
Dawson, Dr. A. J., 49
Dawson, Rev. F. D., 99, 101
Dawson, J. L., 100
Dawson, J. T., 61
Dawson, James B., 90
Dawson, Moore & Chapman, 48

Dean, Dr. John L., 193
Deck, I. J., 68
Decuir, A. M., 144
Delong, John, 34
Dembrinski, Doctor, 121
Denman, W. L., 23
Dennis, Mr., 75
Denny, Judge Sam A., 170
Denny, W. H., Jr., 95
Denny, William, 91
Denson, John, 8
Denson, Shedrick, 8
Denson, Thomas, 7
Dent, Judge B. F., 29, 77
Descendants of the Signers of Texas Declaration of Independence, The, 147
De Soto, 5
Deupree, T. R., 87
De Zavala, Adina, 3, 4, 5, 6, 147-148
De Zavala, Augustine, 147
De Zavala, Julia Tyrell, 147
De Zavala, Lorenzo, 147
De Zavala's Point, 147
Dickerson, Waller, 18, 19, 20
Dickerson, William, 148, 172; children of, 148-149
Dill, Capt. Sam H., 135
Dillard, William, 7, 16, 17
Dillingham, Mrs. H. B., 65, 67
Dodson, George, 66
Dollahite, Y. G., 18
Donecker, Frances, 5, 6
Dorsett, E. L., 57
Doubt, D., 201
Douglas, Mary, 114
Douglas, Texas, 42
Douglass, J. P., 22, 90
Douglass, John, 35
Douglass, Richard, 86, 90, 91, 140
Down, James W., 101
Downes, Frank E., 34
Downes, J. F., 93
Downes, James E., 35, 112, 172
Downes, L. E., 30, 31, 33, 43, 65, 67, 156, 168
Downs, Lodovik E., 19
Drake, John H., 34
Driskill, Henry T., 57-59
Duke, James, ix
Dunlap, Mrs. W. C. (Gregg), 112
Dunlap, Rev. W. C., 112, 113
Dunman, A. J. C., 61
Dunstan, Stephen, 8
Dupree, James C., 31

210

INDEX

Dupuy, Cicero, 66
Dwight, G. E., 8

E

Early, Bishop, 103
Eason, E. O., 77, 78
East Texas Patron, The, 70
Eaton, Richard, 7
Economist, The, 60, 61
Edens, B. F., 81, 132
Edens, Emily, ix
Edens, Judge D. H., ix
Edens, John, ix
Edens, Mrs. John, ix
Edinburgh, Scotland, 165
Edmiston, C. L., 93, 94, 95, 96, 97
Edmiston, Prof. C. W., 69
Edmiston, Jos. F., 31
Edmiston, Rev. Matt J., 31, 43, 81
Edwards, Peyton F., 22, 28
Edwards, Dr. W. H., 49, 90
Egbert, Dan, 124
Elam, A. D., 55
Elam, A. D., & Company, 55
Elam, Roland, 76
Elam, Sarah J., 76
Election results (1860), 46
Elizabeth, Queen of England, 186
Elkhart Creek, 175
Ellis, Christopher, 19
Ellis County, 41
Ellis, H. L., 87, 93, 97
Elwood, 47
English, Arch H., 44, 66, 149; children of, 149-150
English, Elizabeth (Choate), 150
English, Col. George, 149
English, James, 31, 150
English, James D., 34
English, Capt. John, 66, 150-151; children of, 151
English's Ferry, Va., 150
Erwin, Chas., 8
Erwin, John, 8, 30, 109
Erwin, William, 30
Evans, J. R., 31
Evans, Lemuel D., 27
Everett, Mr., 46

F

Fain, Hon. Clem, 74, 141
Fannin County, 13
Fifer, F. F., 93
First Methodist Church, The, 170

First Methodist Society, The, 99
First Presbyterian Church, The, 71, 111, 112-115, 138; also see Tenney Memorial Church
First Presbyterian Church of Marlin, The, 115
First Presbyterian Church of Waco, The, 115, 164
First State Bank of Kerrville, The, 136
Flannagan, James W., 25
Floyd, General, 130
Flynn, Robert, 35
Foik, Father Edward J., 5
Fontaine, Edward, 100
Foot, H. G., 35
Ford, C. E., 49, 92
Forest, Gen. Nathan B., 121
Forrester, Prof., 81
Fort Craig, N. Mexico, 183
Fort Houston, 13, 16, 39, 131, 160, 161
Fort Lacy, 162
Fort St. Louis, 1, 2
Fortune, James, 201
Foster, Samuel O., 91
Foster, W. J., 56
Foster, W. J., & Brother, 50
Fowler, L. M., 100
Fowler, Littleton, 99
Francis, E. M., 111
Franciscan monks, 5
Frazier, Martha, 102
Fredericksburg, Battle of, 123
Fredericksburg, Va., 160
Free Church, The, 40
Freeman, B. G., 118
French Claims, 2, 3
French, W. A. R., 93, 186
Fryar, David, 34
Frymier, B. F., 24, 59, 86, 87
Furlough, R. H., 79
Furlow, Robert, 34

G

Gaddy, W. M., 61, 111, 118
Gage, David, 21
Gallahery, Peter, 8
Galveston, 5, 28, 29, 40, 41, 46, 100, 136, 152, 157, 172, 177, 198
Galveston Mail The, 47, 50
"Gammel's Laws of Texas," 153
Gant, Mr., 9
Gardner, Judge B. H., 29, 163

211

Garfield, James A., 1, 154
Garner, Thomas, 8
Garrett, C. B., 101
Gaston, M. A., 23
Gatewood, George S., 100
Gause & Aldrich, 61
Gause, Catherine Neal (Hall), 154
Gause, Edward Alexander, 60, 69, 70, 154-155; children of, 155
George VI, King of England, 186
George, William E., 100, 101
Georgia University, 129
Gettysburg, Battle of, 123
Gill, Judge W. H., 29
Gillespie, James H., 20, 31, 40, 43, 155, 163
Glenco, 47
Glenwood Cemetery, 94, 133, 162, 169, 185, 187, 193, 198
Glover School, The, 75, 134
Godbey, C. E., 68
Golman, Henry, 12
Gooch, Judge John Young, 29
Goodgoin, Nora, 81
Goodrum, Burton, Place, 81
Goodwin, J. W., 79
Goolsbee, T. B., 87
Goolsby, Gus, 61
Gossett, Andrew Edwards, 8, 18, 35, 44, 90, 146, 152, 153, 154, 187, 200, 201; children of, 154
Gossett, Elijah, 8, 16, 17, 18, 63, 64, 152, 153, 154
Gossett, Elizabeth Stone Edwards, 152
Gossett, James L., 7, 8
Gossett, John V. D., 7
Gossett, Mary Margaret (Murchison), 154
Gossett, Rhoda E. (Mulder), 154
Gossett, Wm. L., 7
Gould's Battalion, 159
Grabenheimer, Henry, 132
Grand Encore, 42
Grant, George W., 19, 20, 63
Grant, Ulysses S., 59, 60
Grapeland, 61, 80, 81, 132
Grapeland High School, The, 78
Grapeland Independent School District, 78
Grapeland Messenger, The, 62
Grapeland School, The, 77-78
Graves, Mrs. 72
Graves, N. B., 111
Graves, Rev., 115

Greely, Horace, 60
Green Parrot Tea Room, The, 94
Green, R. G., 20
Green's Cavalry, 129
Greenville, Tenn, 162
Gregg, Alexander W., 28
Gregg, John, 17
Grey, Jim, 81
Griffin, Ga., 143
Grigsby, John, 17
Grimes, Mr., 32
Grimes County, 22, 47
Grimes, Jesse, 9, 11
Groveton, 73, 191
Grumbles, L. T., 111
Guilford County, N. C., 131
Guytor, C. C., 35
Gwinnett County, Ga., 142

H

Hail, James W., 194
Hail, Nan, 68
Hail, W. E., 34
Haile, S. C., 34
Hale, Miss Eugene, 117
Haley, J., 8
Halifax, N. C., 154, 196
Hall, C. W., 34
Hall, Charles, 55
Hall, Cornelia A. (Bracken), 156
Hall, Frank, 38
Hall, J. B., 100
Hall, James Madison, 43, 52, 86, 155-156, 157
Hall, Capt. John L., 8, 31, 134, 145, 156-157; children of, 157
Hall, Joshua J., 155, 156, 157-158; children of, 157
Hall, Mrs., 38
Hall, Mahala L., 156, 157
Hall, Margaret, 122
Hall, Mary, 38
Hallmark, A. T., 18
Hallmark, Alfred M., 8, 158
Hallmark, George Sr., 8, 17, 18, 20, 158, 191, 192; children of, 158; Will of, 158, 192
Hallmark, George W., 8
Hallmark, James M., 8
Hallmark, John, 7
Hallmark, John B., 8
Hallmark, S. B., 79
Hallmark, W., 18
Hallmark, Wm. C., 79, 158, 159

INDEX

Hall's Bluff, 42, 157
Hall's Hotel, 44, 49, 157
Haltom, Giles, 61
Hamilton, Andrew, J., 27
Hamilton, Rev. Harry H., 115
Hamilton, Gov. Jack, 194
Hamilton, Morgan C., 25
Hancock, Maj. J. R., 192
Hannah, Mrs., 76
Hardwick, Benjamin G., 31
Harper's Ferry, 129
Harring, John G., 98
Harris, H. W., 111
Harrison Circuit, The, 99
Harrison County, 175
Harrison Family, 73
Harrison, G. H., 21
Harrison, Hyman, 87
Harrison, Thomas, 34
Harrison, Col. Tom, 169
Hassell, Rev. A. P., 72
Hassell, Andrew, 71, 72
Hassell, Charles, 71
Hassell, J. Woodrow, 72
Hatten, Stephen H., 19
Hatton, Hugh, 79
Haughton, Cecil, 94
Haupt, Edward, 34
Hawkins, Commander, 88
Hayes, John R., 31
Hayes, W. P., 34
Haynie, John, 99
Heflin, J. R. G., 109, 159
Heflin, James T., 31, 90, 104, 106, 109, 110, 159, 160; children of, 159, 160; speech by, 104-106
Heflin, Lutitia E., 109
Heflin School, The, 71, 72
Heidelberg University, 121
Helms, E. R., 110
Helms, John E., 164
Helms, M., 57, 58
Hemphill, John, 25
Henchett, G. W., 16
Henderson, 44, 46, 61, 101, 103, 104
Henderson County, 11, 12, 29, 139
Henderson Era, The, 54
Henderson, J. Pinckney, 24, 25
Henderson, Judge, 75
Henderson, Thomas B., 31, 86, 90
Herndon, William S., 27
Herrin, J. R., 93
Hester, Addison P., 79
Hickey, N. A., 78
Hicks, T. C., 92

Hicks, W. D., 49
Hill, A. J., 111
Hill, F. H., 31
Hill Robert, 99
Historical Foundation, The, Montreat, N. C., 116
"History and Legends of the Alamo and other Missions of San Antonio," 148
"History of Texas," 176, 193
"History of Texas," by Father Morfi, 2, 3
Hodge, H. A., 100
Hogg, Dr. H. L., 118
Hogg, Joseph L., 21, 26
Holcomb, Willie, 133
Holder, John H., 8
Holland, Judge Sam, 29
Hollis, Mr., 79
Holly Springs, Miss., 181
Holly, Wash., 24, 129
Holmes, Sarah, 76
Hood, Gen. John B., 56, 168; Texas Brigade, 56, 65, 123, 164, 168, 197
Hooper, O. W., 101
Hopkins County, 12
Hord, Jesse, 100
Horton, Gov. Albert C., 188
Horton, Mr., 9
Hotchkiss, D. H., 101
Hough, S. A., 92
Houston, 5, 26, 40, 41, 46, 47, 84, 100; incorporated, 14, 86
Houston, Andrew Jackson, 26
Houston County: boundaries of, 11; committees, 9, 10, 31, 32; Courts, 32, 36, 37, 44, 48, 76; enactment of bill for, 10, 11; first officers of, 17, 18, 19, 20; mail service in, 17; petition for, 7, 8; petition to rebuild courthouse, 30, 31, 32; (1871), 35-37; petition for remission of state tax, 33-35; signers of petition for, 7, 8; State Representatives from, 22-24; State Senators from, 21-22; U. S. Senators from 24-26
Houston County Bar Association, The, 122
Houston County Courthouse, destruction of, 22, 24
Houston County, Deed Records of, 155; Book "A," 30; Book "I," 158; Book "S," 107
Houston County Herald, The, 60

213

Houston County Times, The, 4, 5, 6, 61
Houston & Great Northern Railroad, 76
Houston, Gen. Sam, 11, 12, 14, 24, 54, 110, 111, 153, 163, 177, 188, 194, 199, 200
Houston's Mound, 11, 12, 13, 59
Howard Hospital, The, 199
Howard, J. A., 11
Howard, John, 73
Howard, Volmey E., 27
Howell, A. P., 35
Hughes, C. W., 101
Hughes, Fannie Mae Barbee, 127
Humphreys, Prof., 75, 76, 77
Hunt County, 12
Hunter, Archibald Russell Spence, 160
Hunter, Elizabeth Wyche Lucas, 160
Hunter, G. M., 113
Hunter, Dr. James, 160-161; children of, 160
Hunter, James (R. M. T.), 160
Hunter, Martha (Taliaferro), 160
Hunter, Mary Kate, 161, 163
Hunter, Mary M. (Smith), 160
Hunter, Nathaniel Wyche, 160
Hunter, William, 160
Huntington, W. Va., 187
Huntsville, 5, 24, 42, 44, 46, 47, 67, 136, 186, 193
Huntsville Item, The 54,
Hurricane Bayou, 131, 152
Hyde, James, 35
Hyde, S. V., 35

I

I. & G. N. Railway Company, 136
"Ida Reese," 191
"Independence, The," 88
Independent Order of Odd Fellows, 91-92
Indianola Courier, The, 54
Indians: attack by, ix; Cherokees, 39, 160, 162; Choctaws, 182; Coshattas, 39; Prairie, 39; request mission, 2; Tejas 2; trouble with, 173
Indian Wars, The, 191
Informant, The, 196
Ingram, J. C., 161, 191
Ingram, Tilman, 161
Inman, Johnson & Company, 40
Jonie Village, 11, 13
Irion, R. A., 10, 200

Iron-eye Village, 13
Isbell, Miss, 80

J

Jackson, Gen. Andrew, 150, 182
Jackson, La., 121
Janes, J. A., 34
Jasper, 99
Jasper County, 27
Jasper, Selden L. B., 21, 82, 84, 85, 86
Jefferson County, Miss., 146
Jefferson Medical School, The, 129
Jefferson, Texas, 24, 25, 37, 48
Jefferson, Thomas, 164
Jensen, M. P., 87
Jensen, S. E., 116
Jensen, Mrs. S. E., 116
Jett, Rev. I. N., 116
Jim Smith Memorial Hospital, The, 65
John, Z. B., 55
Johnson, Pres. Andrew, 161, 162
Johnson, Florence Josephine, 161
Johnson, H. C., 8
Johnson, J. W., 100
Johnson, Mary Isabella (Dunwoodie), 162
Johnson, R. S., 90, 92
Johnson, William M., 8, 18, 19, 34, 161-162; children of, 162
Johnston, Albert Sidney, 124
Johnston, Rienzi M., 26, 155
Jones, Anson, 64, 153, 188
Jones, J. R., 110
Jones, John, 31
Jones, M. H., 100
Jones, S. J., 34
Jones, School House, The, 73
Jones, T. H., 87
Jordan, H. R., 35
Jordan, W. L., 68
Jorden, Joseph, 8
Jowers, Ann (Lacy), 162
Jowers, Bettie A. Lamon Hill, 163
Jowers, Mrs. E. W. Gardner, 163
Jowers, Pauline Catherine, 163; also see Pauline C. T. Beeson
Jowers, W. G. W., 21, 22, 41, 132, 162-164; children of, 163
Judges, District, 28, 29
Judicial Districts, 28, 29
Julian Family, 73
Julian, W. D., 93

214

INDEX

K

Kaufman, David S., 27, 64, 153
Kavanaugh, Alfred Leroy, 100, 102, 103
Kavanaugh, Bishop H. H., 102
Keechi, 46
Keechi Mail, The, 46
Keel, C. B., 36, 37
Kelley, Mrs. M. J., 116
Kennard, 71, 73
Kennard, J. R., 29
Kennard Schol, The, 71, 73
Kennard State Bank, The, 66
Kennedy, C. U., 95
Kennedy, D. C., 93, 97
Kennedy, Mrs., 49
Kennedy, Rough, 66
Kennedy, S. E., 16, 17, 19, 31
Kent, T. J., 35
Kerrville, 136
Kickapoo Creek, 10
Kidd's Mills, 47
Kiessling, D. O., 93, 94, 96, 97
Kiessling, Mrs. D. O., 94
Kilpatrick, Rev., 74
Kimberly, James R., 31
King, Adams, 164
King, Adam Columbus, 31, 44, 113, 164, 165; children of, 164
King, Athelia Ann, 114, 165
King, Fanny Glass, 164
King, G. Q., 93
King, Jane Catherine (Bone), 164, 165
King, Lucy Woodson, 164
King, R. L., 95
King, Rev. Samuel Alexander, 113, 114, 115, 138, 164-165
King, Walker, 68, 93
King, Rev. William M., 164
Kingsborough's "Antiquities of Mexico," 148
Kirby Lumber Co., 136
Kirchoffer, Dr., 41
Kirchoffer, John H., 17, 18, 31
Kirkland, _____, 88
Kirkpatrick, John, 36
Kitchens, Mr., 66
Knight, Richard W., 4, 5, 6
Knights and Ladies of Honor, The, 118
Knights of Pythias, 44, 92-93, 123, 157
Knights Templar, Palestine Commandery, 172

Kone, W. W., 111
Kosse, Texas, 144
Ku Klux Klan, 128, 202
Kyle & Aldrich, 55, 124
Kyle, John, 165
Kyle, J. H. B., 81, 165, 166; children of, 166
Kyle, Lou Spencer, 166
Kyle, Matthew G., 124, 165, 166; children of, 166
Kyle, S. B., 166
Kyle, T. J. M., 166
Kyle, W. R. W., 165, 166

L

Lacey, William Y., 82, 85
La Clere, George A., 100
Lacy, Helena, 109
Lacy, J. C., 35
Lacy, M. A., 109
Lacy, Martin, 162
Lacy, W. H. B., 34
La-Fayette Guards, The, 135
La Grande Ga., 129
Lamar, Maribeau B., 14
Lamar, President, 162
Lancaster, Ohio, 193
Landrum, James L., 47
Lane, William, 19, 20
Lansford, C. Gershom, 79
Lapus, Enaske, 8
Lapus, Joseph, 8
Larissa, 195
Larue, E. E., 118
La Salle, 1, 2, 3
Latexo, 132
Lavaca River, The, 1
Lawrence, Ben, 81
Lawrence County, Ala., 195
Leagon, William, 8
Leathers, Joel F., 146
Leaverton, G. W., 34, 55, 109
Leaverton & Hall, 55
Lebanon, Tenn., 182
Lee, A. S., 93, 111
Lee, J. H., 34
Lee, John, 31, 109
Lee, Gen. Robert E., 130, 168
LeGory, A., 166-167, 172; children of, 167
LeGory, C. W., 87, 93
LeGory, Eliza Hortense (Wortham), 167
LeGory, J. G., 95
LeGory, John, 87

LeGory, Mrs. John, 94
LeGory, John B., 167
LeGory, Margaret (Conley), 167
Lehmberg, C. A., 101
Leon, Capt. Alonzo de, 2
Leon County, 22, 59
Leona, 47
Lewis, J., 100
Lexington, Ky., 162
Liberty, Texas, 46, 47
Liberty Stage, The, 46
Linwood, 42
Lions Club, The, 123
Lipscomb, Judge A. D., 29, 61
Lipscomb, James L., 87, 90, 106, 110
Lipscomb, Dr. W. C., 33, 87
Little, Charles, 194
Little, John, 81
Little River Mission, The, 102
Live Oak Seminary, The, 53
Livingston, 46, 85, 102
Lloyd, Rev. R. Gage, 115
Loeske, Louis, 34
London, England, 99
Long, Charles, 61
Long & Downes, 43
Long, Emily (Cash), 168
Long, Hugh, 168
Long, Col. John, 31, 40, 43, 50, 77, 129, 167-168; children of, 168
Long, John A., 81
Long, John B., 28
Long, Lou, 109
Long, Samuel J. W., 31
Long, Vergil, 75, 77
Long, W. H., 116
Long's, Col., Hotel, 49, 50, 168
Longstreet, W. D., 18
Lothrop, Capt, J. K. T., 84, 85, 87; obituary, 88-89
Lothrop, J. L., 85
Louis, King of France and Navarre, 1
Louisiana, 46, 121, 122, 132
Louisville University, The, 193
Love, Andrew C., 86
Lovelady, 76, 77, 115, 118, 170, 171
Lovelady Baptist Church, The, 118
Lovelady, Cyrus, 172
Lovelady Enterprise, The, 62
Lovelady School, The, 76, 77
Lovell, J. M., 6
Lowery, L. J., 80
Lowes Ferry, 27
Lubbock Guards, The, 167

Luker, A. H., 62
Lumpkin, P., 7, 17
Lundy, George Brinson, 56, 168-169; children of, 169
Lundy, Mrs. G. B., 66
Lundy, Mary (Worthington), 169
Lundy, Sallie M. Daniel, 67, 169
Lusk, R. O., 8
Luster, George, 19
Lynch, Rev. Samuel, 48, 100, 102, 104

M

Mail Schedules, 46-47
Mabbitt, Major, ix
Macon, Miss., 183, 184, 198
Madden, James, ix, 17
Madden, Mrs. James, ix
Madden, Hon. James William, 142, 169-170; children of, 170
Madden, Mary, ix
Madden, Mrs. Robert, ix
Madison County, 22
Magee Expedition, The, 173
Magnolia, Texas, 42
Mainer, E., & Sons, 171
Mainer, Ella (Nelms), 170, 171
Mainer & Monday, 170
Mainer, Myrtle, 118
Mainer, N. J., 170-171; children of, 171
Mainer, Rev. T. N., 77, 118
Maness, E. A., 101
Mangum, J. F., 77
Manly, Ervin, B., 100
Mansfield, Battle of, 145
Manzanet, Father Damicean, 2
Maples Family, The, 73
Marion, Texas, 101
Markham, John W., 87
Marler, Rev. W. H., 116
Marlin, Texas, 26
Marshall, 25, 27, 46, 54, 102, 103, 130
Martin, Prof. F. M., 77
Martin, Maj. Jas. F., 132
Martin, John S., 18
Martin, William H., 28
Mary Allen Seminary, The, 114, 153
Masonic Hall, The, 40, 85, 90, 91
"Masonry in Texas," 85-86
Masons, 82, 91, 172, 182
Masters, Elizabeth (Shaw), 171
Masters, Henry, 8, 125
Masters, Jacob, Sr., 7, 171-172, 189;

INDEX

children of, 171
Masters, Joseph M., 8
Masterson, Joseph, 8
Matagorda, 99
Matagorda Bay, 1, 2
Matamoros, 88
Matlock, Thomas, 109
Mathis, John S., 100
Mathes, John W., 49
Matlock, William R., 91
Matthews, Reuben, 44, 81
Maud Pence Memorial, The, 187
Maxey, Samuel B., 25, 26
Mayfield, Earl B., 26
Mayfield, S. R., 31
McAllen, Texas, 72
McCall, Mrs., 154
McCarty, Harvey O., 87, 95
McColl, Mrs. Mary, 69, 70
McCollum, Hon. A. M., 136
McConnell, A. W., 113
McConnell Dry Goods Co., 148, 173
McConnell, John, 31, 35, 50, 86, 90, 91, 110, 172-173; children of, 173
McConnell, John A., 87
McConnell, Martha (Lovelady), 172
McConnell, Mary Jane (Dickerson), 172
McConnell, Maude, 140
McConnell, Miss Otis, 94
McCracken, E. W., 82, 85
McDaniel, H. G., 57
McDonald, Donald, 68
McDonald, M., 31
McDonald, William S., 18, 30
McDowell, James, 92
McElroy, John, 81
McElwee, Rev. W. M., 117
McGill, J. W., 35, 59
McGill, John, 113
McGill, W. H., 61
McKenzie, C. T., 18
McLain, William, 90, 91
McLane, William Z., 19
McLarty, C. U., 101
McLean, Archibald, 174
McLean, Daniel, 173-174; children of, 173
McLean & Davis, 174
McLean George W., 96
McLean James, 174
McLean, William, 147, 173, 174-175; children of, 174-175
McLemore, A. J., 71
McLemore, Dump, 66

McLemore, Mrs. Dump, 71
McLemore, James, 66, 71
McLemore, John, 156
McLemore, Margaret (Hall), 156
McMillan, Joseph, 103
McMillen, John, 102
McNairy County, Tenn., 126
McNeill, H. W., 34
McNeill, Dr. W. L., 49
Meade, Eli, 18
Medina River, The, 173
Menden, Mass., 123
Meredith, Dr. J. W., 45, 49
Meretz, Russia, 134
Meriwether, Ethelinda (Dunlap), 175
Meriwether, Dr. Francis Lewis, 175
Methodist Church, The, 102, 114; Arkansas Conference of, 102; East Texas district of, 99; Mississippi Conference of, 99; Rutersville Conference of, 99
Methodist Episcopal Church, The: Eastern Conference of, 48, 101, 102, 103, 104; General Conference of, 102; Louisiana Conference of, 101; Texas Conference of, 101
Methodist Episcopal Church South, The, 117, 142
Mexia, Texas, 114
Mexican War, The, 88, 122
Miami University, Ohio, 193
Midway, Texas, 47
Millar, J. C., 95, 96
Miller, Emma, 121
Miller, George P., 122
Miller, Rev. J. C., 121
Miller, Rev. J. J., 121
Miller, Mark, 66
Miller, Rebecca F. (Whitten), 176
Miller, Col. Steward A., 22, 31, 34, 44, 140, 175-177, 192
Miller, Dr. W. C., 74
Miller, William T., 82, 85
Milling, Mary, 59
Milling, Robert, 59
Mills, Roger Q., 26
Minza, C. T., 16
Missionary Baptist Church of Christ, The, 107-108, 109
Mississippi, 55, 56, 146
Mississippi River, The, 1, 2, 3
Mitchell, Margaret, 56
Mitchell, Russell Crawford, 56

Mize, W. A., 93
Mobile, Ala., 154
Moffatt, Mr., 94
Monday, C. M., 34
Monday, J. O., 170
Monk, John E., 111
Monk School House, The, 144
Monroe, Col. Armistead Thompson, 31, 43, 55, 73, 76, 90, 106, 125, 136, 137, 177-178, 179, 180
Monroe, A. T., Jr., 177
Monroe, Augustine Garnett, 177
Monroe, Pres. James, 177
Monroe, Jim, 73
Monroe, Sara Jane, 55
Montgomery, 84, 99
Montgomery, John, 31
Moore, Albert, 78
Moore, C. W., 93
Moore, Commander, 88
Moore County, N. C., 174
Moore, D. G., 97
Moore, Elisha, ix
Moore, Eliza (Houston), 194
Moore, G. A., 3, 6
Moore, Judge George F., 31, 176, 178-180, 198
Moore, H. F., 87
Moore, Harvey W., 34, 100, 144
Moore, James, 66
Moore, John, 43
Moore, John C., 7
Moore, John I, 61
Moore, Mollie, 73, 78
Moore, S. M., 194
Moore, William E., 49
Moore, William H., 92
Morfi, Father, 2
Morgan, Dan, 73
Morgan Family, The, 73
Morgan's Battalion, 183
Morley, A., 31
Morris, R. E., 111
Morrow's Grocery Store, 33
Moscow, Texas, 168
Mosely, Rev. Hillery, 114
Mound Prairie, 59
Mt. Enterprise Circuit, 48
Mt. Pleasant, 104
Mt. Zion Baptist Church, The, 106, 107-108, 109
Mulican, O. P., 34
Munger, H. L., 101
Murchison, A. H., 93
Murchison & Arledge, 56

Murchison, Daniel, 112, 155, 180-181; children of, 181
Murchison, Daniel McIntosh, 34, 181-182
Murchison, Gertrude (Lipscomb), 182
Murchison, Mrs. John, ix
Murchison, Kenneth, 34, 59
Murchison, Lucinda Teague, 180
Murchison, M. M., 35
Murchison, Martin, ix
Murchison, Mary Killough, 181
Murchison, Minnie Harris, 127
Murchison, Murdock, 70
Murchison & Rainey, 56
Murchison, S. L., 93, 95
Murchison, Sallie (Arledge), 182
Murchison, Smith, 201
Murchison, W. J., 194
Murchison's Prairie, 11, 12, 13
Murfreesboro University, 182
Mustang Prairie, 7, 16, 123, 124, 146, 158
Myricks, Ernestine, 71

N

Nacogdoches, 6, 30, 42, 99, 153, 162, 172, 178
Nacogdoches Chronicle, The, 54
Nacogdoches County, 7, 10, 12, 21, 22, 24, 28
Nacogdoches Horseback Mail, The. 47
Nacogdoches Stage, The, 46
Nashville, Tenn., 196
Nashville, Texas, 100
Natches, Miss., 99
Natchitoches, La., 173
Nathan, Mr., 17
National Cyclopedia of American Biography, The, 182
Navarro, 46
Navasota, 2, 29
Neal, B. W., 35, 110
Neches, 16
Neches River, The, 2, 10, 11, 12, 13, 42
Neff, Gov. Pat M., 4, 118, 170
Nelms, L. P., 170
Nelms & Mainer, 170
Nelms, Col. Thomas H., 37, 170
Nelson, C. H., 155, 201
Nelson, Horatio, 20, 201
Nelson, Ralph, 63
Neville, D. C., 86

INDEX

Neville, H. W., 20
Neville, James, 8
Nevills, C., 31
Nevills Prairie, 76, 169, 194, 202
Newman, Judge Porter, 116
New Orleans, 41, 46, 172, 174, 182
New Orleans School of Medicine, The, 129
New School Presbyterian Church of Crockett, The, 165
Newton, Allen, 93
Newton, Josie Gossett, 152
New York, 144, 190
New York City, 42, 43, 172, 177
New York College of Pharmacy, The, 198
Norfolk County, Va., 104
Northern Presbyterian Church, The, 114
North Elkhart Creek, 11, 13
"Notice to Travelers," 41-42
Nowlin, Peyton Wade, 187
Nunn, Col. David Alexander, 15, 34, 56, 68, 97, 140, 182, 183, 184, 198; children of, 183
Nunn, Prof. G. J., 61, 68, 70
Nunn, Helen Williams, 68, 183-185
Nunn, Jane (Tubb), 182
Nunn, John, 182
Nunn & Williams, 122

O

Oakland School, The, 72
O'Bannon, Mrs., 33
Ochiltree, Wm. B., 28
O'Daniel, W. Lee, 26
Odell, J. M., 109
Odell, Mrs. J. M., 182
Odell, Judge James L., 59, 92
O'Keefe, J. P., 81
Old Corinth, 73
Old Corinth School, The, 73
"Oldest Inhabitant, The," 38, 40
Old Pleasant Grove, 65
Old Pleasant Grove School, The, 66
Old Rice Cemetery, The, 189, 190
Old Randolph School, The, 65
Old School Presbyterian Church of Centerville, The, 165
Old Shiloh School, The, 67
Oliphant, Joe Bob, 79
Oliver, C. G., 37
Oliver, E. M., 35
Opera House, The, 115
Otts, W. B., 109

Owens, R. B. S., 66, 67
Owens School, The, 67

P

Pace, E. A., 68, 87
Padgitt Brothers Co., 139
Page, Annie (Saunders), 185
Page, Hon. W. B., 61, 68, 87, 123, 185
Paine, Bishop, 101, 103
Palestine, 6, 13, 26, 27, 28, 29, 42, 46, 50, 51, 94, 101, 102, 103, 163
Palmer, Henderson D., 99
Pan-Presbyterian Council, The, 165
Paris, 25, 101, 103, 104
Parker, Benjamin, 8
Parker, Elder Daniel, x
Parker, Daniel, Jr., 8
Parker, Dickerson, 8
Parker, Isaac, 8, 20, 21, 63, 64, 186, 201
Parker J. D., 8
Parker, Mr., 32
Parker, Turner S., 19
Parker's Bluff, 42
Parks, Rev. W. B., 116
Pate, Wm. H., 8
Patterson, Watt, 76
Patton, Bessie Bland, 186
Patton, Frank M., 186
Patton, John J. A., 71
Patton, Mrs. M. E., 71
Patton, Mattie (Taylor), 186
Patton, Hon. Nat, 28, 37, 87, 185-186; children of, 186
Patton, W. M., 33
Paul, Henry J., 62
Payne, O. C., 111
Peacock, Isaac, 156
"Pearville," 80
Peck, Wm. M., 31
Pence, Maud Sims, 186-187
Pennington, 37, 70, 71, 129, 170
Pennington School, The, 70, 71
Pennsylvania University, 160, 198
Perdue, B. O., 87
Perry County, Ala., 137
Perry, Louis C., 94
Peterson, O., 37
Pettitt, John, 18
Pettitt, John G., 31
Phelan's "History of Texas Methodism," 102, 103
Philadelphia, Penn, 129, 137
Phillips, H. B., 100

219

Phillips, Mrs. H. J., 70
Phillips, Samuel, 8
Pickens County, Ala., 166
Pickwick Hotel, The, 95, 132
Pierce, Bishop, 103, 104
Pilsbury, Timothy, 27
Piney Creek, 202
Pitts, Rev. Albert T., 116
Pittsylvania County, Va., 196
Platt, John, 31
Platt, Sam, 144
Pleasant Hill, 81
Polk County, 170
Pollard, E., 31
Polyclinic Hospital, Philadelphia, 199
Pool, Bob L., 101
Porter, Rev. J. D., 116, 117
Porter, James M., 121
Porter Springs, 72, 77, 130
Porter Springs School, The, 72
Posey, F. M., 93, 94, 97
Post Boy, The, 196
Potts, John H., 72
Powell, Edley T., 18, 201
Powell, John, 100, 101
Powers, Richard R., 20
Presbyterian Church of Crockett, The, 187
Presbyterian Church of Marshall, The, 113
Presbyterian Church of Milford, The, 115
Presbyterian Church of New Orleans, The, 113
Presbytery of East Texas, 117
Prewitt, George H., 18, 20
Price, Mr., 78
Pridgen, R. S., 34
Pridgen, Capt. T. J., 72
Prince, Judge John S., 29
Pritchard, Joseph P., 107, 108, 109, 110, 111
Pritchard, Leon, 8
Pritchard, Thomas H., 109, 110
Pritchard, W. D., 56, 172
Provosti, 2
Pruit, C. R., 201
Pruitt, George, 63
Public Works Administration (PWA), 37

Q

Quidnunc, The, 60, 136

R

Race, A. M., 34
Rainey, Dr. Frank, 23, 190
Rainey, Dr. Homer P., 77, 118
Raleigh, N. C., 109
Ramsdale, George, 31
Ramsey, P. T., 101
Randolph, 46, 47, 91, 92, 123, 124, 187, 195
Randolph County, Ark., 102
Randolph County, Ga., 168
Randolph, Cyrus Halbert, 18, 19, 23, 31, 187-188
Randolph, Jesse Nathaniel, 187
Randolph, Judge, 41
Randolph, Senator M. Y., 22
Randolph, Susan (Nowlin), 187
Range, Alfred, 201
Rankin, H. V., 101
Rape, A. J., 77
Raven Hill, 24
Raymond, Mr., 32
Read, Judge Robert Newton, 49, 50, 131, 188-189; children of, 188
Read Schoolhouse, The, 76
Reagan, John, 166
Reagan, Judge John H., 13, 26, 27, 28, 43, 45, 162
Red & White Store, 33
Reding, George W., 7
Reding, Iredell, 7, 8
Reding, John B., 7
Reed, Prof. C. V., 78
Reed, Martin, 34
Reeves, Judge, W. Q., 29, 136
Refugio, 14
Reinhard, Major, 57
Reinicke, J. H., 87
Republic of Texas, 5, 9, 10, 11, 13, 14, 64, 147, 153; House of Rep. of, 7, 9, 10, 11, 64; Masonic lodges in, 83, navy of, 88; Representatives from, 20, 21; Senate of, 7, 10, 11
Reynolds, James, 81
Reynolds, Joseph H., 25
Rhone, Mobley, 18
Rice, Clinton A., 20
Rice, Joseph, Sr., 189; children of, 189-190
Rice, Mrs. Willie (Masters), 189
Richards, James L., 91, 92
Richards, Rev., 81
Richardson, C., 99

INDEX

Richardson, J. D., 90
Richardson, L. C., 50
Riggs, W. H., 34
Riley, William, 8
Rio Grande Valley, 72
Ritz Theatre, The, 195
Roan, H. E., 201
Roan, Mobley, 201
Robbins Ferry, 7, 42
Robert, Salathiel, 178
Roberts, Elisha, 157
Roberts, Geo. W., 34
Roberts, G. W., Bank, The, 73
Roberts, Governor, 178
Roberts, O. M., 188
Robinson, Mrs. Douglas, 177
Robinson, Elizabeth, 47
Robinson, Geo. W., 8
Robinson, Miles, 47
Rogers, A. M., 97
Roman, Bella, 30, 68
Roman de la Garza Grant, The, 156
Roney, W. S., 111
Roosevelt, Pres. Franklin D., 123
Roosevelt, Pres. Theodore, 177
Rose, John, 35
Rowe, Joseph, 14
Rowe, Mr., 80
Runnels, H. R., 54
Rusk, 42, 46, 102, 103, 114
Rusk County, 21 28 101
Rusk Enquirer, The, 54
Rusk, Gen. Thomas J., 24, 152
Russell, Ruben R., 16, 18
Rutersville, 99
Rutersville College, The, 99
Rye, Morgan, 91

S

Sabine County, 22, 27
Sabine River, 12, 13
Sadler, Capt. William T., ix, 16, 21, 22
Sadler, Mrs. W. T., ix
Salem College, N. C., 131
Sam Houston Normal Institute, The, 136, 147, 186
Sampey, W. A., 100
Sampson, Samuel D., 100
Sampson, William P., 100
Sams, L. L., 111
San Antonio, 5, 27, 42, 46, 80, 136, 148, 150, 154
San Antonio Road, 7, 39, 42, 80, 133, 171, 173

San Augustine, 42, 99
San Augustine County, 22, 28, 149
San Felipe, 150
San Francisco de los Tejas, 2, 3, 4, 5, 6
San Jacinto, Battle of, 7, 99, 124, 133, 153
San Jacinto Monument, The, 124, 133, 159
San Pedro, 16
San Pedro Creek, ix
Sansom, Samuel D., 103, 104
Sansom, William P., 103, 104, 150
Santa Fe, N. Mexico, 121
Santissimo Nombre de Maria Mission, 3, 5
Satterwhite, B. L., 93, 97
Satterwhite, B. L., Jr., 95
Savannah, Ga., 130
Sawyer, F. T., 50
Saxon, J. H., 90
Schomaker, John, 82
Schools, see names of
Schopin, Doctor, 129
Schupak, F. F., 87
Schupert, Doctor, 129
Scruggs, Rev. James A., 48, 100
Scurry, Richard, 27
Scurry, Lt. Col. William, 183
Self, Thomas, 133
Selman, Benjamin, 21
Shapira, M. L., 93, 96, 97
Sharp, Major, 116
Sharp, Mrs. Major, 116
Sharp, Sam H., 37
Shelby County, 149
Sheppard, M. L., 111
Sheppard, Morris, 26
Sherdian, John, 173
Sheridan, John R., 93, 116
Sheridan, Col. W. N., 80
Shiloh, 55, 65, 162
Shiloh, Battle of, 135, 166
Shivers, Andrew, 109
Shivers, J. W., 87, 97
Shivers, James S., 93, 94
Shivers, Mrs. James S., 94
Shivers, Mrs. John, 55
Shivers, Mrs. John S., 122
Shivers, R. L., 43
Shook, Jefferson, 100
Shook, Nathan, 100
Shortridge, Judge, 178
Shotwell, J. C., 87
Shreveport, 42, 113

Shreveport Stage, The, 46
Shultz, E. W., 13
Shute, Ira C., 8
Silliman, Rev. A. P., 114
Simms, Allie, 117
Simms, Jefferson, 117
Simms, John M., 117
Simpson, E. L., 34
Simpson, Ellen, 109
Simpson, J. R., 34
"Sketch of Crockett," 39
Skidmore, C. D., 37
Smith, Augusta Louise, 121
Smith, B. B., 31
Smith, C. E., 100
Smith County, 12
Smith County Medical Association, 199
Smith, Ellis, 100
Smith, Prof. Euclid, 75
Smith, F. A., 93, 97
Smith, Fred, 79
Smith, J. H., 87, 93
Smith, John, 31
Smith, John B., 34
Smith, John Ed., 73
Smith, John P., 31
Smith, Capt. John T., 23, 100, 120, 130, 167, 190-191; children of, 191
Smith, Gen. Nathaniel, 160, 161
Smith, W. R., 50
Smith, Prof. Wade L., 78
Smithers, Harriet, 152, 191
Smyth, George W., 27
Sneed, Joseph P., 100
Snelles, Ballin, 8
Snively's, Col. Jacob, Expedition, 176
Soule Commercial College, New Orleans, 132
Southern Presbyterian Church, The, 72
Southwestern Historical Quarterly, The, 171, 176
Sowell, W. H., 111
Spain, W. A., 87
Spanish-American War, The, 137
Spanish Missions, 1-6
Spear, Moses, 99
Spears, Rev. J. L., 115
Spence, Mrs. A. R., 68
Spence, Major John, 68, 122
Springfield Mission, The, 102
Springfield, Texas, 42

Spurlock, Capt. William, 152
Stagecoach Inn, The, 189, 190
Standley, W. C., 8
Standley, Willard, 8
Stanton, Kate, 67
Stanton, Uncle Billy, 67
State Gazette, The, 196
State vs. Hepperla, 51
State Library, 191
St. Claire, Ill., 187
St. Edwards University, 5
St. Joseph's Hospital, The, 199
Stedman, N. A., 198
Steel, Gen. Wm., 183
Steele, D. W., 107, 108, 111
Steele's Academy, 129
Stephen F. Austin State Teachers College, The, 6
Stephens, Rev. John A., 116
Sterne, Adolphus, 21, 22, 30, 83, 171
Stevens, Abel, 99
Steward, Mr., 40
Stewart, Wm. A., 24, 91, 107, 113, 140
Stidham, Adeline (Hallmark), 191, 192
Stidham, Zachariah, 34, 191-192
Stinson's Ferry, 42
Stockton Ranch, The, 132, 137
Stokes Building, The, 61
Stokes, Miss C. C., 94
Stokes, Charles, 61, 92, 192; children of, 192-193
Stokes, Cora (Davis), 193
Stokes, Dr. Edgar B., 93, 192, 193; children of, 193
Stokes, Lucy (Hancock), 192
Stokes, Dr. Paul B., 95, 193
Stokes, Col. William Beeson, 133, 137, 192; children of, 192
"Stop the Murderers," 47
Stout, Callie, 75
Stout, T. H., 75
Stovall, D. M., 100
Stovall, Francis M., 100
Stovall, S. M., 75
Stuart, Dr. J. H., 23, 59
Stubblefield, J. A., 91
Stubblefield, T. J., 34
Sturgis, J. S., 85
Sullivan, Rev. John, 81
Sullivan, S. D., 36
Summers, Thomas O., 100
Summerville, Ga., 135
Summerville, Miss., 182

INDEX

Sumpter, 46, 47, 55
Sweet, Hortense, 95
Syracuse, N. Y., 134

T

Tadmor, Texas, 186
Taft, Pres. William Howard, 170
Tarkington Prairie, 191
Taliaferro, Col. C. C., 55
Tate, Peterson, 8
Taylor, George, 192
Taylor, Isabella A. (Moore), 194
Taylor, Dr. W. T., 50
Taylor, Washington, 79
Taylor, William, 31
Taylor, Judge William M., 21, 44, 48, 76, 86, 90, 91, 136, 140, 193-194
Taylor's Monitor, 194
Teachers, Certification of, 48
Telegraph Mills, 46
Temple of Honor, The, 40, 47
Tenhuacana, 41
Tennessee, 103, 110, 133, 139, 146, 149
Tenney Memorial Church, The, 112, 123, 129, 169; also see First Presbyterian Church
Tenney, Dr. Sam M., 116
Tenney, Rev. Samuel Fisher, 61, 71, 111, 112, 115, 116, 117, 138, 187, 195
Terrell, 94
Terrell, Judge A. W., 179
Terrell, George W., 28
Texarkana, 26
Texas Baptist Association, The, 110
Texas Centennial Association, The, 5, 152
Texas Centennial Historical Board, 5
Texas Forestry Commission, 4
Texas Historical and Landmarks Association, 4, 5, 148
Texas Medical Association, The, 199
Texas Mounted Volunteers, 156, 164
Texas Republican, The, 54
Texas State Historical Association, The, 147, 199
Texas Supreme Courts Reports, The, 176
"Texas and Texans," 197
Texas University, 186; President of, 77, 118, 128
Texas War for Independence, 88,
124, 139, 149, 152
Thirteenth Georgia Regiment, The, 129
Thirteenth Texas Cavalry, The, 135
Thomas, Amelia (Howell), 194
Thomas, B. F., 87
Thomas, J. C., 107, 108, 109, 110, 111
Thomas, James J., 19
Thomas, Dr. M. A., 116, 194
Thomas. Monroe, 194-195; children of, 195
Thompson, Mrs. C. R., 117
Thompson, Caroline (Tunstall), 195
Thompson, David, 195
Thompson, Dolly V., 71, 73, 117; also see Dolly Worthington
Thompson, Mrs. E. A., 117
Thompson, Edward L., 117
Thompson, J. W., 79
Thompson, Miss L. C., 117
Thompson, N. O., 117
Thompson, Porter, 66, 67
Thompson, Prof., 72, 77
Thompson, Sally V., 66, 117
Thompson, Judge Samuel M., 65, 66, 71, 116, 117, 123, 169, 181, 195, 196, 202; children of, 196
Thompson, Thomas W., 66, 67, 117, 189
Thornberg, Alexander C., 20
Titus County, 12
Tobasco, Mexico, 88
Tolbot, Isham, 47
Tompkins, T. D., 18
Towery, C. D., 93, 97, 116
Townsend, Maurice, 31
Townsend, Thomas R., 8
Transylvania Medical College, The, 162
Traylor, Dr. R. S., 95
Trimble, Rev. B. F., 116
Trinity, 85
Trinity Advocate, The, 41, 54
Trinity African Mission, The, 102
Trinity College, 41, 63-64, 126, 152, 201; President and Trustees of, 63
Trinity County, 11, 21, 22, 23, 44, 55, 70, 202; boundaries, 12; creation of, 12
Trinity River, The, 7, 10, 12, 13, 28, 39, 43, 126, 191
Troy, 47

Trube, Harry J., 87, 93, 94
Truitt, Capt. A. M., 149
Tucker, Mary (Kyle), 165
Tucker, Mrs. S. P., 150
Tunstall, Buck, 196
Tunstall, Dolly, 117
Tunstall, Dolly V., 195, 196
Tunstall, William Vicory, 34, 195, 196; children of, 196
Turner, Doctor, 80
Tuscumbia, 53
"Two Centuries in East Texas," 149
Tyler, 3, 26, 27, 44, 46, 103, 104, 169, 198
Tyler County, 102
Tyler Reporter, The, 54

U

United States Congress, The, 45
United States Mail State Line, The, 60
United States Railroad Commission, The, 26
United States War for Independence, The, 124
Universities, see names of
Upshur County, 12
Ursuline Academy, The, Galveston, 147
Utilda, N. Y., 88

V

Vaca, Cabeza de, 2
Van Pelt, Terry, 95
Van Zandt County, 153
Vaughan, B. C., 31
Vaughan, Tom, 65, 123
Vaughan, William, 31
Vaughn, W. E., 92
Vehlin's Colony, 7
Veterans Hospital, The, Kansas, 137
Vicksburg, Miss., 166
Victoria, 99
Virginia, 65, 123
Virginia University, 122, 178

W

Waco, 5, 25, 46, 84, 120, 164, 165, 169
Waco Village, 42
Waddell, W. M., 74, 92
Waddell, Mrs. W. M., 74
Wade, Houston, 84
Wages, J. R., 100
Wagner, F. H., 34

Wagner, F. H., Jr., 109
Wagner, Herbert, 109
Walden, T. E., 87
Walker, H. P., 8
Walker, Martin A., 17, 201
Walker, N. G. M., 23
Walker, R. A., 8, 201
Walker, Judge Richard S., 28
Wall, Nettie (Cooper), 197
Wall, S. G., 110
Wall, Sarah (Holden), 197
Wall, W. F., 31, 43, 90
Wall, Judge William Benjamin, 37, 56, 133, 196-198; children of, 197-198
Wall, Rev. William B., 197
Walling, Jesse, 156
Walling's Ferry, 25
Walsh, Alice, 121
Walton, Rev. J. W., 116
Waltrip, Prof., 78
Ward, Henry W., 20
Ward, Matthias, 24, 25
Warden, Moses, 31, 90, 91, 138
Washington, 14, 42, 64, 83, 89, 100
Washington, County, 9, 53
Washington, D. C., 136; National Cemetery, 177
Waxahachie, 41
Weathered, W. W., 22
Webb, C. O., 87
Weches, 2, 3, 4, 146
Welch, Thomas J., 61, 87, 97
Welch, Thomas J., Jr., 61
Weldon School, The, 81
Wells, Samuel G., 17, 19, 20
Wells, W. C., 93, 94, 96, 97
West, Columbus, 66
West Family, The, 73
West Point Military Academy, 160
Western, Thomas G., 83
Whaling, Moreland, 100
Wharton, Mr., 9
Wharton, The, 88
Wheeler, Judge Royall T., 28, 176
Whipple, W. A., 111
White, Captain, 191
White, Dabney, 61
White, L. W., 92
White Marsh Island, 130
White, Stephen, 8, 17, 18
White, W. M., 8, 9
Whitehurst, A. S., 100
Whitmore, George W., 27
Wigfall, 49

INDEX

Wigfall, Louis T., 25
Wigfall's, General, Battalion, 197
Wilder, Alta Heflin, 160
Wiley, Mr., 66
Wilkerson, Mr., 66
Williams, Bryan T., 183
Williams, Judge Frank Alvin, 29, 61, 198; children of, 198
Williams, J. L., 87
Williams, John A., 81
Williams, Laura (Fisher), 198
Williams, Leonard, 18
Williams, Neethe & Williams, 198
Williams, Samuel A., 99, 104
Williams & Stedman, 198
Wilmington, N. C., 154
Wilson, Francis, 99
Wilson, Mary (Collins), 80
Wilson, Russell, 80, 134
Wilson, Terry W., 101
Wilson, William K., 100, 102, 103
Wilson, Zach, 80
Winfield, L. H., 92
Winfree, E., 87
Wingate, Edward, 57, 58, 59, 139
Wingate, Frank, 57
Wingate, Ned, 57, 58
Wingfield, Billy, 124
Wingfield, J. M., 51
Wise, General, 130
Wisher, John M., 83
Witte Museum Art League, The, 147
Woldert, Dr. Albert, 3, 6, 198-199
Woldert, Alma Edelina (Richter), 198
Woldert, John George, 198
Woman's Confederate Home, The, Austin, 184
Wood, A. J., 79
Wood, Charles, 31
Wood, Gov. T., 188
Wood, W. D., 28
Wood, William 91
Woodard, Dr. F. C., 78
Woodford County, Ky., 164

Woods, Col. George T., 156
Woodson, G. W., 113
Woodson, Dr. J. J., 35, 107, 110, 160
Woodson, Lena, 68, 107
Woodville, 28, 46
Woolam, John C., 100, 102
Wootters, A. H., 87
Wootters, Dr. J. S., 87, 97, 162
Wootters, James C., 34, 86, 90, 110, 168
Wootters, James G., 23
Wootters, Capt. John H., 61, 87
Wootters, R. H., 87
Word, Col. J. J., 161
World War I, 170
Wortham, Albert, 61
Wortham, Cary Ann (Vaughan), 201
Wortham, Maj. John, 7, 17, 31, 63, 64, 167, 199-202; children of, 202
Wortham, William, 90, 155
Wortham's Steam Sawmills, 50
Worthington, Dollie Thompson, 71, 202; also see D. Thompson
Worthington, William Branch, 202; children of, 202
Wright, Mrs. John E., 150

Y

Yarbrough, Joseph R., 8
Yarbrough, Swanson, 8
Yoakum, 44
Yoakum, Hon. Henderson, 176, 193
Yoakum & Taylor, 44
Young, Ella Mainer, 118
Young, J. W., 87, 93, 95
Yucatan, 89

Z

Zavalla Steamer, 88
Zillig, Isaac, 34
Zimmerman, J. C., 75, 90, 91
Zimmerman, John B., 75

www.ingramcontent.com/pod-product-compliance
Lightning Source LLC
Chambersburg PA
CBHW060351080526
44583CB00012B/267